Flash™
ActionScript
f/x & Design

Bill Sanders

 CORIOLIS™

President, CEO
Keith Weiskamp

Publisher
Steve Sayre

Acquisitions Editor
Beth Kohler

Marketing Specialist
Patricia Davenport

Project Editor
Sally M. Scott

Technical Reviewer
Mark Winstanley

Production Coordinator
Carla J. Schuder

Cover Designer
Jody Winkler

Layout Designer
April Nielsen

CD-ROM Developers
Michelle McConnell
Chris Nusbaum

The Coriolis Group, LLC
14455 N. Hayden Road
Suite 220
Scottsdale, Arizona 85260

(480)483-0192
FAX (480)483-0193
www.coriolis.com

Library of Congress Card Number: 00-047429

Printed in the United States of America
10 9 8 7 6 5 4 3 2 1

Other Titles for the Creative Professional

Dedicated to my wife, Delia.
—Bill Sanders

෪

About the Author

Dr. **Bill Sanders** is an experienced script and program developer in a wide range of languages and platforms. He is a professor at the University of Hartford in Connecticut, in the Interactive Information Technology program, where he works with students who are preparing for careers in the wired and wireless environment of the Internet and World Wide Web—and what will follow the current form of the Internet and Web. He has written more than 30 computer books that emphasize clear communication and getting the most out of a computer language or application.

Bill sees Flash as the perfect tool in three key areas of application. First, Flash has the capacity to serve as a robust and lively interactive tool in the development of e-commerce sites on the Web. Its fluid character and responsive development potential make Flash an ideal instrument to make e-commerce sites where designers can build virtual realities that respond to clients' interests and needs. Second, Flash's animated development properties make it the tool of choice for creating online arcade-style games, movie previews, animated cartoons, and online music videos. The potential in this area is becoming ever more obvious, as sound and animation are coordinated in low-bandwidth features on the Web. Finally, and of significant importance for Bill's work, is the use of Flash in developing educational tools that clearly communicate complex concepts and research findings in a nonstatic format that best represents the nature of the phenomena under study. Working with a virtual psychology laboratory and with courses relating to the Internet, Flash has proven to be a flexible tool that can be used to illuminate, involve, and clarify structures and processes.

As owner, developer, and caretaker of Sandlight Productions (**www.sandlight.com**), Bill Sanders maintains a site dedicated to exploring the limits of Flash and ActionScript (**www.sandlight.com/flash** and **www.sandlight.com/actionscript**), along with ongoing interests in creating Web sites that can communicate in ways that no other widely available medium can.

Acknowledgments

Many people helped make this book better than I could have possibly done without their assistance. The Flash group at the University of Hartford, in Connecticut, served as a constant resource. Steve Misovich, Lou Boudreau, Laura Spitz, Dave Demers, and I met weekly to plumb the limits of Flash. Everyone helped and learned from one another and had a great time doing so.

Leslie Cabarga lent a good deal of artistic design to the creations in the book and on the CD-ROM. A talented California Flash designer in his own right, and creator of **www.flashfonts.com**, Leslie provided fonts and artwork across three time zones. Another West Coast Flash talent is Mark Winstanley, who served as Technical Reviewer for the project. Mark checked and doublechecked to make sure the action scripts were done correctly and often added enhancements.

The people at Macromedia were gracious in their support in providing beta software and assistance. The technical folks at Macromedia, including Eric Wittman, Brad Bechtel, Matt Wobensmith, and Jeremy Clark, provided invaluable technical assistance and great tips. The Flash 5 beta group are a talented lot who were very generous in their assistance. Colin Moock, Amit Pitaru, Mark Clarkson, and Nigel Chapman were especially insightful in their help. Leona Lapez and David Brent Meyer at Macromedia supplied documentation and software that helped considerably.

Sally Scott, Michelle McConnell, and Beth Kohler at The Coriolis Group made everything come together from the inception to the completion. Colleen Brosnan served as a thorough and sharp-eyed copyeditor.

Margot Maley Hutchison at Waterside Productions is responsible for the initial idea of the book, and her work with Beth Kohler launched the project.

Contents at a Glance

Table of Contents

Foreword

Flash 5 is the Future of the Internet

To say that Flash 5 is the future of the Internet is a very bold statement but a very true one nonetheless. I've been involved in Flash since its earliest days as a mere novelty to motion vector graphics. Seeing it evolve into the massive powerhouse of Web production it has become today—Flash is essential to every facet of Web development—is nothing short of awe inspiring.

I was one of the early beta-testers of Flash 5 who helped put it through its paces and iron out any rough spots in the system. While doing that, I also reviewed the technical aspects of this book and helped Bill Sanders make sure everything here is right on the money in terms of technical accuracy and presentation.

This book is a wonderful guide through the world of Flash 5 Action Scripting, and my hat goes off to Bill Sanders for writing such a compelling and thorough text on this brand-new JavaScript–like language. Conceived by Macromedia to integrate with Flash 5, it leaves any other visual/interactive web application language in the dust, without even breaking a sweat.

As with any new application, especially one involving a new programming language, plenty of questions need to be answered about how and why certain elements work the way they do. In this book, Bill guides you through this new language by presenting a well-laid-out text description of the new functions, as well as great examples to show them in real-world action. The very basic concepts are presented early in the book, so if you're new to scripting in Flash you'll be able to get up to speed on how to use the fundamental scripting features in Flash 5.

Even if you're a veteran Action Scripter from Flash 4, it's worth reviewing the basics since so many elements have changed in Flash 5. After presenting the basics, Bill builds on these concepts to take you deeper into the world of this powerful language. Soon you'll be creating scripts that track arrays of items in a virtual shopping cart; altering the panning and volume of sound output; creating virtual calendar systems; and much, much more. Bill has even included a comprehensive breakdown of the newest functions so that, once you know how the Flash 5 syntax applies to the tried-and-true programming concepts you know so well, all advanced programmers will be able to jump right in.

This book has something to offer the Flash developer at every skill level, and I feel that everyone who reads it will come away feeling enlightened; they will raise their Action Scripting knowledge to the next level—and beyond!

Happy scripting!

Mark Winstanley
mwinstanley@flashcore.com
MultiMeteor.com
FlashCore.com (The Los Angeles Macromedia Flash Users Group)

Introduction

Flash 5 has revolutionized itself. In going from Flash 3 to Flash 4, ActionScript took a major leap from a small set of actions to a recognizable scripting language. Now, in Flash 5, ActionScript moves into the realm of a full-fledged object-oriented scripting language. ActionScript has retained its ability to help novices learn to script with point-and-click and, now, point-and-drag placement of commands. The new ActionScript is actually easier to learn. Experienced programmers can now type in ActionScript without having to point-and-click on the desired action, operator, object, or property. All of the ActionScript can be typed in like any other language. Flash 5 gives everyone a choice.

Flash 5 has a new "look and feel," and it has an ActionScript Editor with two modes. In the Normal mode, you double-click or drag the actions and associated parameters into the script. If you prefer, you can press the plus (+) button to open a menu to select your script actions and parameters, as in Flash 4. Access to the ActionScript Editor is located in a button at the bottom of the stage so that it's easy to open and put away. As part of the new Object Actions Panel, the ActionScript Editor has a whole new presentation from that of Flash 4, but it retains enough features of earlier versions so that the transition is clear and simple. In addition, you can make the editing area the size of your screen so that seeing the whole script all at once is no longer impossible. In the Expert mode, you have all of the flexibility you may want. You can either start typing in ActionScript as you would in a text editor, or you can use any of the script entry options available in the Normal Mode. It's the best of both worlds.

Why ActionScript?

A much-admired designer once asked me, "Why bother with ActionScript? Using the standard Flash 5 tools, I can create anything I want." Actually, he was using ActionScript but did not realize it. In simple jump statements such as Go To And Play [or gotoAndPlay(f)], he had an ActionScript command in use. More important, using ActionScript with Flash 5 is not an either/or proposition. When you need ActionScript in Flash 5, you *really* need it, as evidenced in every Go To And Play command. ActionScript interacts with a Flash movie created with non–ActionScript elements in Flash 5. In one creation, I made graphical control sliders for a movie that had been done entirely without

ActionScript. However, because you cannot make slider controls or make them control anything without using ActionScript, I left the movie as it was, created the script to simulate slider controls, and linked the controls to the frames in the movie. ActionScript works *with* a standard Flash 5 movie, not against it or instead of it.

Finally, some tasks done in the conventional manner with Flash 5 can be done more easily and more practically with ActionScript. For example, tweening is a pervasive and important part of Flash. In some cases where fine adjustments are necessary to get a motion just right, however, changing the value of a variable, property, or object in ActionScript can be a lot easier than retweening until a movement looks as it should. For designers who wonder how some Flash sites have jaw-dropping animation, scrolling text, and dazzling interactive interfaces, the answer probably lies in good design enhanced by ActionScript. As clients demand more Flash enhancements to keep their Web sites lively and competitive—as well as connected to a back-end link to server-side applications—understanding ActionScript becomes more important. Fortunately, Macromedia has made ActionScript easy to learn, yet powerful enough to satisfy the demands of designers and emerging interactive technology.

Who This Book Is For

First, I wrote the book for Flash 5 users who want to enhance their Flash movies by adding ActionScript. The book is not for the novice who is learning Flash for the first time. It is intended for Flash 3 and Flash 4 users who are transitioning to Flash 5 and want to learn ActionScript. No previous programming or scripting background is necessary for this group, but you do need to know enough Flash to create a simple Flash movie.

Second, the book is designed for programmers who want to add ActionScript to their arsenal of languages quickly. All programming and scripting languages have common elements, and ActionScript is no exception. Programmers familiar with languages from Basic to C++ to JavaScript are easily going to be able to adopt and use ActionScript with Flash designers. JavaScript programmers will find the transition almost seamless because the new ActionScript looks almost identical to JavaScript. In fact, I found it to be better than JavaScript as an object-oriented language because there is no separate version for different browsers. You write it once, in one way, and both Netscape Communicator and Microsoft Internet Explorer interpret it in the same manner. As an implementation of an object-oriented language, JavaScript has a thing or two to learn from ActionScript. Nevertheless, key important differences exist between JavaScript and ActionScript, and you need to know what they are and how to take advantage of ActionScript's unique characteristics.

Third, the book is for Flash 4 ActionScript users. With almost twice as many actions, a brand new user interface and addressing system, new objects, arrays, functions, operators, and build-your-own functions, Flash 5 ActionScript is a horse of a very different color than ActionScript in Flash 4. The focus for this group is one of transition and enhancement. As with all changes, you may find some elements of the old Flash 4 ActionScript preferable; after you've become familiar with Flash 5 ActionScript, however, you are going to prefer it. You will soon discover that it is easier to get the results working with ActionScript in Flash 5 movies than with Flash 4. You will find yourself with a very powerful scripting tool.

A Sip at a Time

For those new to scripting or programming, the task of learning can seem daunting. No reason exists to attempt to learn ActionScript all at once, however, especially if ActionScript is the first scripting or programming language you've attempted. Take it in small doses. Try out the examples, then try altering them a little, and have some fun with what you learn. You need to pay attention to certain details, such as making sure you provide instance names for movie clips and variable names for text fields and do not use reserved words for variable names. You don't have to be a math whiz to write ActionScript. You do need to take everything a step at a time, however. Compared to other programming or scripting languages, most ActionScript is written in short, simple scripts rather than long, complicated ones. It is modular in that some scripts are in buttons, some in frames, and others in movie clips.

Rather than looking at ActionScript or this book as a mountain to be climbed, therefore, look at it as a guide and resource that can be taken at your own pace.

How This Book Covers ActionScript

I wrote this book in expository English. It is not written in the shorthand of computer science or engineering or even in the language of a technical writer. The book is a conversation with the reader about using ActionScript. The beginning of the book presents the fundamentals of scripting languages and builds from that point. As the book progresses, explanations and examples guide you through ActionScript. I doubt that you can read the book for more than 10 minutes before you will want to create a movie to try using a newly acquired piece of ActionScript. So when using this book, turn on your computer, load Flash 5, and be prepared to use and learn ActionScript.

Learning utilities and projects accompany very short script examples. These examples show how an ActionScript of one sort or another is to be written, along with example values and parameters. A *learning utility* is a Flash 5 movie that has as its sole purpose the demonstration of one or more ActionScript features. For example, one shows how all of the different button events work. Although each button fires the same event in the movie, the purpose is to show how the different events work with the buttons. *Projects* are movies using the accumulated ActionScript materials within a chapter that have a real-world application. Some applications are simple, such as taking input in a text box and rearranging the data before sending it to a database in a server-side application. Others are more elaborate, such as a bar chart that makes a proportional graph no matter what data set is entered. All of the learning utilities and projects are designed to help you understand a focused part of ActionScript. Except for the introductory chapters that cover the foundational aspects of ActionScript, each chapter has at least one learning utility and one project.

All of the learning utilities and projects are on the accompanying CD-ROM. If you don't feel like following the instructions in the book and want to create the movies with the ActionScript from scratch, open the FLA files on the CD and deconstruct the script. By typing in the script yourself, however, you will quickly discover some common errors. A script may not run as it is supposed to run and you may be frustrated at times, but you will learn more about creating action scripts and learn it more quickly if you do it yourself. Another trick is to load the FLA file as a library and then just type in the script without redrawing the graphic elements. Whatever way works best for you is the one to use.

Throughout the book I use the same terms that Macromedia employs. However, instead of using the greater-than symbol (>) to trace a path through a menu hierarchy, I use a vertical line or "pipe." For example, Modify|Instance means to first press "Modify" on the menu bar and then select "Instance" from the Modify menu. I think it is clear, and I use it throughout, including in context menus. For keyboard shortcuts, I use the familiar Ctrl/Cmd sequence to differentiate between Windows PCs and Macintosh computers. The Ctrl is shorthand for the Control key used on the Windows PC, and Cmd is shorthand for the Command key on the Macintosh—the one with the apple outline. The Macintosh has a Control key, but it tends to be used like the right button on a Windows PC mouse, so when a reference is made to the Macintosh Control key, it needs to be spelled out. The Alt/Option shorthand refers to the Alt key on the Windows PC and the Option key on the Macintosh.

Throughout, layers are always listed in the order in which they appear in the movie, but sometimes it makes more sense to discuss them in a different order. Sometimes the Background layer, which always appears at the bottom, is the first layer you want to deal with when developing the program. Layers are therefore discussed here in the order that makes most sense for developers.

In Flash 5, you may also set your own keyboard shortcuts, and each action has an Esc sequence. Because it is impossible to predict which keyboard shortcut a user wants to use, actions and other script words are listed as they appear in the ActionScript Editor. Choose your favorite way of getting them there.

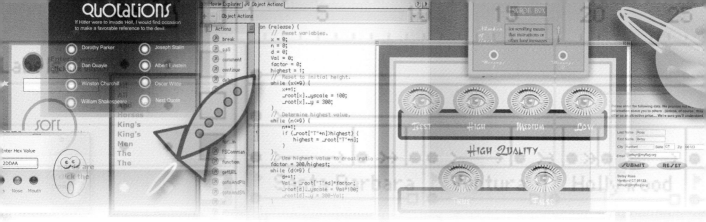

Chapter 1

Supercharging Flash with ActionScript

ActionScript is a scripting language that enables developers to "supercharge" their Flash movies. This first chapter introduces you to some of the basic objects used with ActionScript and explains how each type of Flash element is connected to ActionScript.

What Can You Do with ActionScript?

If you've had any experience with Flash, you've probably used at least some ActionScript. If you've inserted a Stop command in a keyframe or had a button initiate a Play command, you've used ActionScript. ActionScript is designed around Flash, and all of its commands relate to some object in a Flash movie. For example, the Play and Stop commands in ActionScript relate to playing or stopping a movie clip or the timeline. In another scripting or programming language, these same commands may be more general and may require more information before they can be implemented. With ActionScript in Flash, the Stop command in a frame means just one thing—stop the movie at this frame. No muss. No fuss. ActionScript is so simple and basic that you may not even realize you've used it, unlike other scripting and programming languages.

After you've gained a basic understanding of these ActionScript commands, you may soon start asking, "What can I do in Flash without ActionScript?" The answer is, "Not much," especially if you're designing interactive Flash movies. Even a great Flash movie can be a fairly passive affair. Web surfers find that the action is fun to watch, but they are not involved; they sit on the sidelines looking at all the dazzle on the screen and then click to go somewhere else.

With ActionScript, you are able to provide Flash with decisions that involve the user. You set up a set of conditions, the user chooses from the options given, and the Flash movie responds accordingly and appropriately. For example, you may put in some ActionScript that allows the user three tries to get the right answer. After the third time, the movie sends him to the "RefresherCourse" to learn more about the question before having another shot at getting the right answer. The RefresherCourse is simply the label on a frame with information about the question. The three tries are just a frame loop (or scripting sequence) using ActionScript to count the number of tries before sending the user to the frame named RefresherCourse.

Likewise, if you want to design an arcade-style game, you need some way to make the Flash movie respond quickly and accurately to a whole array of events. Plain old Flash movies with no ActionScript respond to absolutely nothing. ActionScript enables Flash to know the location of the mouse pointer; the location of other objects on the screen; and the relationship among the player's actions, the objects, the time left, and the player's skill level. It can also keep score at the same time. ActionScript can do all of this with aplomb.

If your primary use of Flash movies is for Web-based pages, ActionScript can act as an intermediary as well. As a user enters data into a Flash movie, that data can be passed to a Web page and used in the Web page, or vice versa. You can pass form data from a Web page to a Flash movie. Even more important, you can gather information with ActionScript and pass it directly to a server for database storage and retrieval. This provides your Web site with a dynamite

Flash interface in which users can enter their names, addresses, and credit card numbers, which are then passed on to a Web server where orders are processed.

Scripting and programming language designers are always amazed when they learn users end up doing more with the language than they intended. Although ActionScript was designed primarily to provide user interactivity in a Flash movie, the extent and type of interactivity is left to the imagination of the Flash movie designer.

Thinking ActionScript

In previous versions of ActionScript, all scripting was confined to a small window where actions had to be selected from a menu. You could see only a small portion of the script, and, while you could write some interesting scripts, the task was a bit awkward. In Flash 5 ActionScript, that language has metamorphosed into a full-fledged object-oriented scripting language. It is very similar to JavaScript, but writing a script is aided by point-and-click script entry. For advanced users, the Expert mode allows you to enter code just as you would in a text editor with the added convenience of pointing and clicking options for different actions, functions, operators, and objects. The ActionScript Editor, now in an Object or Frame Panel, helps you learn ActionScript and then gets out of your way once you become proficient.

ActionScript Is Modular

ActionScript is a modular programming language. This means that the scripts are little modules that do particular things, such as stop or play a movie. Each module stands alone but is related to the rest of the Flash movie. Essentially, you put ActionScript into buttons, movie clips (MCs), and frames; when the Flash movie comes to a frame or MC, or the user activates the button, the ActionScript executes. This does not mean that ActionScript scripts cannot be sophisticated and complex. They can be. Usually, however, all you have to do is to write a little ActionScript in the button, MC, or frame to accomplish what you need.

For people who have never programmed before, this is good news. Essentially, it means that you don't have to learn a large, complex language all at once. You can learn what you need as you go along and use it in the buttons, MCs, and frames of your Flash movie. When you want your Flash movie to do more, you learn a little more ActionScript. More experienced programmers will find that learning ActionScript just involves understanding where and how to use familiar programming structures, such as conditionals, arrays, and loops.

ActionScript Uses OOP

A surprise for programmers (and a good concept for nonprogrammers to understand) is that ActionScript uses Object-Oriented Programming (OOP). Without going into the technical aspects of OOP (and perhaps calling down the wrath of the gods of computer science), the approach focuses on treating all of the elements in a program as an object. A scene, a frame, a text box, a drawing, and a symbol are all ActionScript objects. The objects have *attributes* that can be altered by action scripts, and each object has a *unique ID* that can be referenced by ActionScript. For example, you may have an MC named "Cecil." "Rotation" is a property (attribute) of the object named Cecil. ActionScript can tell Cecil to rotate 90 degrees (see Table 1.1).

Objects can live in a hierarchy. An object can be made up of several other objects. For example, an MC may be made up of symbols, drawings, buttons, and even other MCs all on different layers. Some of those objects may consist of still other objects. Consider the following:

- *Zoo*—Main timeline root

- *Lion*—MC on the main timeline

- *Teeth*—MC that is part of the Lion MC

- *White*—Property of Teeth MC (Color white is hexadecimal FFFFFF)

The object named "Zoo" is on the main timeline or the root level. Zoo contains an MC named "Lion." In turn, Lion is made up of (among other things) an object named "Teeth." If an object is changed, other objects change as well. For example, suppose the object Teeth has its color property changed from white to gold. The Lion object will now have gold teeth instead of white ones. In turn, that will change the way Zoo looks as well. Originally, Zoo had a lion with white teeth, and now the lion sports gold caps. Zoo just doesn't look the same. In ActionScript, the order—or hierarchy—of the zoological examples may look as follows:

```
toothColor=new Color(_root.lion.teeth);
toothColor.setRGB(0xFF9900);
```

The change could have been made by a script in a button, a frame, or a different MC, or it could have been by the MC named "Teeth." As long as the object is the right kind (an MC), any other objects that can contain ActionScript can send commands to others. However, they must address the correct path and follow the other rules of syntax. In this example, the hierarchy is

```
_root.lion.teeth
```

ActionScript in any hierarchy can change what happens in any other hierarchy. One object's ActionScript can affect itself or another object's behavior or characteristics. For example, an object that resides as a "child" of an MC on

Table 1.1 Movie clip properties.

Object	Attribute	Unique ID	ActionScript
Movie Clip	Rotation	Cecil	"Cecil, rotate 90 degrees"

the main timeline may have an ActionScript instructing an object that is the "grandchild" of a different MC—and thus in a different hierarchy—to go to and play Frame 34. Just for good measure, it may command it to double in size as well. Frame 34, in turn, may contain additional ActionScript that instructs an object belonging to yet another MC to whistle "Dixie."

Working with ActionScript and objects in a hierarchy is not as complex as it may seem. Instead of writing one huge program that is 29,876 lines long, OOP in Flash is modular and is made up of short action scripts living in frames, buttons, and MCs. When making a Flash movie, whether you use ActionScript or not, it is important to organize all of the parts and to plan how different keyframes are used. Working in an OOP environment also requires planning and actually assists you in effectively orchestrating your Flash movie using ActionScript. Think of ActionScript as a basic, yet effective, OOP language to make your work simpler, not more tedious.

Where Do Action Scripts Go?

In the simplest terms, action scripts are embedded in instances of MCs, buttons, or frames, but many different conditions can change the status of an MC, button, or frame. Before you begin scripting, you need to understand the actual circumstances of MCs, buttons, and frames under which ActionScript can be added to your Flash movie.

Movie Clips

Movie clips in Flash 5 can now have their own scripts. In previous versions of ActionScript, only buttons and frames contained scripts. Because MCs are the only objects whose properties can be changed with action scripts, they are by far the most important objects in Flash 5 and for use in ActionScript. Other objects can be changed by jumping to various points on the timeline where tweened objects are in the process of change or objects appear in a new configuration in a keyframe. However, only MCs have properties that may be addressed and changed with ActionScript. To make an MC, use the following steps:

1. Select File|New (Ctrl+N [Windows]/ Cmd+N [Macintosh]) to open a new Flash page.

2. Select the rectangle on the Tools bar. Draw a rectangle on the page, and select it using the Arrow tool from Tools. (Drag the Arrow tool around the entire rectangle so that you don't get just part of it.)

3. Select Insert|Convert to Symbol, or press F8. Select Movie Clip as the behavior, and name it "MyMC." Click on OK.

4. Select Window|Panels|Instance or Ctrl+I/Cmd+N. When the Instance Panel appears, write the instance name "sample" in the Name window. (See Figure 1.1).

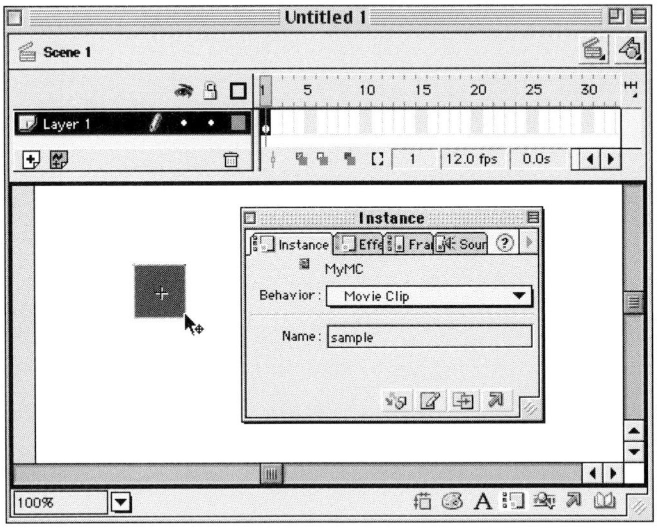

Figure 1.1
Use the Instance Panel to provide an instance name to a movie clip.

Your MC is ready for action. Figure 1.1 shows the new MC along with the Instance Panel that is so crucial in getting everything to work correctly. The instance name in the Name window is actually more important than the symbol name located above the Behavior pulldown menu.

Buttons

Prior to Flash 5, buttons were the only symbol object where scripts could be placed. Even though MCs now accept ActionScript, buttons still play a key role with ActionScript. As Flash users know, a Button symbol may not look like a button at all. A Button symbol can be part of a larger graphic waiting for the user to do something before making a change in the movie. For example, a Button symbol could appear as a person sitting with other people at a conference table. When the button-person is clicked on, the Flash movie jumps to a frame that tells something about the person's function.

To create a Button symbol in Flash, follow these steps:

1. Select File|New (Ctrl+N/Cmd+N) to open a new Flash page.

2. Double-click Layer 1 in the Timeline Inspector, and rename it "Real-Button." When a layer is double-clicked, the name can be changed.

3. Select the Circle tool, and draw a circle on the stage.

4. Click RealButton in the Layer column of the Timeline Inspector. The circle just created will be selected.

5. Select Insert|Convert To Symbol or press F8.

6. Select Button as the Behavior type, and key in the name "RealButton" in the Name window. (See Figure 1.2.) (By clicking the radio button next to Button in the Behavior column, the new symbol will automatically have

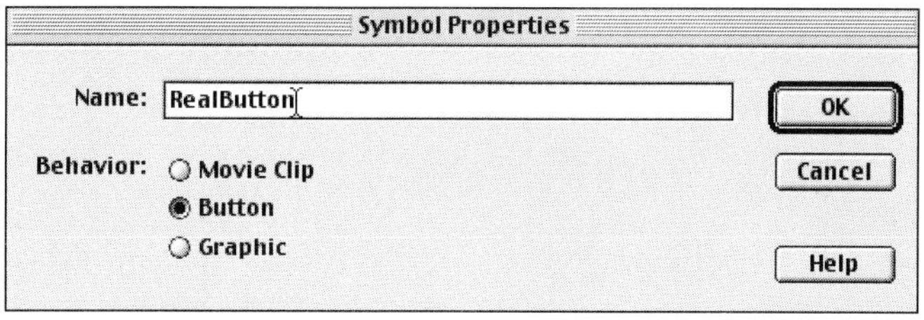

Figure 1.2
Symbol Properties dialog box creating a button symbol.

Up, Over, Down, and Hit frame groups in the Symbol Editor. They're not important for ActionScript, but they provide a clue to some of the conditions the mouse can be in to trigger an ActionScript.)

You can also select one of Flash's premade buttons by selecting Window| Common Libraries|Buttons.fla on the menu bar. A Buttons library window appears with several buttons from which to choose. Selecting one will make it appear in the library window's preview pane. Drag it to the stage, and it's all ready to be used. You can drag as many copies of the same button as you want. Each one is called an *instance*. When you use more than one instance of a symbol, however, put each instance on a separate layer. (Flash will work with more than one instance on a layer, but managing multiple instances on a single layer can become problematic.)

Instance Properties

In dealing with symbols, an instance of a symbol refers to a specific use of a symbol. Buttons are essentially instances of a symbol with button characteristics. The basic properties of a button are few, but very important for ActionScript. To view an instance's properties, first select the instance and then choose Modify|Instance from the menu bar. Alternatively, you can select Window|Panels|Instance or Ctrl+I/Cmd+I. All of these procedures open the Instance Panel. Figure 1.3 shows the Instance Panel with a typical button. Note the differences between the Instance Panels in Figures 1.1 and 1.3

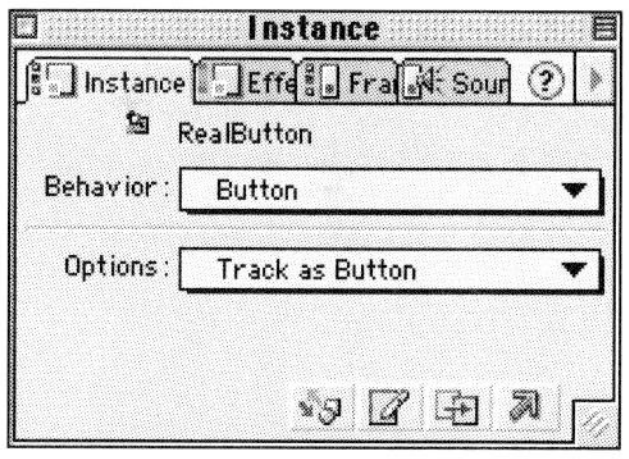

Figure 1.3
The appearance of Instance Panel with a button symbol instance.

In Figure 1.3, note that Button is selected in the Behavior menu, and the Track As Button is selected in the Options menu. Such elements are extremely important for ActionScript. The selection of Button in the Behavior dropdown menu is the key to an instance actually working like a button. When a symbol is initially developed, the same choices are made. However, even though a symbol may have been defined initially as a Graphic, Button, or Movie Clip, any instance can be used with a different type of behavior if you are careful.

In looking at Figures 1.1 and 1.3, the most important feature to note is the Show Object Actions icon in the lower right corner (arrow icon). By clicking on that icon, any ActionScript associated with the button is made available for creation or examination. Figure 1.4 shows a typical (and very simple) script written in ActionScript.

Figure 1.4
Actions are part of a button
instance's properties.

For a quick exercise on the importance of a button's properties, try the following experiment:

1. Create a button as described earlier. Use the name "RealButton."

2. Open the Instance panel.

3. In the Behavior pulldown menu, select Graphic. The button symbol instance is now behaving as a graphic instance. Select the graphic instance.

4. Click on the Object Actions icon to open the Object Actions window, and select one of the actions in the ActionScript Editor. You will see that all of the actions are "ghosted" and cannot be selected or used.

Although the icon in the Symbol window still shows a button, the instance has been changed so that it is now an instance of a Graphic symbol, and Graphic symbols do not have action properties. In other words, you cannot use a Graphic symbol to create ActionScript. An instance's properties *must* include the behavior of a Movie Clip or Button to have actions triggered by a mouse event.

Just as an instance of a Button symbol can be transformed into another symbol, the opposite is also true. If you create a Graphic or Movie Clip symbol and then change the instance's property to button behavior by selecting Button in the Behavior column, you will see the Object Actions icon come alive in the ActionScript Editor. Figure 1.5 shows a symbol named "Graphic." The Actions in the ActionScript Editor are live, however, meaning that the instance is truly a button, and ActionScript can be included in the instance. Movie clips can also be transformed in the Instance Panel.

Changing Instance Properties in a Movie

In a Flash movie, objects can change. For those familiar with Flash, such news comes as no surprise; however, symbol instances can be changed from Graphic instances to Button instances or Movie Clip instances on the fly. For example,

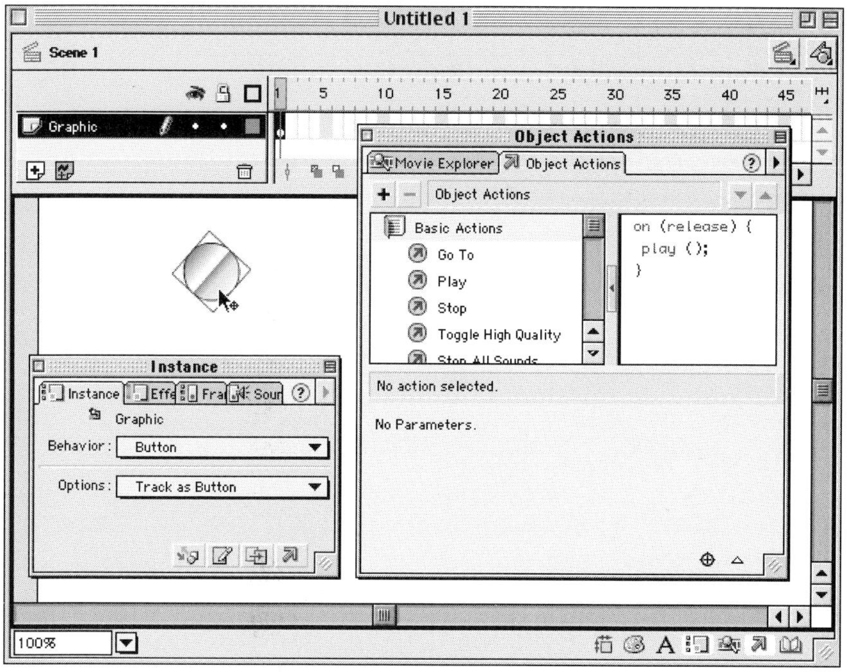

Figure 1.5
A Graphic symbol changed to a Button.

a Graphic instance in Frame 1 can be transformed into a Button instance in Frame 10, and then to a Movie Clip instance in Frame 40. Making such changes is *not* a good idea, however. I point this out because some changes are made unwittingly, and unwanted results may crop up when doing so.

Frame Properties

The third source area for action scripts is *frames*. Keyframes, empty keyframes, or just simple plain vanilla frames all have live Actions tabs in the Frame panel of the ActionScript Editor. However, the Actions in keyframes, including empty keyframes, are the only ones that count. ActionScript programs placed in simple frames become "owned" by keyframes. Try the following experiment to see how actions are affected by keyframes:

1. Select File|New on the menu bar, or use Ctrl+N/Cmd+N. A clean page appears with a single layer named "Layer 1" in the timeline. A keyframe is in the first frame.

2. Rename Layer 1, "FrameTest." It is always a good habit to name everything you use in Flash with a relevant label. Using labels when writing ActionScript is even more crucial.

3. Click on Frame 40 to select it. The frame turns dark when selected.

4. Select Insert|Frame from the menu bar, or just press the F5 key. Now you have 40 frames to work with.

5. Select Frame 20, and choose Modify|Frame from the menu bar. You can also use Ctrl+F/Cmd+F for the same results. The Frame panel appears.

6. Click on the Object Actions icon in the lower right corner of the stage window, and click Basic Actions directly under where you see Frame Actions. Double-click on Stop in the Actions menu. Figure 1.6 shows how your timeline now appears.

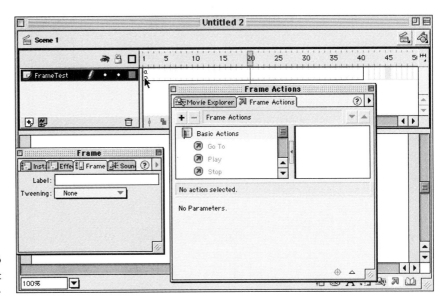

Figure 1.6
Entering ActionScript through a frame.

In Figure 1.6, note the small letter "a" above the initial keyframe. This means that the frame contains ActionScript. However, the script was entered in Frame 20. Now to complete this experiment, do the following:

1. Enter a keyframe in Frame 10. Click on Frame 10 and press the F6 button, or select Insert|Keyframe from the menu bar.

2. Select Frame 20 and then Modify|Frame from the menu bar. The Frame panel appears.

3. Click the Object Actions icon. In the Actions window, you will see no ActionScript. It's disappeared.

What's happened is no big mystery, but it is important to understand when using ActionScript. Whenever ActionScript is entered between keyframes, the script becomes owned by the closest keyframe to the left of the frame where the script is written. If you inspect any of the other frames between keyframes where script has been entered, you will see the same script in any of the frames. If you change the ActionScript in Frame 5, the keyframe to the left of Frame 5 also changes. Likewise, if the ActionScript in any of the other frames between the two keyframes is changed, all of the frames between the keyframes have their scripts changed as well. If the keyframe's ActionScript is modified, all of the frames to the right of the keyframe are changed as well until the next keyframe.

The lesson here may appear to be that all scripts between keyframes or the end of the timeline take on the script of the keyframe to their left. Although logical, this conclusion is erroneous, however. If this were true, Flash would become an impossible environment for ActionScript. Actions are launched only by keyframes. Otherwise, all of the frames until the next keyframe would independently initiate duplicate actions. For example, in the previous experiment with frames, the Stop action was placed in the frame and became the property of the keyframe to its left. Suppose your Flash movie called for a halt (Stop) at a keyframe that was restarted by a button with a Play action. If several frames initiated another Stop action until the next keyframe, the movie would hiccup along, and the user would have to click the button constantly with the Play action. Therefore, although you can place ActionScript in plain vanilla frames, only keyframes can initiate an ActionScript.

Programmers, Think of Gosub, Goto, and OOP

If you come from a programming background, jumping around in a program may be anathema to good programming practices and structure. However, a well-orchestrated set of modules controlling where the movie jumps is relative to the Flash timeline, not the program structure. After all, the programming is all located in the objects and positions in the timeline. When it comes time to move out of the timeline sequence, a good Gosub is best executed with a clear label. Likewise, a clear label is an essential property of objects in scripting as well.

Label Your Frames

The properties of frames are relatively simple compared to buttons. In the Label window of the Frame panel, frames can have one of the following basic behaviors:

- Label
- Comment

To enter a label, select the keyframe you wish to label, and type in the desired wording. For comments, do the same thing except preface the wording with a double slash (//). Effective use of labels is the key to getting along with frames when using ActionScript. When writing scripts, a common action is to go to a particular frame and do something. Addressing the frame correctly is crucial. If you use clear labels, your scripting life is made much clearer and cleaner. For example, Figure 1.7 shows a label named "BusStop," giving a clue to what may happen when the user jumps to that particular frame. In writing ActionScript, you can instruct the Flash movie to jump to BusStop instead of Frame 83 (or was it Frame 82? Or maybe 84? Or how about 48?).

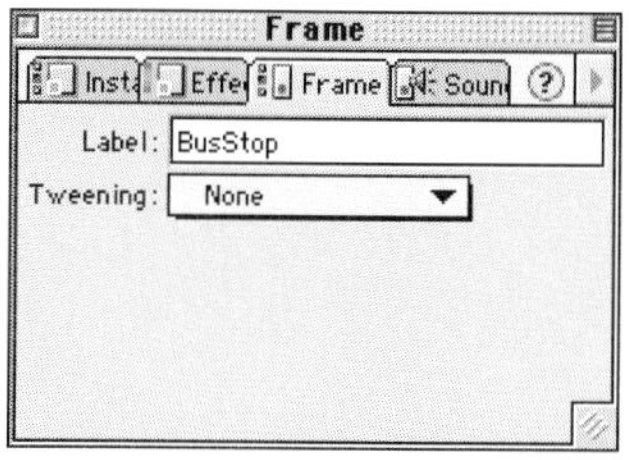

Figure 1.7
A Frame label.

Comments in Frames

Comments are meant to help you remember what's going on in your program as you develop it. They have no effect on what the program does. Like labels, though, they must go into the Frame Properties window. Because they are entered in the same window as labels, you need to keep an eye on which radio button for Behavior is selected. Figure 1.8 shows a timeline with both labels and comments in the BusStop layer. The comment merely reminds the programmer what happens when the timeline goes to the next keyframe.

How Do You Write Action Scripts?

For nonprogrammers, ActionScript is about as easy as programming or scripting can be. For programmers, ActionScript is an initial shock. Like free-range chickens, programmers are used to the wide-open spaces of a text file where programs or scripts are typically developed. By comparison, ActionScript programs are created by clicking and adding actions and scripts in bits and pieces.

Frame and Object Actions Window

The Frame and Object Actions window is context sensitive, which means that it changes depending on whether you have a frame or object selected. The window contains the ActionScript Editor where you enter your code. You can open the window by selecting Window|Actions from the menu bar. You can also use Ctrl+Alt+A/Cmd+Option+A to open the panel, or click on the Objects window icon in the lower right corner of the stage window or Instance Panel. For the actions to be *alive* (working), an MC, button, or frame must first be selected. There are various ways to enter actions and other elements of ActionScript; just select the one you prefer.

- *Drag and Drop*—Select the script you want, and drag it from the script menu to the ActionScript Editor.

- *Double-Click*—Double-click on the script element, and it appears in the ActionScript Editor.

- *Menu-Method*—For those used to entering ActionScript in Flash 4, click on the plus (+) sign on the left side of the ActionScript Editor, and select the script you want from menu options that appear.

- *Type In*—For those who like the free range of a text editor and come from a programming background, the Expert Mode may be best suited for their style. Just type in the code with no help (or interference) from the other methods.

- *Combination*—In the Expert Mode, you can use any of the preceding combinations. Flash 5 provides the best of all worlds for entering ActionScript.

Normal Mode

Entering script in the Normal Mode is recommended for getting started. When you enter script in the Normal Mode, the parameters are clearly laid out for each script element, whether it's an action, function, operator, property, or object. For example, Figure 1.9 shows the Basic Actions menu and the parameters laid out for helping the developer put in the correct parts. Some conditions in the parameters can be tricky. For example, when using a label instead of a line number, the label is put into quotation marks. The pulldown menus in the ActionScript Editor put in quotes automatically when you select Frame Label in the pulldown menu. Figure 1.9 also shows the location of the pulldown menu to select Normal or Expert Mode.

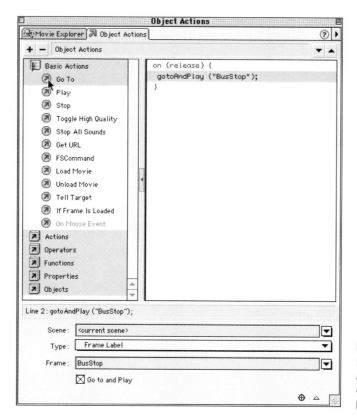

Figure 1.9

In the Normal Mode, the ActionScript Editor provides assistance with getting the parameters correct.

In the Normal Mode, the ActionScript Editor adds a Basic Actions folder that contains more than half of the actions from Flash 4. If only these actions are selected, you can safely export the file to a Flash 4 format. Among the other five folders in the Actions Menu, an Actions folder contains a far wider selection of actions; the added actions, functions, properties, and objects are presented in the Flash 5 format that the ActionScript editor now uses.

The Normal Mode automatically installs a Button action when a button object is selected, and it installs a Movie Clip action when an MC instance is selected. In the example in Figure 1.9, the "Go To" action was selected from the Basic Actions folder, and the **on(release)** code was automatically installed. For longer scripts, this feature can get in the way because each time you enter a new action, a new "on" or "onClipEvent" statement appears. Many times, you will want several actions and functions in a single mouse or MC event, and you may find it awkward to remove the many "on (release)" segments that you must pull out of the script.

Expert Mode

By selecting the Expert Mode, you give up the guidance of the Normal Mode, but then you are not hampered by unnecessary help. You do get *some* assistance for what is required by the script element you selected. For example, if you select the gotoAndPlay action in the Expert Mode, you will see the following:

```
gotoAndPlay ( frame );
```

The reverse text lets you know that you must enter some "frame" information, but it does not put labels in quotes or provide other information about the parameters. For example, if you plan to play a frame in a different scene, you must designate the scene as follows:

```
gotoAndPlay ("Scene 5", "hit" );
```

At the same time, though, you do not get the unwanted button or MC event handlers added. You put them in on your own. Once you become proficient with ActionScript, the parameters will become a bit more obvious. Until that time, however, getting help in the Normal Mode saves time and frustration.

Event Options

Chapter 6 covers the different options for handling events with the mouse, but here I'd like to point out some options that will always come up when you are using a button script. Besides "Release," you are given six other options for the mouse event to launch the script. In addition, if you select the "Key Press" checkbox, you can then use different keys to initiate the script. If you select more than one checkbox, multiple actions can set off the script. For all intents and purposes, the "Release" option is a mouse click. As soon as the mouse button is in the "up" position, it is clicked. Figure 1.10 shows how the options appear in the ActionScript Editor.

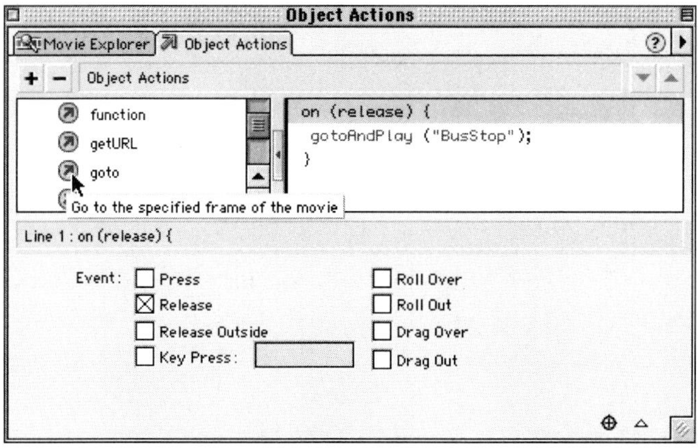

Figure 1.10
The parameters pane changes with a change in the action selection.

Just as buttons have different event-handling conditions, so do MCs. The default condition for onClipEvent is "load," which means to run the script as soon as the MC is loaded. You have several other options for events involving MCs, however. Figure 1.11 shows some different options.

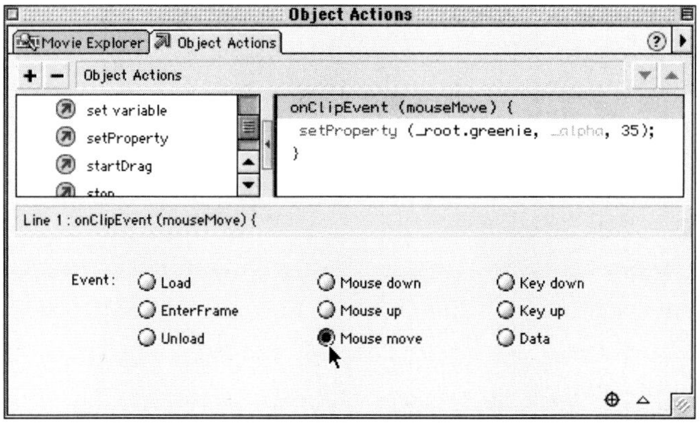

Figure 1.11
Different events are available for a movie clip than for a button.

Notice that with an MC event, the "mouseDown" and "mouseUp" terms are used instead of "onPress" or "onRelease." Until you're used to the subtle differences, use these user-initiated scripts in the Normal Mode. One trick is to get the more difficult, trickier material done in Normal Mode, and then shift to the Expert Mode when you have the more complex code where you want it.

Editing Expressions

Flash 4's Expression Editor has been integrated into the body of Flash 5. Many of the features of the Expression Editor are now part of what happens when you drag an action and its associated parameters into the ActionScript Editor. When you edit expressions in the ActionScript Editor, you can do it using either the Normal or Expert Modes. In the Normal Mode, the editing takes place in the bottom portion of the Editor where you make changes to the parameters for the action, property, function, operator, or object. When you bring the various script elements into the ActionScript Editor, you are given its parameters to help you get the script done correctly. Chapter 2 covers the different types of data you will work with in ActionScript, and much of the work you do with expressions will depend on the nature of that data.

Movie Clips, Paths, and ActionScript

Movie clips are the only symbols whose properties can be read or changed by action scripts. Although buttons can contain action scripts, action scripts cannot directly alter buttons. Graphic symbols cannot have their properties read or changed by action scripts, nor can they contain scripts. Frames can contain ActionScript; however, frames do not have properties that can be altered except for changing the current frame or using a call to a frame in an MC.

Independent Timelines

Movie clips have their own timelines and can keep on playing even if the main timeline is stopped. As objects, MCs are simply little Flash movies that have a life of their own and can influence and be influenced by other MCs or the main timeline as well as by buttons and frames with scripts. ActionScript serves as the orchestrating ingredient in Flash movies so that different parts (objects) of a movie can work together.

Paths

To deal with the different levels in a movie, ActionScript needs a way to address objects on the same timeline or in different timelines. The *path* from one object to another refers to its position (level) relative to another object. Fortunately, Flash ActionScript has adopted the same addressing system used for URLs in Web pages and JavaScript. In the Zoo example earlier in this chapter, the objects exist with three timelines:

- *Zoo*—Main timeline

- *Lion*—Lives on the main timeline but also has its own timeline

- *Teeth*—Lives within the Lion's timeline but also has its own timeline

Flash 5 has a dual addressing system. The old system used with Flash 4 still works, and you may use it. To address an object, you must first go to the main timeline, and then to the Lion's timeline to reach the Teeth timeline. Following URL addressing levels, you would write

```
/Lions/Teeth
```

to address Teeth from an absolute level. The logic is that Teeth exist in the Lions that exist in the Zoo. Because Zoo is on the main timeline, no name is used to reference it, just the slash "/". (I like to think of it as a compound pulldown menu: Zoo|Lions|Teeth.)

To address an object that is the parent (as the Lion is to Teeth), you use the "../" symbol to indicate that the reference goes upward. To go to the main timeline "Zoo" from the MC Teeth nested in the MC Lion, therefore, you would write

```
../.. /
```

Each "../" goes up a level of reference.

Flash 5 has introduced an addressing system that is simpler and more in line with OOP discussed earlier in the chapter. At the top of any hierarchy is the main timeline. In the old system of reference, a simple "/" sufficed as a preface to indicate the object was at the main timeline level. In the new reference system, a special name—**_root**—always means the main timeline. In our example, "Zoo" is the main timeline, and it is referenced as **_root** in the new system of reference. To point to Teeth, the address is

```
_root.Lions.Teeth
```

In addition, variables, methods, and properties are part of an object. After identifying the object, more elements may be added. For example, you may have a "roar" in the "Teeth" MC and call it "sound." The address to the sound may look like the following:

```
_root.Lions.Teeth.sound
```

Throughout the remainder of the book, the hierarchy of reference is used constantly, especially as more complex movies are developed in Flash and ActionScript. Take a second to review it so that the system is familiar. Later in the book, when a script shows a compound level of reference to a variable, property, or object, you won't have to keep flipping back and forth through the hierarchy.

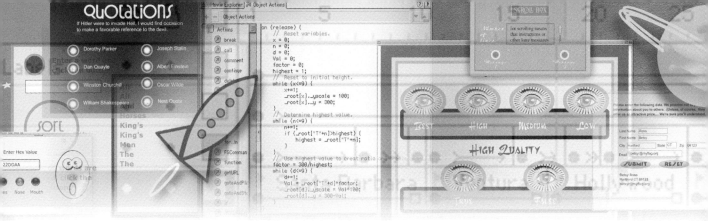

Chapter 2

Variables and Data Types

ActionScript, like all scripting and programming languages, uses data. Understanding the nature of the data, and understanding the containers for the data that ActionScript uses, are foundational steps in mastering the language. Learning how to use ActionScript's unique method of entering script is another important step.

What's a Variable?

One of the fundamental components of any kind of programming is the *variable*. As the name implies, variables change—they vary. Probably the best way to think of a variable is as a box of different things. In programming, variables store data of different sorts with different values. For example, a pet store can be considered a variable because its contents may change. Initially, the pet store (variable) may sell only puppies. Wanting to expand, the owner of the pet store may decide to offer kittens, fish, birds, and lizards as well as puppies. The pet store (variable) is the same store with the same name, but it has a different mix of animals. Therefore, its quality has changed.

For programmers, an important characteristic of Flash ActionScript is the contextual nature of variables. Languages such as C++ have *strongly typed* characteristics that require declaring not only a variable, but also the type of variable. Is the variable going to store text, integers, or floating point numbers? ActionScript, like virtually all scripted languages, does not require such declarations. ActionScript automatically deals with different types of data stored in variables.

Naming Variables

The name you select for a variable should give a clue to what the variable does. Names such as "VariableA," "VariableB," and so forth are virtually useless. Names such as "ItemCost" and "Tax ," however, tell you what the variable contains and make the variables easy to find, remember, and use accordingly. If you use shortcuts when naming variables in longer scripts or complex movies and call them "a," "b," and "c," always go back and provide descriptive names before you start working on other parts of your ActionScript. In Flash, clear variable naming is even more important because the scripts are short (generally) and scattered all over the place. For example, you may want to find or change the value of a variable that resides in a frame that is part of a movie clip embedded in another movie clip. You think you're going to remember what the variable "k" does in that maze? Probably not.

Variables must be a single string of connected characters, with no spaces between the words. Variable names such as "Pet Store" or "John Smith" are not acceptable; however, "petstore," "Pet_Store," or "PetStore" are. Moreover, ActionScript is not case sensitive. If a variable is named "PetStore," you can use "PETSTORE" or "petstore" to call the variable's current value. However, "Pet_Store" will not be recognized as the same variable as "PetStore" because it contains an extra character—the underscore. This lack of case sensitivity makes it easier when you want to call a variable by name, but make sure that you don't use names such as "BIGSTORE" and "bigstore" for your variables in the same button or frame. You may think they are different, but ActionScript won't.

Another naming convention you need to consider in naming variables is the use of reserved words or keywords. The keywords in the ActionScript vocabulary cannot be used as labels, variable names, or function names. These 16 key-words are as follows:

- break
- continue
- delete
- else
- for
- function
- if
- in
- new
- return
- this
- typeof
- var
- void
- while
- with

Two more terms—**true** and **false**—are Boolean literals, which also cannot be used. Names of actions, built-in functions, and other terms that you may confuse with scripting words should be avoided as well.

Arrays

A special type of variable called an *array* is now part of ActionScript's structure. (It was not in Flash 4.) Scripting languages, such as JavaScript, use built-in, single-variable arrays to create much of the structure of Web pages, including images and forms. Essentially, arrays are numbered variables with one or more dimensions. As such, they are considered *objects*. Objects are a collection of properties, and those properties are the array elements. For example, a simple, or one-dimensional, array named "Fruit" has four elements and looks like the following:

```
Fruit[0] = "apples"
Fruit[1] = "oranges"
Fruit[2] = "peaches"
Fruit[3] = "pears"
```

Tables of data are often generated in arrays and addressed in terms of the variable name and the number specifying a series of numbers for multiple dimensions. Table 2.1 shows how a two-dimensional array can easily address the table matrix.

Table 2.1 A two-dimensional array.

Column 1	Column 2	
Row 1	Var(1,1)	Var(1,2)
Row 2	Var(2,1)	Var(2,2)

To address the first column in the second row, the array variable Var(2,1) provides a visual, orderly way of arranging data. That is why arrays are very popular among programmers. Later in this chapter, you will see how to create an array in the discussion of Objects.

Data Types in ActionScript

Strings

The easiest way to think of strings, initially, is just as *words* or *text*. In programming, you will often see strings used as messages. For example, a string in a variable can be

```
Airplane = "Cessna Cardinal"
```

The variable is "Airplane," and the string *literal* is "Cessna Cardinal." A literal is the raw data that goes into a variable. The type of airplane can change, but a Cessna Cardinal is always going to be a Cessna Cardinal—the literal. Sometimes, a string can be a numeral, such as

```
StreetNumber = "250"
```

The variable "StreetNumber" is just another string literal that consists of numeric characters. In fact, just about any alphanumeric string of characters is a string. The phrase "string of characters" means that it can contain most punctuation marks and spaces as well as alphabetic characters and numbers. (Note that "Cessna Cardinal" includes a space.) Characters and numbers can be used in any combination. Strings, such as the following, have to make sense only to the designer and Flash; the user doesn't see them or have to understand them:

```
MixUp = "Juan2Tree4"
```

An important fact to keep in mind about strings is that they are not numbers. You can spot a string because it has quotation marks around it. In the earlier StreetNumber example, the number "250" is in quotation marks. If "250" were added to "250," the result would be "250250," not "500." Quotation marks around a literal usually mean that it's a string literal.

Expressions

Expressions are considered *compound* because they contain more than a single element. In ActionScript, a simple logical expression looks like the following:

```
Total = 7 + 5;
```

The value of "Total" is 12. The expression is compound (the 7 and 5 make it compound), but the value of "Total" is 12 because it is not broken down into its component properties. However, why type in "7 + 5" when you know it's 12? Programmers generally do not enter such a simple expression. The concept of expressions begins to make more sense if you look at the following:

```
Total = ItemCost + Tax;
```

The variable "Total" is the total value of two other variables. You may not know the value of the variables because they are *variables*. Variables change. Rather than having to keep track of what's in the variable, ActionScript does it for you and calculates the total. For example, consider the following script using variables and expressions:

```
ItemCost = 12;
Tax = ItemCost * .08;
sum = ItemCost + Tax;
```

The first variable—"ItemCost"—is defined with a literal having the value 12. The second variable—"Tax"—is an expression using the value of the first variable multiplied by .08. (The .08 represents an 8 percent sales tax rate.) The third variable—"sum"—uses another expression that is the total of the first two variables.

So far, the expressions have been relatively simple in order to illustrate how they are used in action scripts. Expressions can be very complex, especially when you have several variables that must interact with each other. The good part is that no matter how complex an expression is, the computer has to do all of the calculations. When you use complex expressions, however, always organize and label all of the parts clearly. Flash 5's ActionScript Editor assists you in creating valid expressions. A more in-depth discussion of operators that work with ActionScript to make compound expressions is included in Chapter 4.

String Concatenation

When two or more strings are joined together, the process is known as *concatenation*. All concatenations are treated as expressions. In ActionScript, the add operator, +, or the string operator **add** joins strings. The expression

```
Both = "Johnnie" + "Sally";
Both = "Johnnie" add "Sally";
```

results in "JohnnieSally." The value of the variable "Both" becomes "Johnnie-Sally." Concatenation is very useful when putting together strings that go together, such as first and last names. You've probably filled out forms in which you enter your first name in one field and your last name in another. Using concatenation, the names can be joined. Because a space is needed between the first and last names, the concatenation has to add a space, as shown here:

```
WholeName = "John" + " " + "Davis";
```

Two plus (+) signs are needed. The first one joins "John" and the space (two quotation marks with a space between them), and the second joins "Davis." The output is then "John Davis" instead of "JohnDavis."

Additional operators used with strings are discussed in Chapter 4.

Boolean Expressions

Boolean expressions can also be used in ActionScript. The results of a Boolean expression in Flash are "0" (No, False) or "1" (Yes, True). Named after George Boole, a brilliant British mathematician, Boolean expressions have a unique character. (See **http://encarta.msn.com/find/Concise.asp?ti=058D1000** for a brief biography of Boole.) For example, the following variable—"Bigger"—declares that 10 is greater than 15. Because that's not true, the variable "Bigger" is "false."

```
Bigger = 10 > 15;
```

The literal is the expression "10 > 15," not "0" or "1." Programmers are well aware of the value of Boolean expressions. Nonprogrammers may see little value in such expressions initially, but they will come to appreciate them.

Boolean Objects

Boolean literals are very smart. If you assign a Boolean value to a variable such as,

```
BooVar= 9 < 10;
```

the result is "true" but it can also be interpreted as a "1." For example, if you type

```
BooVar= 9 < 10;
Total=BooVar + 20;
```

your variable "Total" is 21. To control your Boolean results to specify a value or a string, you may use the Boolean objects. The Boolean object acts as a container for the Boolean properties. Three Boolean objects are available in ActionScript:

- **new Boolean()**—Acts as a container for the Boolean property
- **toString()**—Converts Boolean literal to string "true" or "false"
- **valueOf()**—Returns the Boolean primitive

The following script uses all three objects.

1. The variable "booVar" provides a name for the Boolean object with the contents of the Boolean literal "true" or "1" because 8 is greater than 7.

2. The variable "s" then stores the string literal of "booVar," which is "true."

3. The variable "v" stores the primitive value of "booVar," which again is the Boolean literal of "true" or "1."

4. The variable "textVal" uses the plus sign (+), which works like **add** for concatenation. Because adding a string to anything else returns the string and the number as a string, the outcome should be "true2."

5. When the Boolean literal is treated as a value, the results should be 3 (1 + 2 = 3) and stored in the variable "realVal."

```
booVar = new Boolean( 8 > 7);
s=booVar.toString();
v=booVar.valueOf();
textVal=s + 2;
realVal=v + 2;
output=textVal + newline + realVal;
```

The variable "output" is a text field so that the results show on the screen. The "newline" function serves to add a "carriage return" so that the results are sorted out and clear in the text field.

```
true2
3
```

For nonprogrammers, Boolean expressions may not seem very useful; as you begin using them, however, you will discover their value. At the end of this chapter, the learning utility uses a Boolean to change the automatic rounding down in the integer function that truncates any decimals in a number. (See also the "Integers" section in this chapter.)

Numbers

Numbers are pretty straightforward. Unlike strings, numbers must be written only as such. Any nonnumeric characters can cause problems unless they have been defined as a variable. A variable defined as a number *is* a number and has all the properties of a number.

Numbers can have positive or negative values. You can create a variable that includes both positive and negative numbers, such as

```
Nuts = -5 + 15;
```

or

```
ReallyNuts = -5 + -15 + 3;
```

Integers

Integers are simply whole numbers with any decimals lobbed off. In creating variables, you do not have to declare what type of variable you are using (integer or floating point). To create integers, however, you must tell the variable that the numbers are to be treated as integers. An integer is declared as such by using the integer function. For example, to create an integer, you may write

```
whole = int(AllStuff / Parts);
```

Rounding Up

If you want to round numbers up when the decimal is .5 or greater and round them down for the rest of the values (.049 or less), you can do it using Boolean expressions. At the end of this chapter, I've included a learning utility to show you how. Remember, you have a computer that is really good at dealing with numbers, and you should make it do what you want.

The expression "AllStuff / Parts" means that the variable "AllStuff" is being divided by a variable named "Parts." No matter what the outcome of the expression, the function turns the results into an integer with the decimals deleted. Thus, a value of 17.9 is rounded down to 17. (If you had 17.84563, it also would be rounded to 17. The number of decimals after an integer has no effect on rounding.)

In a Flash movie, you frequently use integers when you script loops. (See Chapter 5 for a full discussion of loops.) Because loops are generally stepped in single units, some designers make sure that all of the steps are integers. Likewise, frame numbers are integers (there's no Frame 7.5). If you use calculated values with frame numbers, turning the outcomes into integers assures the correct frame.

Real Numbers (Floating Point)

To avoid losing those added decimals and to have greater accuracy, most programmers use real—or *floating point*—numbers. The default character of numbers in ActionScript is floating point. Also, unless an integer function is used, integers return to floating point values when further calculations are made. The following shows an example:

```
whole = int(AllStuff / Parts);
SplitWhole = whole / 7;
```

If the result of dividing the variable "whole" by 7 resulted in a fraction, the variable "SplitWhole" would include the decimal values even though "whole" and "7" are integer values.

Objects

Anything that is a collection of properties in ActionScript is considered an *object*. You can create your own objects, or you can use predefined objects. All properties have a name and a value. For example, **_rotation** is the *name* of a property that can have a positive or negative *value* between 0 and 360. Objects may also have *methods*—or actions—to perform a calculation or create a transformation. For example, previously you saw that the Boolean object **Boolean.toString()** contained a method that transformed a Boolean literal into a string. In Chapter 8, you will find a full discussion of objects, and different objects are introduced throughout the book as appropriate. Here, array objects are introduced.

Arrays

Arrays are objects containing several properties. For the general use of arrays, you can think of them as numbered variables. Each element of the array is a property with its value being the string, Boolean literal, or number equated with the array element. Each element in an array is numbered from 0 to the length of the array minus 1. A six-element array may look like the following:

```
Friends[0]="Delia";
Friends[1]="Richard";
Friends[2]="Bill";
Friends[3]="Melanie";
Friends[4]="David";
Friends[5]="Patrick";
```

To create an array, use the Array object. For example, the preceding array, "Friends," could be created with the constructor **new Array** in either of the following formats:

```
Friends=new Array("Delia", "Richard", "Bill",
    "Melanie", "David", "Patrick");
```

Alternatively, the array could have been created by typing

```
Friends=new Array(6);
```

and then designating each element as before, beginning with

```
Friends[0]="Delia";
. . . .
```

The real value of arrays is appreciated when you use a loop to enter or send data. The Array object has the methods shown in Table 2.2 associated with it.

Table 2.2 Methods associated with Array objects.

Method	Description	Example	Outcome
concat ()	Concatenates two or more arrays.	`group=friends.concat(neighbors)`	The new array "group" is made up of the array "friends" and the array "neighbors."
join( )	Array elements converted to strings and concatenated with separator.	`pair= new Array ("Joe", "Mae")` `together= pair.join(" * ")`	"together" contains the string "Joe * Mae."
length	Returns length of array with no arguments.	`trio=new Array("King", "Queen", "Prince")` `royal=length.trio`	The variable "royal" has a value of 3.
pop( )	Eliminates the last element of the array with no argument.	`landers=new Array ("Spock", "Bones", "Sulu", "Smith")` `Zapped=landers.pop()`	"Zapped" contains "Smith," and "landers" contains only Spock, Bones, and Sulu after pop action.
push( )	Adds element to the end of the array and returns new array length.	`usTwo= new Array ("Moe","Larry")` `oneMore=usTwo.push("Curly")`	The variable "oneMore" has a value of 3, and "usTwo" now contains Moe, Larry, and Curly.
reverse( )	Reverses the order of array elements.	`right= new Array("Juan", "Chuey", "Teresa")` `right.reverse()`	The array "right" now reads Teresa, Chuey, Juan.
shift( )	Eliminates the first array element and returns it.	`adios=new Array ("rap", "swing", "opera")` `digIt=adios.shift()`	After shift, "adios" contains "swing" and "opera," and "digIt" contains "rap."
slice(start, end)	Does not modify array, but takes a substring (slice) of the array beginning at "start" and up to—but not including—"end." To get all of the array after "start," leave "end" blank.	`pizza=new Array("mushrooms", "anchovies", "olives")` `piece=pizza.slice(0,2)`	Variable "piece" contains "mushrooms" and "anchovies." "Pizza" is unchanged.
sort ( )		`bakeArray=new Array("Muffins", "Bear Claws","Donuts","Pie")` `chooseEm=bakeArray.sort()`	The variable "chooseEm" contains "Bear Claws," "Donuts," "Muffins," and "Pie"—in that order.
splice(start, deleteN,v0, v1...vN)	Deletes specified number ("deleteN") of elements beginning with "start" and/or adds elements beginning with "v0" and up to "vN."	`weather=new Array("rain", "snow","sleet","tornado")` `weather.splice(3,1,"nice day")`	After the splice, the fourth element—"tornado"—(remember that the numbering begins with 0) is removed, and "nice day" is added to the array "weather" so that it contains "rain," "snow," "sleet," and "nice day."
unshift(v0)	Without removing anything, places new element at the beginning of the array and returns the new length.	`pigHouse=new Array("straw", "wood", "brick")` `a=pigHouse.unshift("steel")`	Array "pigHouse" is now "steel," "straw," "wood," and "brick"—in that order. Variable "a" = 4.

Movie Clips

The final data type in ActionScript is the movie clip. Unlike other data types, it is the only one that references a graphic. Like arrays, movie clips (MCs) have their own methods that can be used with the MovieClip object. In later chapters, as various concepts are introduced, more MovieClip objects will be introduced. MCs are more often the target of another object's action commands than they are the source for issuing an action command to another object. MCs can issue actions only to other MCs or go to a specific frame. The following are examples of MovieClip objects. In these examples, the instance name "flame" is a reference of the MC:

```
flame.gotoAndStop( 8 );
flame.gotoAndPlay(6);
flame.play();
flame.stop();
flame.nextFrame();
```

> **Note:** The most important element in an MC is its instance name. More mistakes are made in ActionScript because developers forget to include an instance name. That name need not be the same as the MC's label, but it must be included. Use the Instance Panel to put in instance names for all of your MCs as soon as you finish creating them.

Creating and Placing Variables

Now that you have an idea of the data types, you need a way to get them into an action script and use them in Flash. Flash tries to make this easy with the ActionScript Editor in the Actions panel, but variables are also associated with text fields. To show how each works, I've included an example using both types of variable placement and setting. So pull out Flash, and follow these instructions:

1. Create a new page in Flash.

2. Double-click on Layer 1, and rename it "Sales Tax."

3. Select Window|Panels|Text Options from the menu bar to bring the Text Options panel to the screen. Create a text field by selecting the Text tool from the Tools window. With the text field selected, choose "Dynamic Text" from the pulldown menu in the Text Options panel. (If the Text panel is on the screen but on a different tab, click on the Text Options tab.)

4. In the Text Options panel window, select HTML and Border/Bg checkboxes.

5. In the Variable window, type in the word "result" (without the quote marks). Congratulations. You've created a variable name associated with a text field.

Figure 2.1 shows the completed Text Options panel.

Placing a text field on the stage is a great utility and learning tool with variables. When the Flash movie runs, you can see what's going on in your action scripts by assigning different values to the text field variable (named "result" in this example). Because no ActionScript is written, the next step is to place an action script in the ActionScript Editor. (The ActionScript Editor is in the Frame/Object Actions panel.)

Figure 2.1

Naming a text field for variable input or output.

1. Click on the keyframe in Frame 1.

2. Select Window|Actions from the menu bar or Ctrl+Alt+A (Windows)/ Cmd+Option+A (Macintosh) to open the Frame Actions window and the ActionScript Editor.

3. In the left pane of the ActionScript Editor, you will see Basic Action and Actions folders, among other folders. Click on the Actions folder to open it.

4. Double-click on Set Variable from the Actions list.

5. At the bottom of the ActionScript Editor in the right panel, you will see Variable Name and Value. (See Figure 2.2.) Using the following script, set the remaining variables and their values. *All* of the values are expressions, so be sure to check the Expression checkbox to the right of the value window.

```
ItemCost = 12;
Tax = ItemCost*0.08;
result = ItemCost+Tax;
```

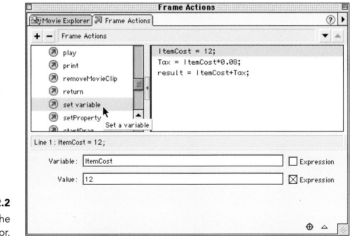

Figure 2.2
Setting variables in the ActionScript Editor.

After all of the variables and their associated values are entered, test the script. Select Control|Test Movie from the menu bar or Ctrl+Enter/Cmd+Return. Notice that one of the variable names used is the one assigned to the text field ("result"). By assigning the value of the other variables in the script to the "result" variable, the calculated outcome appears on the stage when the Flash movie runs.

Testing the ActionScript

For those who are new to programming, one of the most frustrating experiences is forgetting to put in some little character or adding the wrong character so that the program doesn't run as expected. Typos are killers in coding, so be very careful and proofread your scripts. (Experienced programmers get the same little "bugs," but they seem to do so in much more complex programs and with more ingenuity than beginners. Just remember, *people are smarter than computers*. However, *computers are always smarter than programmers*.)

First, see if you can figure out what should appear on your screen. Here's how to break it down:

- The first line places the literal 12 into the variable "ItemCost." Result = 12.

- The second line multiplies "ItemCost" (12) by .08. Result = .96.

- The third line adds the contents of line 1 to the result of line 2. Result = 12.96.

Because the text field has been assigned to display the variable "result," you should see "12.96" on your screen when you play the Flash movie. By selecting the frame you used for your script, you can double-check the script. All objects and frames that contain scripts appear in the ActionScript Editor when selected. Be careful not to select multiple objects, however, because if you do, no script appears. If the movie does not work as you expect, it is easy to see the ActionScript Editor. Figure 2.3 shows how the completed movie looks from the stage. The empty rectangle is the text field where the script shows the results. You must select Control|Test Movie or Ctrl+Enter/Cmd+Return because you cannot test it on the stage without using Test Movie.

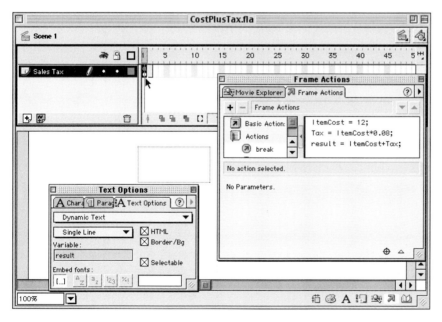

Figure 2.3
The completed movie and ActionScript in the Frame Inspector.

Global Variables

A variable has a *scope* that encompasses either the whole movie or just segments of it. Before Flash 5, the ActionScript variables were global. As long as the addressing was done correctly, you could access any variable on any level and in any scene. The same is true in Flash 5 but only with *global variables*.

Global variables are the default variables established using the Set Variable action. For example, all of the variables in the script in the previous section are global.

All timelines share global variables if the proper paths to them are referenced. A global variable buried in a button script three levels down in a hierarchy of movie clips has the same status as one in the first frame on the main timeline. Every object can affect and be affected by the changes in a global variable. When you need to coordinate several objects with information from a single variable, global variables can be very helpful. When you use the same variable name in different places, however, you can get confused about which value has been assigned the same variable. For example, a common loop variable is "i" because it has conventionally been shorthand for "increment." If the same loop variable is used in two different scripts inside the same timeline, the value of the variable may have been changed in one loop, yet it affects another loop. So, although global variables have important uses, they can also be a problem.

Local Variables

Local variables are ones declared using the **var** statement inside of a script. When a variable is declared using **var** between the curly braces ({ }) of a script, only changes within that script affect the variable's value. For example, whenever a button is used to launch a script, it creates a block of code contained within curly braces. It is possible to localize the variables in the buttons by making all of the variables in the button local. The following shows an example of a script with local variables:

```
on(release) {
var retail=50;
var wholesale=30;
var markup=(retail - wholesale);
output=markup;
}
```

Several different buttons can use the same variable names in their scripts, as can scripts in movie clips and frames. However, other than the variable "output," which is a global variable, none of the local variable's values are changed or accessed by other scripts.

Changing Values in Variables with Buttons

Changes that take place in variables can occur in hundreds, thousands, or even millions of calculations before you actually see the results of the variable on the screen. Other variable changes, such as game scores, are displayed immediately. In games, each point gained by the player is shown instantly on the screen. The following examples all use text fields as variables so that you can see the output of the ActionScript.

Because buttons can host action scripts and can be affected by user actions, buttons are dynamic sources for changing variables. The Set Variable command for a button in ActionScript is different from setting variables in frames or in text fields. When you select a Set Variable action for a button, an event handler is always included. (The full range of event handlers is discussed in Chapter 6.) Figure 2.4 shows what you see in the Actions list when you select Set Variable using a button.

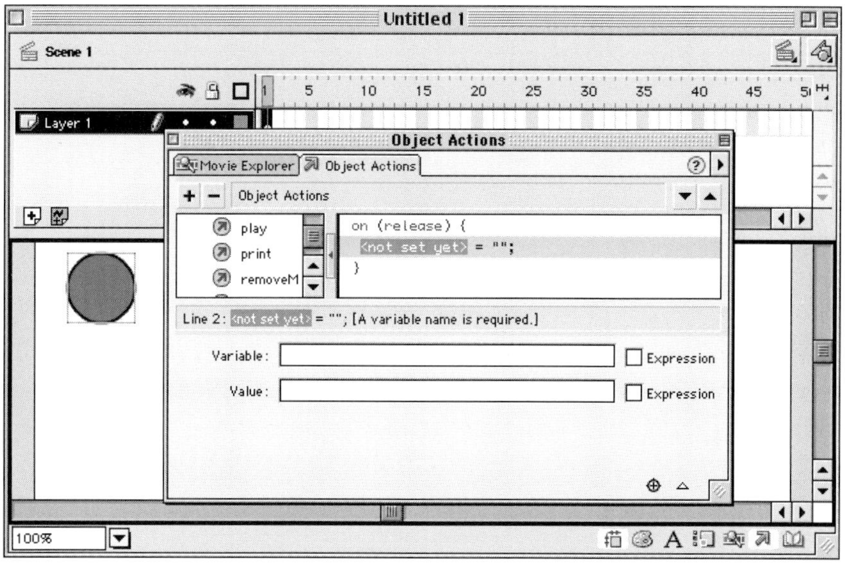

Figure 2.4

Initial ActionScript for a button when the Set Variable action is selected. Note that the event handler—**on (release)** —is automatically attached.

Buttons with Text Fields (Button I/O.fla on CD-ROM)

This movie uses scripts in three buttons to demonstrate how to manipulate data entered into a variable through text fields. The layers include the following:

- Concatenate Strings

- Add Numbers

- Test Boolean

- Output Window

- Input Windows

To see how buttons work with variables, follow these instructions to create a page and its associated ActionScript:

1. Create a single Button symbol, and name it "ChangeVariable" (you can also just borrow one from the Library).

2 Create three instances of the button, one each in these layers: Concatenate Strings, Add Numbers, and Test Boolean.

3. Add an Output Windows layer, which will contain the text fields.

4. Add an Input Window layer where users can change values and watch the results. Note that there are two input windows.

Figure 2.5 shows the stage, timeline, and all of the objects on the page. Note that each layer has only a single frame.

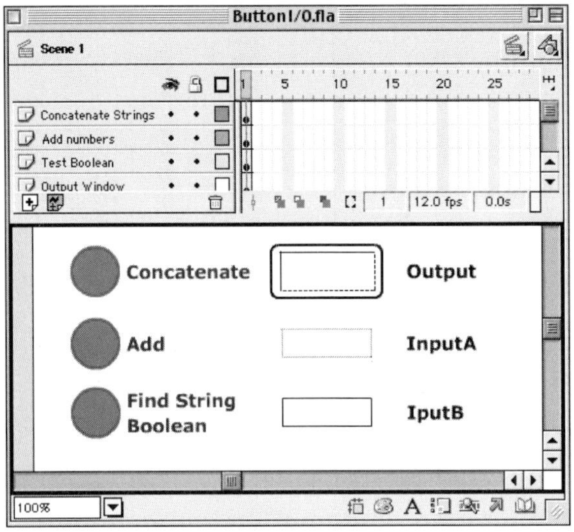

Figure 2.5

Button and text areas on the stage for testing variable changing using buttons.

Each of the three buttons uses the ActionScript Editor Set Variable action. The on (release) portion of the script is automatically added to any button script when you add the Set Variable action to the Action list in the ActionScript Editor. Follow these steps to create the scene:

1. Create a symbol by drawing a button on the stage and selecting Insert| Convert To Symbol from the menu bar or pressing F8. Alternatively, you can create a button in the Symbol Editor by selecting Insert|New Symbol from the menu bar or Ctrl+F8/Cmd+F8 and drawing the symbol in the Editor.

2. In the Symbols Properties dialog box, select Button as the behavior. Type in a name in the Name window. This example uses the name "ChangeVariable."

3. Select Window|Library or Ctrl+L/Cmd+L to open the Library window. Drag an instance of the button to the stage for each of the button layers (Change String, Change Number, and Test Boolean).

4. Select each button, and enter the ActionScript in the ActionScript Editor. If the Actions panel is not on the screen, open it by selecting Window| Actions or Ctrl+Alt+A/Cmd+Option+A. As you select each button, the script you enter automatically becomes the script associated with the selected button.

Concatenate String Layer

The Change String layer is used to create a ChangeVariable button with the following action script to demonstrate how a string variable is changed by the user input.

Button—Concatenate String (An Instance of ChangeVariable Button)

```
on (release) {
    a = inputA;
    b = inputB;
    output = a + b;
}
```

Either the **add** operator or the plus sign (+) can be used to concatenate strings. The plus operator is context sensitive so that it differentiates between numbers and strings. The action script sets the variable named "output" (the variable name given to the text field) to concatenate two strings in variables named "inputA" and "inputA" (two more variables created from text fields).

Add Numbers Layer

The Add Numbers layer is used to create a ChangeVariable button with the following action script to demonstrate how a number variable is changed by the user input.

Button—Add (An Instance of ChangeVariable Button)

```
on (release) {
    a = Number(inputA);
    b = Number(inputB);
    output = a + b;
}
```

The action script is almost identical to the Add String button except that data entered into a text field needs to be converted from text to a number using the **Number** function. You can enter a number as a string literal in variables to get the sum or some other mathematical result instead of concatenating the variables. Just use the **Number** function to change the text into real numbers. Later, you will see that using **parseInt()** and **parseFloat()** allows you to change a string or text field data into exactly the type of number, integer, or floating point, respectively. (See Chapter 4 for more details on operators.)

Test Boolean Layer

In the Test Boolean layer, the outcome of a Boolean expression is either "true" or "false." If the variable "inputA" has a larger value than that in "inputB," the output is "true." Otherwise, the output is "false." The following action script demonstrates how this works.

Button—Test Find String Boolean (An Instance of ChangeVariable Button)

```
on (release) {
    a = inputA;
    b = inputB;
    output = a> b;
}
```

If you enter a number, you can get some interesting results. For example, if you enter the value "8" in "inputA" and "10" in "inputB," the output is "true." Because 8 is *less than* 10, you may have expected an outcome of "false." However, because both values are treated as strings instead of numbers, the first value character "1" is treated as the value to be compared to the character "8." If both strings had been transformed into numbers using the **Number** function, your results would have been "false."

Output Window and Input Window Layers

The Output Window layer sets up the movie clip for displaying the outcome of a particular action script.

1. Create your text fields using the values in Table 2.3. Remember that all text field variable associations are entered in the Text Options panel (see Figure 2.1).

2. Open the Text Options panel by selecting Window|Panels|Text Options or pressing Ctrl+T/Cmd+T. Create the text fields by selecting the Text tool from Tools and selecting Input text from the top pulldown menu. Provide the variable name in the Variable window.

3. Set text alignment in the Paragraph panel. The Paragraph panel is in the same panel window as the Text Options and Character panels.

After your Flash movie is completed, select Control|Text Movie or Ctrl+Enter/Cmd+Return to see what happens. Try a number of different values including

Table 2.3 Text Options panel and names.

Variable Name	Border/Bg	Text Alignment
Output	None	Right
Input1	Yes	Right
Input2	Yes	Right

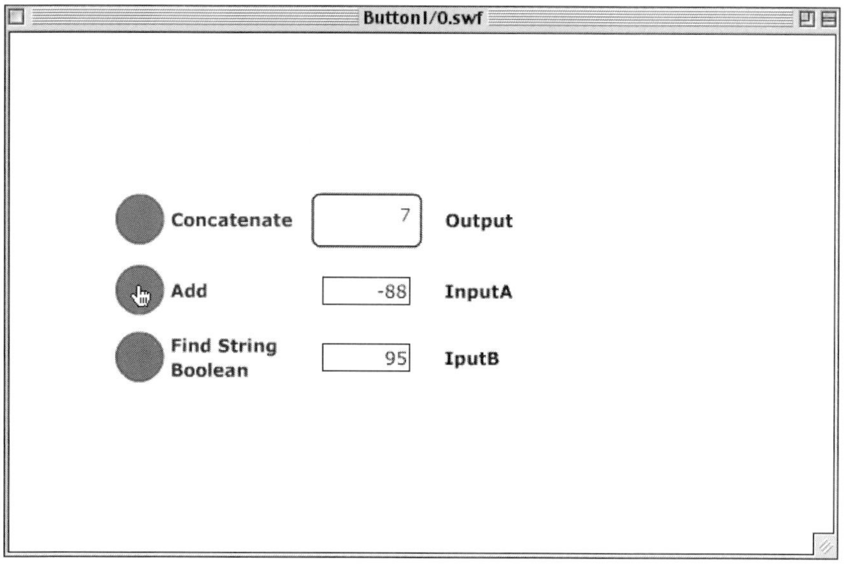

Button1/0.swf

Concatenate	7	Output
Add	-88	InputA
Find String Boolean	95	IputB

Figure 2.6
Buttons and text areas on the stage used for changing variables in the movie.

negative values. Figure 2.6 shows how it should look when it's completed and working correctly.

Try out as many different combinations as you can. For example, take the values in Figure 2.6 and select the Concatenate button. Also see what happens when you press the Test Boolean button with different values and arrangements. Remember that buttons do not contain variables; they contain the actions that set and change variables. The variables themselves are contained in the timeline. All of the variables in the example are global because none are prefaced by the **var** statement. If you have any problems with the movie, take a look at it on the CD-ROM. Open the FLA file and check the various parts.

Frames and Setting Variables

Frames can use data that is generated either by other frames or by buttons, and they can retrieve data from text fields. In the previous example that used buttons to change variables, only a single frame was needed to stress the button. In this next example, many frames are used, but no buttons. Only the frames contain action scripts, and the results are then displayed on the screen. Figure 2.7 shows the basic screen with one selected script visible in the ActionScript Editor.

String Booleans

Because Boolean expressions are one of the fundamental data types, you should learn a little more about using strings with Boolean expressions. In the previous example, the Boolean expression used the greater-than (">") operator with strings. In Flash 4, the greater-than operator worked *only* with numbers. In Flash 5 ActionScript, however, the ">" symbol works with all data types, not

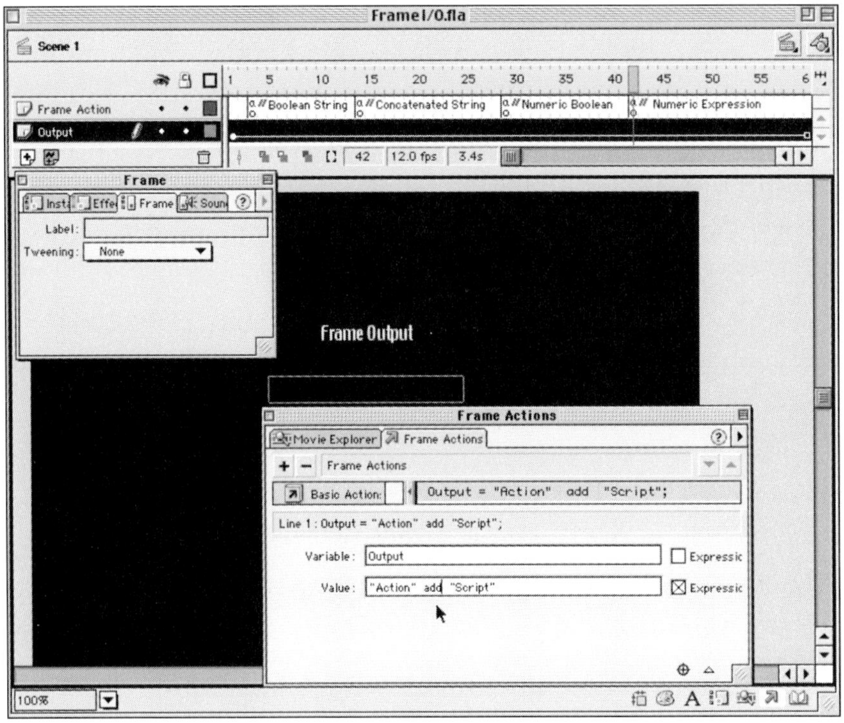

Figure 2.7

Only the frames contain action scripts. The output of those scripts is displayed in the text field on the stage.

just numbers. The exclusive string operator for "greater than" is **gt**. For example, in Flash 5,

```
"Smith" gt "Jones"
```

or

```
"Smith" > "Jones"
```

states that the value of the string "Smith" is greater than the string "Jones." Because the value of strings in Boolean expressions is based on the position of the first letter of the string in the alphabet (A = 1 and Z = 26), the string "Smith" is greater than the string "Jones." Therefore, the expression returns a value of "true," as you will see in the following example with frame action scripts.

Output Generated in Frame Scripts (Frame I/O.fla on CD-ROM)

This next script shows different output generated by frames appearing in an "output window" made up of a single text field. It contains the following layers:

- Frame Action

- Output

Each keyframe with an action script is flagged with a comment. Comments are used instead of labels because it is not necessary to address a frame label in this example. The movie simply runs through the frames to fire off the different action scripts where the keyframes are tagged with the little "a." After you have your layers in place and labeled, you are ready to enter your action script.

1. Add a layer to the existing layer. Name the top layer "Frame Action" and the lower layer "Output."

2. In the Frame Action layer, click on Frame 60. Drag the mouse pointer downward so that Frame 60 is selected in both layers.

3. Insert a frame by using Insert|Frame from the menu bar or pressing the F5 key. Both layers should now have 60 frames.

Now you're set to enter the action scripts and other movie objects.

Frame Action Layer

In the Frame Action layer, you insert the keyframes, as follows:

1. Click on the appropriate frame number and select Insert|Keyframe, or press the F6 key.

2. Double-click on the keyframe to bring up the Sound panel and Frame Actions window. Click on the Frame tab to open the Frame panel.

3. In the Label window, type in the comments indicated for each frame, preceded by double slashes (||).

4. Insert the accompanying actions in the ActionScript Editor.

Following are the comments you should enter for each frame and the script for each frame.

Boolean String (comment)—Frame 3

```
Output = "Smith" > "Jones"
```

Concatenated String (comment)—Frame 14

```
Output = "Action" + "Script"
```

Numeric Boolean—Frame 29

```
Output = -80 > 5
```

Numeric Expression—Frame 42

```
Output = 10 + -7 + 4
```

Output Layer

The Output layer contains text fields and labels for those fields, but no keyframes. However, the text fields have variable names that are used for the output data generated by each of the frame's action scripts. To enter information in this layer, put your Timeline cursor at the beginning of the timeline, and select the Output layer.

1. Select Modify|Movie, and click on the Background Color well (a small box or window) to bring up the color swatches to select a background color (black was chosen for the background in Figure 2.7). Click on the color well on the Character panel to choose a color for the text (the yellow font contrasts with the black background, as can be seen clearly in the file on the accompanying CD-ROM).

2. Select Input Text from the Text Options panel and type in the Variable name window "Output" (without the quote marks). Click on the Border/Bg checkbox.

Addressing Variables on Different Timelines

Whenever you create a new MC, you create a new timeline. Later in this book, you'll learn how to use similar path structures with Tell Target and other commands commonly used for communicating across timelines.

In Flash 4, a *slash syntax* was used to trace a path to a movie clip and its variables. Slashes were inserted after each level in a hierarchy, and the variable was preceded by a colon in the following format:

```
/mc1/mc2/:variable
```

Movie clips that are inside another timeline use a different path. For example, going up from an MC within an MC inside your main timeline would reference a variable as

```
../../:variable
```

Note: The Flash ActionScript Editor is a great tool for helping you insert your script correctly. Nevertheless, be careful when using it. All of the values in the preceding frame scripts are expressions. When you enter numbers and words in the Value window in the ActionScript Editor, be sure that you select the value as an expression by clicking the expression checkbox to the right of the Value line.

The slash syntax is still available in Flash 5, but a much better addressing system is now available—the *dot syntax*. The dot syntax will be familiar to those who work with Object-Oriented Programming (OOP) or JavaScript. For those new to scripting, I believe you will find the dot syntax simpler and more intuitively sensible. Each object has properties, which are listed following the main object in order of hierarchy. For example, if an MC contains another MC with a variable you wish to address, the path will be as follows:

```
mc1.mc2.variable
```

Instead of a colon (:) before the variable as in the slash syntax, another period or "dot" is placed to maintain consistency. Methods, functions, and properties associated with an MC may be placed in the same hierarchy. For example, using the dot syntax, you can write

```
airplane.propeller._rotation= 75
```

"Airplane" is an MC that contains another MC named "propeller." The rotation property in the propeller MC is set to a value of "75."

In moving up a hierarchy, instead of using the "../" format, you can use "_parent" for each step upward. For example,

```
_parent._parent.variable
```

moves up through the parent of the MC to its parent and to the main timeline. Generally, it is easier to address any object on the main timeline using **_root** to indicate the top level of any hierarchy. So instead of

```
_parent._parent.variable
```

the line

```
_root.variable
```

addresses the variable on the same level.

To see some working examples of addressing different timelines, the next utility MC shows how to get variables from different levels. Figures 2.8, 2.9, and 2.10 show the essentials of a main timeline that contains an MC with its own timeline.

Following Paths (DataPaths.fla on CD-ROM)

One of the most important features to understand in Flash 5 is how objects on different timelines communicate with one another. This next movie demonstrates how an MC communicates with the main timeline and vice versa. The movie contains the following layers and MCs with scripts:

- Mainline

- Movie Clip: Indie

- DataLine

- Buttons

- Output

The movie DataPaths shows how different objects in a movie use information from different timelines. An action script in a frame in an MC sets a string variable's value. A button on the main timeline contains an action script that sends the MC's value to a main timeline text field where it is then displayed on the screen. A button in the MC defines the value of a text field on the main timeline.

When the button is activated, the value appears in the same text field in the main timeline. Finally, a button on the main timeline generates a value in a text field variable on the same timeline. Each button has a different path to do essentially the same thing—use a text field to show string literals on the screen.

Mainline Layer

The Mainline layer—the top layer—is used for setting a variable in a single frame on the layer. It is also used as a starting point for creating another MC. To do this, you follow these steps:

1. Create an MC by selecting Insert|New Symbol from the menu bar and selecting Movie Clip for the behavior. Name it "indie." You are now in the Symbol Editor.

2. In the Symbol Editor, create a Button symbol with a width and height of 47 points. Name it "Mbutt."

3. Select Window|Panels|Info to open the Info panel. Select the Button Instance, type in "47" for "W" and "H" in the Info panel. Use the same technique for the other buttons in the movie. (See Figure 2.8.)

4. Create action scripts for the Button and MC frames as follows.

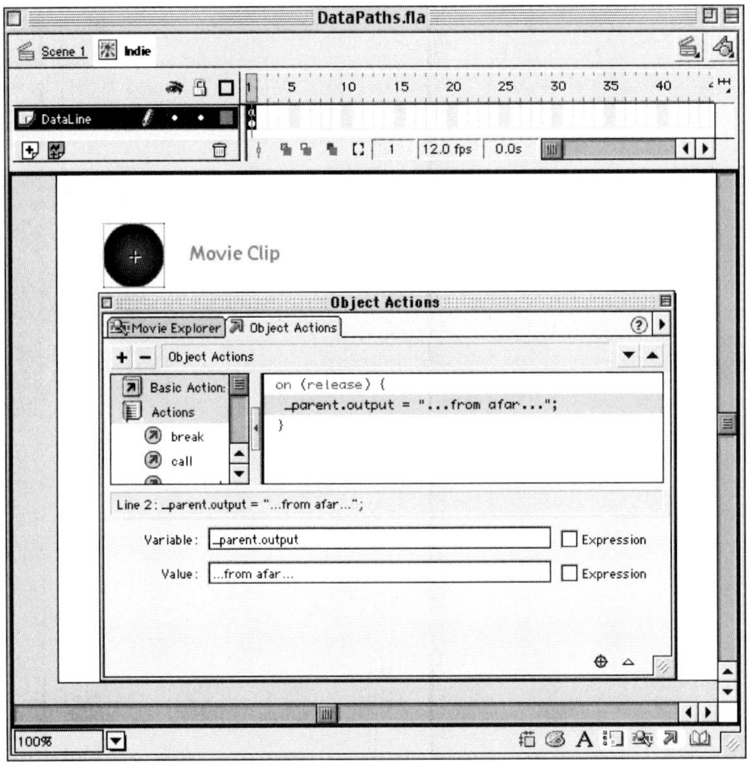

Figure 2.8
The movie clip in the Symbol Editor.

Button Indie (MC)—Mbutt

```
on (release) {
    _parent.output = "...from afar...";
}
```

Main TimeLine (Comment)—Indie (MC)—Frame1

```
iData = "Label your MC!!";
```

Main TimeLine (Comment)—Frame1

```
Data = "Main TimeLine Frame";
```

5. Click on "Scene 1" in the upper left corner to return to the main time-line. You will see the button you created as a movie clip. Select Window|Panels|Instance or Ctrl+I/Cmd+I to open the Instance panel. Enter an instance name for the MC. *This is a crucial step!* In Figure 2.9, the instance name (in the Name window) is the same as the symbol name in the Symbol column; however, they do not have to be the same. If more than a single instance of the same MC symbol is used in a movie, the symbol and instance names should *not* be the same. Click on OK to close the window and return to the main timeline.

6. Set up the frame to be used in the movie.

7. Double-check your Button and MC frames scripts, and proceed to the Buttons layer.

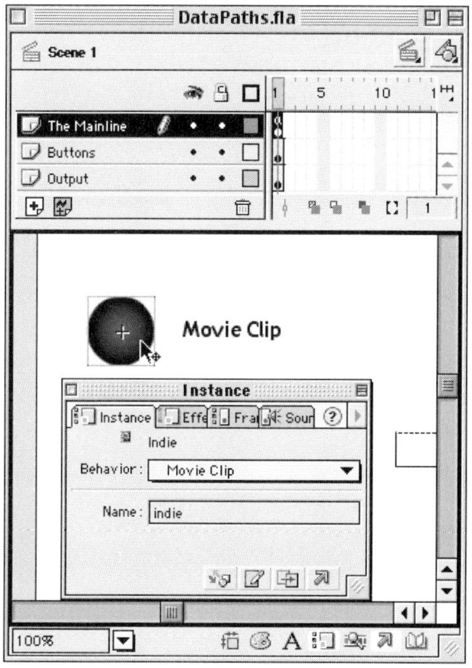

Figure 2.9
Be sure to enter an instance name for movie clips that are referenced in an action script.

Buttons Layer

As the name implies, the Buttons layer is used for the buttons on the main time-line. The first thing to do is to create two symbols with a height and width of 47 using the Info panel as described in Step 2 of the previous section. Figure 2.10 shows the completed buttons and their labels. Name one Button symbol "Main" and the other "Remote."

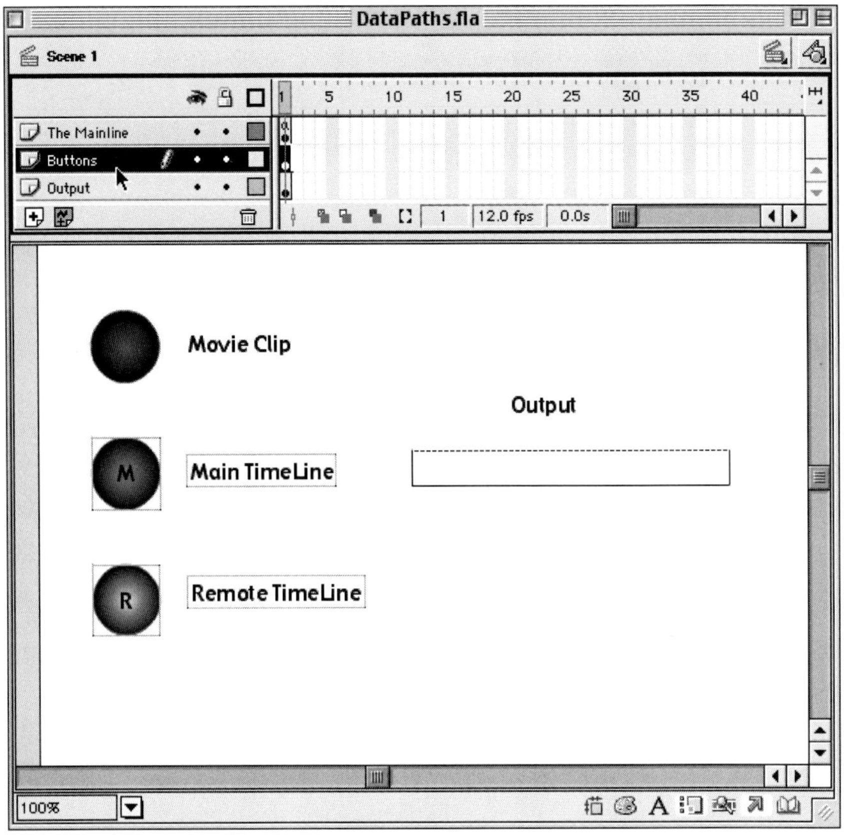

Figure 2.10
Create two additional buttons in
the Buttons layer.

Button—Main

```
on (release) {
    Output = Data;
}
```

Using the Text tool, type this label to the right of the button: "Main TimeLine".

Button—Remote

```
on (release) {
    output = indie.iData;
}
```

Using the Text tool, type this label to the right of the button: "Remote TimeLine."

Output Layer

The Output layer uses a text field with a variable association, as shown in Table 2.4.

Above the text field, set the Text Field modifier from the Toolbox to Off, and type in the label "Output." Your movie is ready to test.

When you test the movie, you will see different messages appearing in the main timeline's output window. The button in the MC announces, "From afar...," reminding you that the variable is from the timeline of the MC. Second, the button labeled "Main TimeLine" sends the Main TimeLine frame, which tells you that the data came from the script in the main timeline's frame. Finally, the Remote button displays, "Label your MC!" from a frame in the MC's timeline, not from the main timeline.

Learning Utility: Fixing the Dropped Decimals

In Chapter 4, you will be using conditional statements to make decisions in action scripts. However, one of the uses of Boolean literals is to make a comparison and take a course of action without using a conditional statement. (Of course, Boolean expressions are widely used with conditional statements as well.) The ActionScript is very short; it contains just three lines, and only one of the lines performs all of the calculations. However, you will quickly see that it does quite a bit. With it, you can round up fractions if the decimal is .5 or greater and down if it is .5 or smaller. Remember that the current **int()** function only rounds down, making 2.99 worth 2. (In Chapter 8, you will see how the Math object, using Math.round, performs the same function.) Figure 2.11 shows the completed movie stage.

Learning Utility: Make a Rounded Integer (RoundUp.fla on CD-ROM)

To see how a Boolean expression can be used to respond to different conditions, this next movie improves on the **int()** function to round a number with a decimal up or down. It contains the following two layers:

* Output

* Input

Table 2.4 Text Options panel and names.

Variable Name	Border/Bg	Text Alignment
Output	None	Right

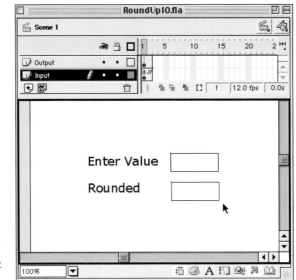

The movie itself is quite simple to set up. First, you create the Output and Input layers, using the information shown in Tables 2.5 and 2.6. From the top layer, drag your mouse down over the second frame to select both frames, and select Insert|Frame or press the F5 key. This movie needs only two frames to work.

Output Layer

Table 2.5 Output Text Options panel and names.

Variable Name	Border/Bg	Text Alignment
Output	None	Left

Input Layer

Table 2.6 Input Text Options panel and names.

Variable Name	Border/Bg	Text Alignment
Input	Yes	Left

Calculate (Comment)—Frame 1

Enter "Calculate" as a comment in Frame 1. The number of parentheses you use is very important. Every open parenthesis "("must have a closing parenthesis")."

```
fraction = Input;
whole = int(fraction);
output = whole + ((fraction-whole)>=.5);
```

After you're finished, test the movie by using Ctrl+Enter/Cmd+Return. The movie cycles fairly fast because it has only two frames, which means that the script is almost always in a steady state of refresh. Whenever you put in a number with a fraction, the script will quickly round it up or down. Here's how it does that:

1. The first line takes the first input variable, a number with a fraction entered by the user.

2. The number with a fraction is next converted into an integer, rounding fractions down.

3. The integer is added to the Boolean expression. The decimal is extracted by subtracting the integer from the original value. (The integer is always equal to or smaller than the real number—the one with the fraction— because **int()** rounds them down.) The Boolean expression states that the decimal is greater than or equal to .5. If that statement is true, the expression returns a value of "true" or "1"; if not, the result is "false" or "0." Because you just want to round up numbers with fractions of .5 or greater, the value is added only when the Boolean expression is true. Otherwise it adds a "0", and the number remains at the integer value it has when converted by the **int()** function.

OBJECT User Identity Entry and Storage for a Database (DataEntry.fla on CD-ROM)

Flash is essentially a powerful tool for making movies that can be run on the Web and that will dazzle Web surfers, but it can also be used to store information about Web surfers in a database that can be used by the Web site. Following is an example of a movie that uses buttons and text fields to take data, put it into a database that "records" on your screen—one record at a time—and clears the forms using a Reset button. It contains the following two layers:

- Buttons

- Forms

Figure 2.12 shows the basic stage with six data entry forms (text fields), two buttons, and an output database form (text field.) The Submit button takes all of the data entered and puts it into another form while slightly changing the data arrangement. To do this requires the use of the **chr(N)** function. (All of the other functions needed for ActionScript are discussed in Chapter 7.) When you need to reformat text using ActionScript, some characters have to perform a function normally accomplished by human touch. For example, when you're typing and you want to start a new line, you have to press the Enter/Return key on your keyboard. Because ActionScript can't perform this manually, it has to use the **chr(N)** function, in which N is a number. The functional code for a new line is **chr(13)**, and it is useful for putting in a line break where you want. (You can also use the "newline" statement for the

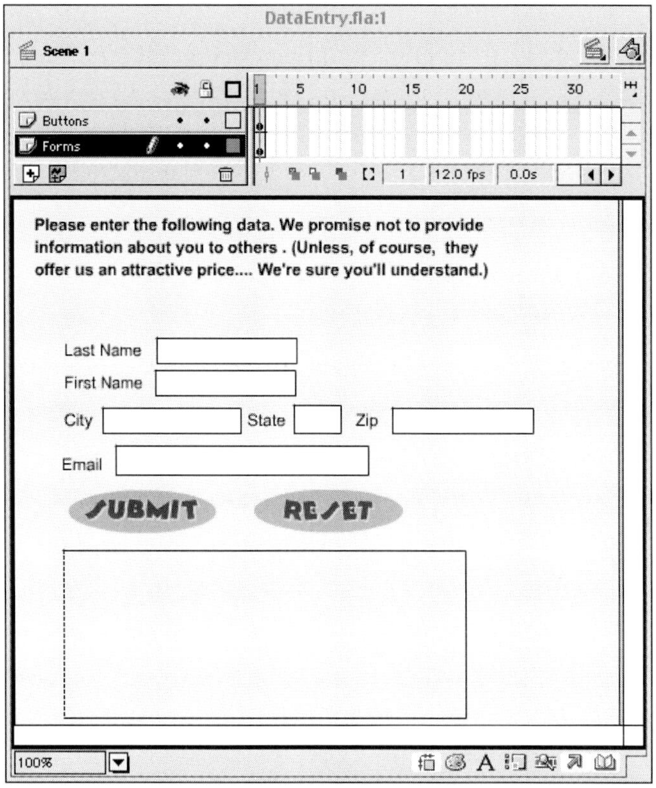

Figure 2.12
Two-layered set-up with forms and buttons for data entry.

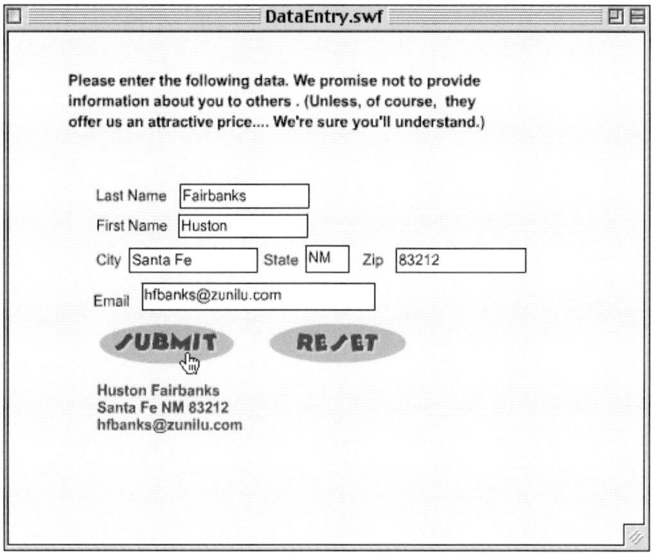

Figure 2.13
The output is rearranged for better clarity and organization.

same type of line break.) Figure 2.13 is an illustration of how a new line is inserted after the last name and the ZIP code; **chr(13)** is concatenated with the strings from the forms in the action script Submit button. The Reset button just goes through all of the forms and enters null values.

Buttons Layer

The Submit and Reset buttons do all of the scripting work for this movie. The Submit button takes the data entered in the top text fields and puts it into the bottom text field in a slightly different arrangement. The Reset button puts null values into all of the text fields to clear them out. Here is how you do this:

1. Create two buttons with the names, "Submit" and "Reset."

2. Use the Text tool to place the label on the button. First, draw an oval, and then type the label on the oval.

3. Select the drawn oval and text. Select Modify|Group from the menu bar or Ctrl+G/Cmd+G from the keyboard to group the two.

4. With the group still selected, press F8 to turn each into a symbol.

Button—Submit

The variables associated with the text fields are put into new variables. The last and first names are reversed in order and placed into the variable "name." Then the city, state, and ZIP code variables are combined in "address." The string concatenation operator "+" is used to create the larger strings stored in the new variables. Both **chr(13)** and **newline** are used to create carriage returns. Finally, the output window named "database" uses the plus sign (+) once again to concatenate the string variables and adds the email variable.

```
on (release) {
    name = fname  +  " "  +  lname  +  chr(13);
    address= city  +  " "   +  State  +  " "  +  zip  +  newline;
    database=name + address + email;
}
```

Button—Reset

Leaving the values blank in the ActionScript Editor Value window causes a null result. The following script empties the text fields by putting absolutely *nothing* in each one.

```
on (release) {
    lname = "";
    fname = "";
    city = "";
    state = "";
    zip = "";
    email = "";
    database = "";
}
```

Forms Layer

The text fields in the Forms layer are very straightforward. Each has a variable name approximating its association with the data. Every text field except the database field contains a Border/Bg so that a user can enter the data. When I created the database text field in Table 2.7, I selected a bold dark brown font, just to give the output a different character. You can make your text field a unique color by selecting a color from the Character panel when you begin to create the text field. For all of the text fields where you have the user enter data, always use the Input Text format selected in the Text Options panel. When you place labels next to the text fields, be sure to select Static Text in the Text Options panel.

Table 2.7 Database text fields.

Variable Name	Border/Bg	Text Alignment
Lname	Yes	Left
Fname	Yes	Left
City	Yes	Left

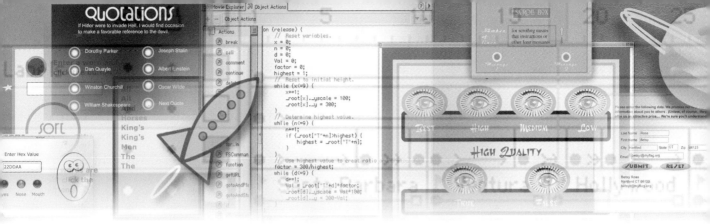

Chapter 3

Basic Actions

This chapter provides an overview of basic actions in ActionScript. A summary of each action is given, together with an example of how the action may be employed. The primary focus of this chapter is how to integrate ActionScript with Flash movie objects.

Half Flash and Half ActionScript

The true essence of using ActionScript is to integrate it thoughtfully into a Flash movie. You could spend several hours working out a tweening path using ActionScript, but the tweening tools in Flash are far more effective and easier to use. By the same token, you are much better off using ActionScript than creating a convoluted workaround in a Flash movie. Using action scripts in Flash movies makes sense when the best features of ActionScript complement the other elements of the movie. In this book, the Flash movies are a combination of standard Flash objects integrated with ActionScript. This chapter covers an essential feature of that combination.

Chapter 2 explained how variables are used in text fields, button scripts, and frame scripts. It also discussed the use of descriptive comments in keyframes to help designers easily understand what the frame scripts contain. This chapter stresses the importance of labeling frames for controlling the timeline of a Flash movie. Each component of the movie can control other components by starting and stopping the actions in the frames, and a simple task such as labeling a frame is part of an orchestrated plan in your movie. ActionScript in both buttons and frames can fire off or halt actions in the Flash movie; therefore, part of the preparation for an effective movie is planning how and what your action scripts will impact.

Setting Up and Labeling Frames for ActionScript

Imagine a highway map that uses only numbers instead of names. Instead of using "Omaha, Nebraska," the sign just reads, "To 23421." Pretty confusing, isn't it? By the same token, frames in ActionScript need to be clearly labeled in order to use them effectively. Instead of being directed to "Frame 7" (a perfectly legitimate assignment), it's far easier to find a frame that is labeled "Right," "Wrong," or "Is that your final answer?"

Here's how you label a frame:

1. Select the frame you want to label by clicking on it. It will turn black.

2. Select Modify|Frame, double-click on the frame, or press Ctrl+F (Windows)/Cmd+F (Macintosh) to open the Frame panel.

3. In the Label window, type in the label you want to use and click on OK. Figure 3.1 shows a labeled frame.

Figure 3.1

Labeling a frame.

In Chapter 2, you saw how to put comments on frames, but you cannot use comments as targets for action scripts. If you do not label a frame, you can still use its frame number as your target, but then your frame roadmap is like the highway map where the city names have been replaced by numbers. It's still functional, but it is far more difficult to remember where you're going. In developing a movie, you will find that frames may shift to different numbers when you insert new frames or keyframes. For example, Frame 20 may become Frame 27. If you use labels as targets, however, you can do all the shifting you want, and it will not affect the target frame.

Go To and Stop or Play (SBLimit.fla on CD-ROM)

This next example uses the following layers:

- Buttons N Labels
- Train
- Smoke
- Track
- Headline
- Backdrop

Two of the most important actions in Flash are the **gotoAndPlay** and **gotoAndStop** actions. Because Flash is built around a timeline, the ability to move to different positions in the timeline lets the designer establish action scripts in any frame and then direct the movie to any of the scripts when the conditions warrant. The two actions are limited and easy to use and understand.

- **gotoAndStop** ("**FrameName**" or **Number**)—The ActionScript directs the movie to go to a specified frame and to halt until the movie receives a Play command. When you select Go To from the Basic Action menu, the default script is

  ```
  gotoAndPlay (1);
  ```

  To change from the default **gotoAndPlay**, you must click on the Go to and Play checkbox at the bottom of ActionScript Editor with the script selected. When the checkbox is blank, the script automatically changes to **gotoAndStop**.

- **gotoAndPlay** ("**FrameName**" or **Number**)—The ActionScript directs the movie to a specified frame and plays whatever is in the frame. If no action scripts are in the frame, the movie keeps on playing.

To illustrate how Go To works, I made a simple Flash movie that shows a train on a trip from Santa Barbara to San Diego. Each of the stops is a frame, and buttons simply tell the train to go to the different stops. Figure 3.2 shows the movie's layers, and Figure 3.3 shows the stage for the movie.

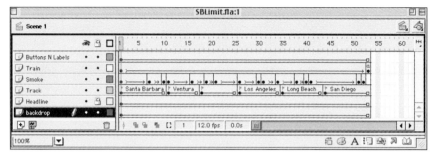

Figure 3.2
The labels on the Track layer are
used in Go To actions.

Figure 3.3
A Flash movie with Stop actions
in the frames and Go to and Stop
actions in the buttons.

The train faces the viewer, and, as the timeline begins, the train is a little speck
in the background. As the timeline comes closer to San Diego, the image (a
graphic symbol) gets bigger. The Smoke layer provides some animated smoke.
The R/R button at the bottom center of the stage simply contains a Play action
to start the timeline again after a Stop action in the last frame of the Train
layer. Each of the city buttons contains a script to Go to and Stop at the cities
represented on the buttons and frames. Figure 3.4 shows the generic script for
all of the city buttons. (Note that the label is from the Frame Properties dialog
box in Figure 3.1.)

Layers

First, provide a backdrop consisting of a block of color and/or scenery. Next,
drop in the headline, "Santa Barbara Limited" using a graphic. Both layers

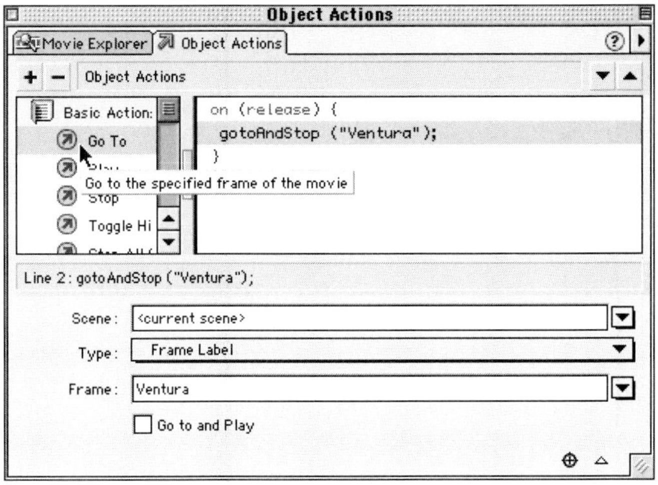

Figure 3.4
A pulldown menu on the right side of the Frame window shows the names of all labeled key-frames. Note the Go to and Play checkbox on the bottom of the panel is not checked.

should extend out to 53 frames, so click on Frame 53 and press the F5 key. The Track layer must be done next. All of the labeled keyframes you will be using are in this layer. When inserting Go To actions in the buttons, as shown in Figure 3.4, the pulldown menu with the frame labels must be in place. Insert the keyframes about every 10 frames so that the labels can be seen on the timeline. None of the frames on the Track layer have action scripts.

In the Buttons N Labels track, create six city buttons and a single R/R button, as follows:

1. Create a separate city button drawing for each of the cities. Draw a single button and copy it five times.

2. Label each button with the city name, and select Modify|Group from the menu bar or press Ctrl+G/Cmd+G on the keyboard.

3. Select each button drawing and convert it into a button symbol by selecting Insert|Convert To Symbol on the menu bar or by pressing the F8 key and selecting Button as the behavior in the Symbol Properties dialog box.

4. Select a button and click the Show Object Actions icon on the lower right of the stage to open the Object Actions panel or Ctrl+Alt+A/ Cmd+Option+A.

5. In the Basic Action folder, select Go To at the very top of the selections by double-clicking on it.

6. When you select Go To, the default is **gotoAndPlay(1)**. To change that to **gotoAndStop(1)**, click the Go to and Play checkbox at the bottom on the ActionScript Editor.

7. In the Type pulldown menu in the ActionScript Editor, select Frame Label. Below the Type pulldown menu, open the Frame pulldown menu where you should see the name of all of the labeled frames. Select the frame name to match the city name on the selected button. Repeat this process with all six city buttons.

8. Create another button with the R/R symbol on it. Select the button, and open the ActionScript Editor. Double-click on Play in the Basic Actions folder in the Actions menu. The **play( )** action has no arguments, so you do not have to do anything else. Also note that you are automatically provided with ActionScript code to initiate the play action when the button is pressed. (That's the **on(release)** code.)

9. Finally, draw a train track relative to the size of the smallest and largest train representation. You may want to take a close look at the movie on the accompanying CD-ROM to get an idea of how to create the perspective.

The Train layer contains both an animated train and the tracks. The train—a graphic symbol—is made from a graphic in a font-set. The last frame of the layer contains ActionScript. Here's how you do this:

1. Insert a layer by clicking on the Add Layer button in the Layer list.

2. Insert a frame in Position 54 of the timeline by clicking on the frame position and selecting Insert|Frame or pressing the F5 key.

3. Place the playhead in the first frame. To get the image of the train, either create a drawing and convert it into a graphic symbol or transform a train image font into a symbol. (Just select the font or drawing and choose Insert|Convert To Symbol from the menu bar or press F8.)

4. Move the playhead to the last frame, and insert a keyframe by choosing Insert|Keyframe or pressing the F6 key.

5. Leave the playhead in the last frame and select the keyframe. Open the ActionScript Editor by clicking the Open Actions Panel button in the lower right side of the stage. In the Basic Actions folder, double-click on Stop to insert a stop action in the frame.

6. Select Window|Panel|Info to open the Info panel. Select the train symbol and increase the "W" and "H" values by a factor of 10. (Just remove the decimal points for a quick tenfold increase.) The train should now be 10 times larger than it was originally.

7. Move the playhead to Frame 1 and double click on the frame. The Sound panel opens. Click on the Frame tab to open the Frame panel or

use Ctrl+F/Cmd+F. In the Frame panel, select Motion from the pulldown Tweening menu. You should now see a smooth, animated size change from the original image.

8. To make the tracks, place the playhead in the last frame. Mark the position of where the tracks should go (at the edges of the cowcatcher), and then move the playhead to the first frame. Draw track lines from the train image in the first frame to the marks you made in the last frame. Finally, draw the ties across the track (see Figure 3.2). Look at the FLA file on the CD-ROM as well to get a better picture of the tracks.

The Smoke layer contains an animated smoke plume in a movie clip (MC). You insert it as follows:

1. Select Insert|New Symbol... from the menu bar, or press Ctrl+F8/ Cmd+F8. In the Symbol Properties dialog box, select Movie Clip as the behavior and name your new MC.

2. Create the MC so that the size of the smoke plume is proportional to the train in Frame 1. Animate the smoke plume by using three or four keyframes and redrawings of the smoke image. Use the magnifier while doing this because the size of the plume in Frame 1 is fairly small.

3. Insert a Smoke layer, and drag the smoke MC to the stage in Frame 1 from the Library window. Once you are finished, click on the Scene 1 icon in the upper left corner in order to exit the symbol editing mode.

4. Insert a keyframe into the last frame by selecting Insert|Keyframe from the menu bar or pressing F8. Move the playhead to the last frame.

5. Enlarge the smoke MC to a size proportional to the train in the last frame, and position it relative to the train's smokestack.

6. Double-click on the first frame to call up the Frame Properties dialog box. Select the Tweening tab.

7. In the Tweening menu, select Motion, and click on OK to tween the small to large smoke plume. In the example on the CD-ROM, several tweens and loop changes are made to provide a more natural smoke, but a single tween using the MC belching smoke will do the job.

Your movie will now show a train off in the distance that rushes forward and then stops in the size indicated for the last frame in the timeline. (See Figure 3.5.) By pressing any of the buttons, the ActionScript changes the size of the train and smoke symbols to a "distance" relative to where the "city" is on the timeline. This ActionScript is quite simple, but it illustrates the relationship between the objects in the Flash movie and how action scripts can be created to control the objects.

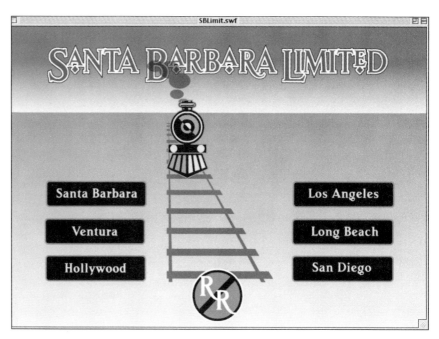

Figure 3.5
The button's ActionScript that moves the train to different labeled frames also controls the completed movie.

Play

Occasionally, an ActionScript may use both Stop and Play actions, which contradict each other. For example, what happens if a movie includes a **gotoAndStop** action to a frame that has a **Play()** script? Will it stop or keep on truckin'? Conversely, what occurs when a **gotoAndPlay** action goes to a frame with a **Stop()** action? Will a **gotoAndStop** action cause the movie to stop at a frame with another Go To action, or will it go where the target frame's action commands? In a nutshell, here's the rule: *Any Go To action automatically executes the action in the target frame.* This means *any* Go To action—whether it is a Stop or a Play action. This can be a little tricky because you may want the action to go to a certain frame and stop there until a Play action is fired. If the target frame has its own action script, however, that action script will be executed no matter what. So if you Go To and Play a Frame with a Stop action, the movie stops. Likewise, if you use a **gotoAndStop** action at a Frame with a Play action, the movie just keeps on going.

This next movie is designed to show you what happens with different frame conditions using the Go To action.

Stop or Play and Buttons (StopAtPlay.fla on CD-ROM)

This next movie shows the effects of scripts in frames and stop or play commands associated with Go To actions. The two layers in this movie are:

- Stop or Play

- Buttons

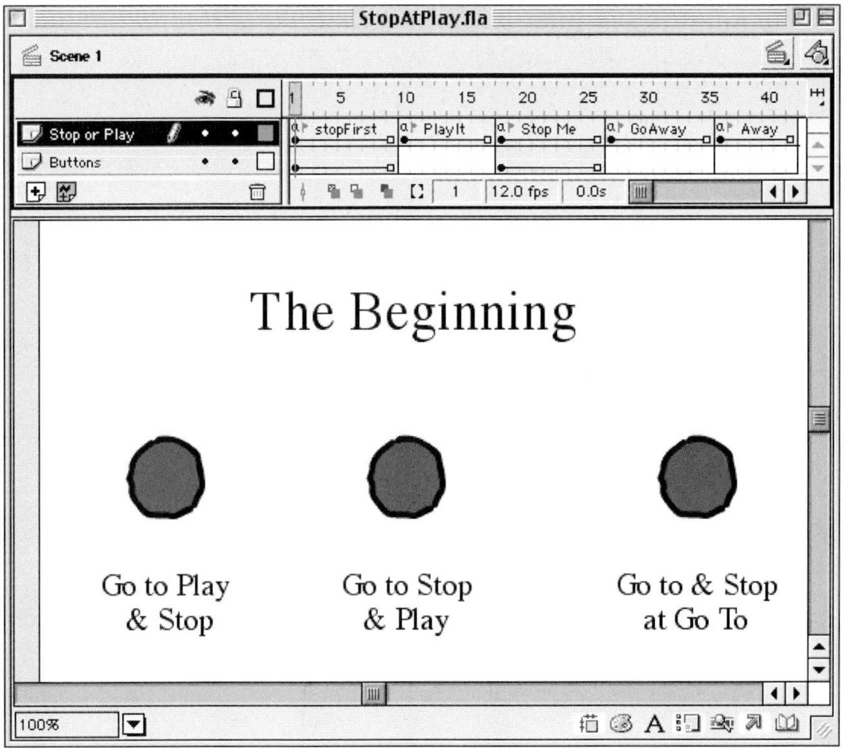

Figure 3.6
The primary buttons for the movie are at the beginning of the movie. Watch carefully what happens when each button is pressed.

The Stop or Play layer contains five keyframes with actions. Each is labeled as shown in Figure 3.6.

Stop or Play Layer

On the first layer, the keyframes are labeled as indicated and contain a text message added at the keyframe. The following labels and messages are used in the frames.

Frame 1—stopFirst (label)

Put a text message on the page that reads, "The Beginning."

```
stop();
```

Frame 10—PlayIt (label)

The message on the page is "This is the Play Place."

```
play();
```

Frame 18—Stop Me (label)

The message on the page is "You are stopped."

```
stop();
```

Frame 27—GoAway (label)

The message on the page is "Go Away!"

```
gotoAndPlay ("Away");
```

Frame 36—Away (label)

The message on the page is "Away."

```
stop();
```

Buttons Layer

Buttons are organized by the frame grouping. The buttons in Figure 3.6 are all identified by a functional label beneath each button and are referenced as such. The first frame (stopFirst) has three instances of a button symbol named ButtonUp:

GotoAndPlay & Stop

```
on (release) {
    gotoAndStop ("PlayIt");
}
```

GotoAndStop & Play

```
on(release) {
    gotoAndPlay ("StopMe");
}
```

GotoAndStopat Go To

```
on(release) {
    gotoAndStop ("GoAway");
}
```

The buttons in the Stop Me and Away frames are additional instances of the ButtonUp symbol. They simply contain a Play action and are labeled "Click to continue."

Click to continue

```
on (release) {
    play ();
}
```

Watch carefully when you run this movie. Scrutinize the movie as the message that begins in the PlayIt frame coasts by until the movie reaches the Stop Me keyframe. (Select the Go to & Play button.) However, you will never see the message "Go Away!" (see Figure 3.7). Why is it clearly in the movie, but never viewed?

To solve the mystery of the missing message, consider the ActionScript in the Go Away frame:

```
gotoAndPlay ("Away");
```

As soon as the movie encounters the keyframe with the ActionScript, it executes the action command and never stops to display the frame itself. As a result, when the sample movie encounters Go to and Play ("Away") in the Go Away frame, it immediately jumps past the frames that display the "Go Away!" message.

Back and Forth between Frames and Scenes

Besides going to a specified frame by number or label, you may also write script that sends your movie one frame ahead or back. In the previous section, you saw how movies that jumped to a frame would either play or stop. If no script is in a frame when a Go to and Play action is issued, the movie keeps playing. If a Go to and Stop action is selected, the movie stops. However, no matter whether the action is Stop or Play, any action script in a frame is initiated by a go to that frame.

Next and Previous Frames

This next set of actions goes just one frame forward or backward and stops. In most respects, these action targets are like a **gotoAndStop** statement. Unless script is in the frame, the movie stops. Because this action moves the playhead one frame either forward or backward, regardless of whether it's a keyframe or not, unlabeled frames can be navigated relative to a timeline instead of to a specific frame number or label. The action itself is quite simple and unique in that no "Go To" of any kind is mentioned. For example, in the following button script, the command to go to the previous frame specifies only the target:

```
on(release) {
    prevFrame ();
}
```

The script for going to the next frame is equally simple:

```
nextFrame();
```

Either action can be used in an MC, button, or frame. Using this in a frame without a conditional statement probably would not have a purpose. With conditional statements, however, moving one frame forward or backward could be very useful.

Next and Previous Scenes

ActionScript also contains a set of targets to the next or previous scene. The action statements are almost identical to those for frames, but the next or previous scene constitutes the targets. A move to the next scene in a button script would look like the following:

```
on(release) {
    nextScene ();
}
```

Going to a scene where the movie had just been uses a similar statement:

```
prevScene ();
```

Going to another scene has interesting consequences. If you go frame by frame, the first frame number of the new scene is 1 plus the frame number of the previous scene. For example, if the last frame in Scene 1 is 30, the first frame in Scene 2 will be 31 and can be referenced as such. So the statement,

```
gotoAndPlay(31)
```

would go and play Frame 1 of Scene 2. You could also use the statement,

```
gotoAndPlay("Scene 2",1)
```

to go to the same frame. Obviously, it is much easier to go to the first frame of the next scene using the **nextScene()** action.

Frame labels are accessible across scenes anywhere in the main timeline. Flash will search all scenes in the main timeline to find the one referenced in an action script. Suppose you have 15 different scenes, and you keep score at Frame 27 in Scene 11. Remembering the address "Scene 11", "Frame 27" can be very confusing, but a labeled frame named "Score" is easy to find from any scene and any frame in the movie. This next movie shows the different ways to move backward and forward through two scenes along with their frames. It also shows the many ways to target a specific frame in a different scene.

Finding the Frame and Scene (FrameScene.fla on CD-ROM)

This movie has two scenes. The first scene contains two layers, and the second scene contains one layer, as follows:

- Output (Scene 1)

- Buttons (Scene 1)

- Copy Here (Scene 2)

Output Layer (Scene 1)

For both the Output and the Buttons layers, first place a frame at Frame 15 to bring both layers out to the fifteenth frame. Most of the scripts are on the buttons, but the Output layer has a Stop script in Frame 1.

```
Stop();
```

Place a text field large enough for two digits next to a Frame Number label, as shown in Figure 3.8. Select Input Text from the drop-down menu in the Text Options panel to set the field, and type the variable name, "output," in the variable name window. Table 3.1 shows the specifications for the text field.

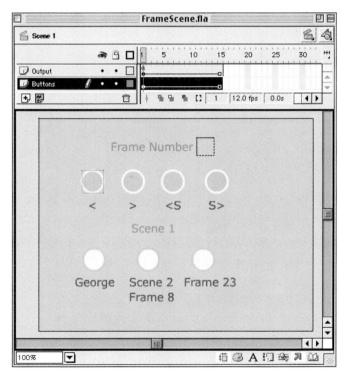

Figure 3.8

Scene 1 contains buttons for moving back and forth between frames and scenes.

Table 3.1 Text field properties.

Variable Name	Border/Bg	Text Alignment
output	No	Right

Buttons Layer (Scene 1)

The bulk of the movie is in the Buttons layer. The first line of buttons will be copied and pasted in the second scene. Each button is labeled with a symbol to simulate direction and scene movement.

Button(<)

All of the buttons contain local variable codes to show the current frame. Using **_root**, any frame on the main timeline in any scene is displayed as a value relative to the first frame in the first scene. The **_currentframe** property returns the current frame of a specified MC or the main timeline through **_root**. Whenever you move the frame, therefore, you can see it in the text field "window." The (<) button moves to the previous frame.

```
on(release) {
    prevFrame ();
    var a = _root._currentframe;
    output = a;
}
```

Button(<S)

Move to the previous scene.

```
on(release) {
    prevScene ();
    var a = _root._currentframe;
    output = a;
}
```

Button(S>)

Move to the next scene.

```
on(release) {
    nextScene ();
    var    a=_root._currentframe;
    output = a;
}
```

Button(George)

Move to a frame named "George." Note that there is no reference to a scene, even though the frame "George" is in the second scene.

```
on(release) {
    gotoAndPlay ("George");
    a = _root._currentframe;
    output = a;
}
```

Button(Scene 2 Frame 8)

Move to the eighth frame in the second scene. This address will also end up at the "George" frame. Because the scene number is specified, the frame number is the absolute one for that scene rather than one relative to the beginning of the movie.

```
on(release) {
    gotoAndPlay ("Scene 2",8);
    a=_root._currentframe;
    output=a;
}
```

Button(Frame 23)

Move to Frame 23. Without specifying a scene number or a label name, one other way to go to "George" in Frame 8 of Scene 2 is to specify the value returned by the current frame property, which counts from Frame 1 in Scene 1 through subsequent scenes.

```
on(release) { {
    gotoAndPlay (23);
    a=_root._currentframe;
    output=a;
}
```

Copy Here Layer (Scene 2)

Scene 2 has been created to demonstrate navigation between scenes and is very simple, as shown in Figure 3.9.

Scene 2 is easy to make because most of it is a cut and paste from Scene 1. Follow these steps:

1. From the menu bar, select Insert|Scene. It is automatically named "Scene 2" and has the same movie dimensions as the first scene, including stage size and background color.

2. Select the Pointer tool from the Toolbox, and drag it around the four top buttons, their labels, the output window, and the label above it. Select Edit|Copy from the menu bar or use Ctrl+C/Cmd+C.

3. In the upper right corner of the stage, click on the Clapper box icon to change to Scene 2.

4. Click on Frame 15, and press the F5 key to bring the first layer out to 15 frames. Rename the layer "Copy Here."

5. Select Edit|Paste In Place to put the copied material from Scene 1 into Scene 2. Add a label to the bottom of the stage so you'll know you're in Scene 2.

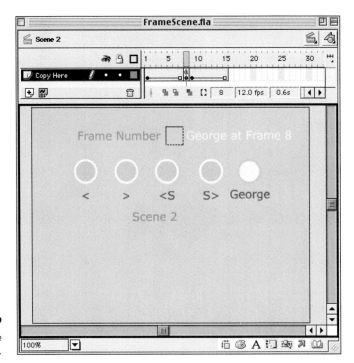

Figure 3.9
Scene 2 has most of the
characteristics as Scene 1.

6. Add a keyframe at Frame 8. Type in "George at Frame 8" with the Text tool next to the text field as shown in Figure 3.9. Add a stop script in the frame:

```
stop();
```

7. Add a keyframe in Frame 9, and delete "George at Frame 8." This eliminates the message from appearing anywhere except when the timeline is at Frame 8 of Scene 2.

8. Add a button with the label "George" next to the four transferred from Scene 1.

```
on(release) {
    gotoAndPlay ("Scene 2", "George");
    a=_root._currentframe;
    output=a;
}
```

Because this movie is primarily instructional in nature, use it to help answer questions about how to use different ActionScript actions to navigate between scenes and frames. Experiment with it and try out different combinations to see what happens.

Targeting Frames on Different Timelines

Going to frames on the same timeline, even in different scenes, is relatively easy. However, going from one timeline to another, although not difficult, requires a bit more thought and planning. Movie clips have their own timelines, and to make an MC go to a certain frame you need to address the MC by its *instance name* and path. To have a movie on a different timeline go to and play or stop at a given frame, precede the action by the object's path. An MC can be ordered to go to and play or stop on any of its own frames on its timeline. For example, the following script tells the MC that has the instance name "driver" to go to a frame called "Starting Line" and begin playing.

```
_root.driver.gotoAndPlay("Starting Line")
```

This next movie shows how three different buttons on the main timeline can tell an MC to go to different frames—by name or by number—and begin playing after being stopped. Remember that if the main timeline is stopped, any MC may still play, and the buttons are on one timeline and the MC on another.

Controlling Different Timelines (PlayAway.fla on CD-ROM)

This next movie has buttons that control a bouncing ball on a different timeline. Only two layers are in the movie—one on the main timeline and one in the MC.

- MainTimeLine
- Bouncer (MC)

The movie is fairly simple, with three buttons on the MainTimeLine layer and an MC with the Bouncer layer. You will make an MC that has a bouncing ball created with tweening frames, put the MC on the main timeline, and then create three buttons that can place the ball where directed on the MC timeline. Figure 3.10 shows the main stage, and Figure 3.11 shows the MC in the Symbol Editor.

Bouncer (MC)

The movie and MC are both simple ways to illustrate how ActionScript works with addressing objects on different timelines.

1. Open a new movie, and select Insert|New Symbol from the menu bar. Select Movie Clip in the Symbol Properties dialog box and name it "Bounce." Click on OK to enter the Symbol Editor.

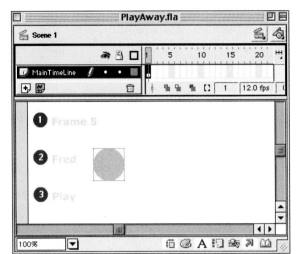

Figure 3.10

The main stage with the buttons containing script to control the MC, also shown.

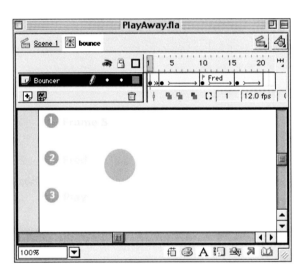

Figure 3.11

The MC in the Symbol Editor. Note the keyframe labeled "Fred" and the tweening symbols in the timeline.

2. In the Symbol Editor, draw a ball using the Oval tool from the Toolbox. Click Frame 20, and press F5 to bring the layer out 20 frames. Rename the layer "Bouncer."

3. Insert three keyframes in Frames 3, 10, and 15. Move the playhead to the first frame.

4. Click on the keyframes, and move the ball to a different position for each keyframe.

5. Click on Frame 1, and open the Frame panel by selecting Window| Panels|Frame from the menu bar. In the Frame panel, select Shape from the Tweening pulldown menu. Blend should be Distributive and Ease = 0 on the Frame panel. Repeat the same process for the other keyframes. Test the MC to make sure the ball moves when the movie runs.

MainTimeLine Layer

Return to the main timeline by clicking the Scene 1 icon in the upper left corner. Next, drag an instance of the "Bounce" MC to the stage. Position it as shown in Figures 3.10 and 3.11. Select the MC, and open the Instance panel by selecting Window|Panels|Instance or Ctrl+I/Cmd+I. In the Instance Name window, type in the name "ball" (without the quote marks). You will use this instance name in all of your references.

Next, you need to create three buttons. In the example, I used three buttons from the Buttons.fla common library—"Go to 1," "Go to 2," and "Go to 3." I then made changes in the Symbol Editor to change the labels to "Frame 5," "Fred," and "Play." (Just double-click on each original button and make the changes in the Symbol Editor.)

Button (Frame 5)

The first button simply sends the MC to Frame 5. The path, beginning at the main timeline, identifies the MC by its instance name and then specifies the action.

```
on(release) {
    _root.ball.gotoAndStop(5);
}
```

Button (Fred)

The second button simply demonstrates that remote timelines can be easily used with labeled frames.

```
on(release) {
    _root.ball.gotoAndStop("Fred");
}
```

Button (Play)

The final button resumes the action on the remote timeline after it has been stopped by either of the first two buttons.

```
on(release) {
    _root.ball.play ();
}
```

Going to and playing or stopping remote timelines is much easier in Flash 5 than in Flash 4. As you will see in later chapters, and as you saw to some extent in Chapter 1, the format of Object-Oriented Programming makes it very easy to find a path and issue an action to other timelines.

Actions from an External Script

If you have certain code that you use repeatedly in scripts, I suggest that you write it once and then access it whenever you want to use it in a script. You can write ActionScript code in any text editor, such as Note Pad (Windows) or Simple

Text (Macintosh.) For example, you may have an especially complicated sorting routine that you've written in ActionScript, and you don't want to have to rewrite it every time you want to use it in a movie. Flash 5 introduces the **include** action that can be used to open a script written in an external text file. The format is fairly straightforward. For example, the following button script opens a text file named "remote.as." (The ".as" extension is recommended but not necessary.)

```
on(release) {
    #include "remote.as"
}
```

The path to the external file is the same as for any URL. In the preceding example, because the external file is stored in the same directory as the SWF (Shockwave Flash) file, no special directory list needs to be included.

In using the **include** statement in a button or MC script, do not include an event handler in the external text file. Any event handler, such as **on(release)**, brings in the code itself from the text file and launches it. An additional event handler negates any action from taking place. For example, if you wanted a button to send the movie to a frame named "Score," you would put the following in the text file and nothing more:

```
gotoAndStop("Score");
```

The button script would have just the event handler and the **include** action to call the text file with the script in it.

Learning Utility: Two Languages, One Layer, and One Timeline

Using ActionScript to control the position of the playhead on the timeline enables you to be in complete charge of your movie. The following project is a learning utility to see how much hopscotching can be done on a single layer in a timeline. The project is a children's number-learning game in both English and Spanish. The purpose of the game is to learn to count in two different languages. Because I am bilingual in Spanish and English (but only up to the number 5), this project fits my linguistic talents perfectly.

The user selects whether to count in Spanish or English. The word for the number appears in the left text field, and the number itself is in the right. The user first selects one of two buttons. As the movie continues, a third button appears on the stage that allows the user to jump to the next number in the selected language. (Yes, grouping all the frames of the same language would have been easier and more sensible, but the purpose of this movie is to demonstrate the ability of ActionScript to control all aspects of the movie.)

Figure 3.12 shows the start page layout of the stage along with the necessary layers and most of the labels in the frames.

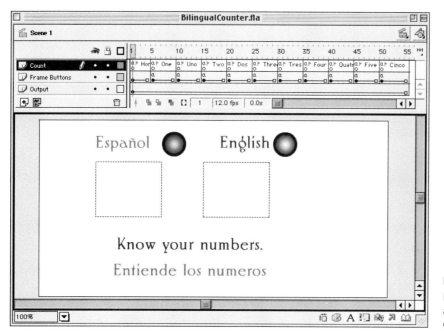

Figure 3.12
Layer and foundation layout for alternating the keyframe advance on the timeline.

PROJECT Learning Utility: Counting Game (BilingualCounter.fla on CD-ROM)

This learning utility shows how two different paths may be taken in a movie; one path is in English, and the other is in Spanish. Three layers are used:

- Count

- Frame Buttons

- Output

Count Layer

The Count layer has a series of keyframes that place variables into the two text fields. To use them, do the following:

1. Click on Frame 55, and insert a frame by selecting Insert|Frame from the menu bar or pressing the F5 key. Beginning with Frame 5, insert a keyframe at five-frame intervals by clicking on the frame and selecting Insert|Keyframe or pressing the F6 key.

2. Label the first keyframe (Frame 1) "Home," and put a Stop action in the ActionScript Editor.

3. English and Spanish alternate in the keyframes sequentially from one/uno to five/cinco. The order of labels for the remaining keyframes is One, Uno, Two, Dos, Three, Tres, Four, Quatro, Five, and Cinco.

4. Each keyframe has two actions, both of which set the numeric value in the text field variable "Number" and the word for the number into the text field variable "Word." For example, the number "3" is placed into the "Number" variable, and the word "Tres" in the "Word" variable. All values are string literals because no calculations are required. Each keyframe has the title of the word value in its label (see Figure 3.13).

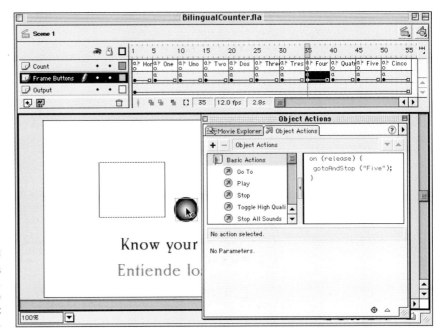

Figure 3.13

Each labeled keyframe shows a page with a third button. The third button contains the script to jump to the next appropriate keyframe.

5. Select Modify|Frame, Ctrl+F/Cmd+F, or double-click on each keyframe. Select the Actions tab of the Frame Properties dialog box. In the Action-Script Editor's Actions folder, double-click, "set variable" and insert the following code using the number and word indicated by the frame label. For example, the first English frame (One) would have the following action script:

```
number = "1"
word = "One"
```

All frames have the same relative code.

Frame Buttons Layer

Create a layer, and place it directly below the Count layer. To put in all of the necessary keyframes and buttons, you do the following:

1. Add keyframes directly under those in the Count layer. Each keyframe is set at five-frame intervals.

2. In each keyframe, double-click on the "Stop" action from the Basic Action folder in the ActionScript Editor in the Action panel. In the Editor, you will see the action

   ```
   stop();
   ```

3. Select the first keyframe. Create two buttons of different colors. (I made green and silver 3-D buttons.) Save one as "Engbutton" (English button) and the other as "Spbutton" (Spanish button). The rest of the buttons for this movie are instances of these two buttons.

4. Place instances of each button on the stage. Label one "Español" and the other "English" using the Text tool. (See Figure 3.12.) Access the ActionScript Editor and enter this script with the Español button selected:

   Español Button

   ```
   on(release) {
       gotoAndStop("Uno")
   }
   ```

   and this script for the English button:

   English Button

   ```
   on(release) {
       gotoAndStop("One")
   }
   ```

5. In the remaining keyframes in the Frame Buttons layers, each Spanish frame requires a button that jumps to the next Spanish frame (Dos, Tres, Quatro, and Cinco), and each English frame requires a button to jump to the next English frame (Two, Three, Four, and Five). For example, in the Tres keyframe, the button would require the following action script:

   ```
   on(release) {
       gotoAndStop("Quatro")
   }
   ```

Align the buttons and double-check to make sure you haven't mixed up the English and Spanish versions.

6. When you get to keyframes Five and Cinco, put in a "Good job!" or "¡Que bueno!" text message at the top of the screen. The button script for both Cinco and Five is as follows:

```
on(release) {
  word = ""
  number = ""
 gotoAndStop("Home")
}
```

The script clears the two text fields and sends the movie back to the first frame, Home.

The Output layer consists of two text fields and two text labels (shown in Figure 3.12). Table 3.2 shows the properties for the two text fields.

Using the Text tool, type the following in the center of the page below the text fields: "Know your numbers" and "Entiende los numeros." The project is now complete. Give it a test run by selecting Control|Test Movie from the menu bar or just press Ctrl+Enter/Cmd+Return. Figure 3.14 shows one of the screens that appears when completed.

Table 3.2   Text field properties.

Variable Name	Border/Bg	Text Alignment
number	None	Center
word	None	Center

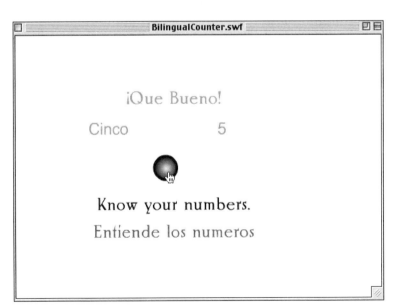

Figure 3.14

When the script is run, the user sees the output on the screen. She can select the bottom button to go to the next number in English or Spanish, depending on which language she originally selected.

Project: Dynamic Menu Creation

Compared to the learning utility, this project is very straightforward and practical. In this project, you create a dynamic menu for showing Web customers an assortment of products for sale. In addition, your menu should try to keep customers focused on the site and not stray out of the online store. In many ways, the dynamic menu is exactly like an HTML menu using frames. A menu bar stays put over to the side of the movie, and the user can quickly navigate to any desired product groupings. The important feature is to keep the navigation tool (the menu bar) in sight at all times. By using a little ActionScript and good organization, it's not difficult.

Figure 3.15 shows the basic layers, buttons, menu, and the front page used for our example. Note that in the top layer, all of the keyframes contain labels and action scripts. All of the buttons—including the Menu button at the top of the menu bar—contain action scripts to go to one of the keyframes. (Look for the little flags and the "a" symbol to tip you off to labels and action scripts even if you cannot read the labels.)

Figure 3.15

Initial page, layers, buttons, menu, and front page of a fictional e-commerce site.

PROJECT Beginning an E-Commerce Site (ecommerceMenu.fla on CD-ROM)

This next movie uses a menu to select one of several selections in a simulated e-commerce site. Three layers are used:

- Selections
- Buttons
- Menu Bar Bg

Selections Layer

The Selections layer is the heart of the movie. Although it needs to be only six frames long, I used more so that some of the labels would be visible. The purpose of this layer of the movie is to organize—not animate—the movie, so that different messages can appear on the page in different frames. (All of this section uses the key shortcuts. It's a lot faster.) To do this, follow these instructions:

1. Select a frame at least six from the beginning, and press the F5 key to insert a frame.

2. Insert five keyframes by selecting the frames and pressing the F6 key.

3. Beginning at Frame 1, label the keyframes "Home," "Computers," "Network," "Monitors," "Printers," and "PDAs." Each frame is labeled by selecting the keyframe and typing in the label in the Frame panel *while the frame is selected*. As you label each frame, add an action script as described in Step 4.

4. Open the Basic Actions folder in the ActionScript menu, and double-click on "Stop" for each frame while it is selected. Each frame has the following script:

   ```
   stop();
   ```

5. After the Buttons and Menu Bar Bg layers have been placed, select each keyframe, beginning with the one labeled "Home," and add the information you want on the page using the Text and Drawing tools. Place any graphics that you have imported. Once that is complete, the layer is done.

Multiple Keyframes

If you're going to group all of the keyframes together, drag the mouse over the frames, and press the F6 key to create multiple keyframes all at once.

Menu Bar Bg Layer

On the Menu Bar Bg layer, you can place a black symbol on the page to separate the menu bar from the content. (See Figure 3.16.) You do this by using the Rectangle tool to draw a vertical rectangle the length of the page and wide enough to accommodate the buttons. After you have it positioned and sized correctly, click on the Lock column of the layer column.

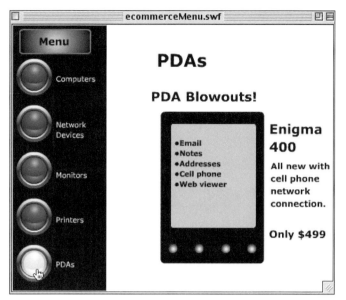

Figure 3.16
The menu remains on all pages
of the movie.

Buttons Layer

The Buttons layer must be above the Menu Bar Bg layer, or the background of that layer may cover it up. The buttons' job is to have the movie jump to the appropriate frame so that the information on the content portion of the stage can be viewed. You accomplish this as follows:

1. Select a button by opening Window|Common Libraries|Buttons.fla from the menu bar (I used the Push Button Yellow button for this example).

2. Drag an instance of the button from the Libraries Button.fla window to the stage. Open the Info panel by pressing the Show Info button at the bottom of the stage—the first button on the left. Select the instance of the button.

3. You can size it in half by going to the Info panel and changing the "W" and "H" (width and height) values to half of what appears in the related windows. When the new values are in place, your button will be half its original size.

4. Select the button and, while holding down the Alt/Option key, drag the button to duplicate four copies. You now have five copies of the button at the desired size.

5. Draw a sixth button, and label it "Menu." Label each button by using the Text tool to write the related product group next to the button.

6. Select each button and, in the ActionScript Editor, enter a script for each button that will jump to the appropriate keyframe. The following script shows the actions required:

Selection Buttons

```
on(release) {
    gotoAndStop("Computers")
}
```

Use the keyframe label name in your script; not the label for the button!

7. Select the Menu button, and insert the following action script:

Menu Button

```
on(release) {
 gotoAndStop("Home")
}
```

The menu button provides the option of returning to an introductory page. A return button to the home or core page is essential in a movie using a menu. Otherwise, the user can feel lost or trapped and will avoid the site in the future.

This chapter covered the most important step in learning how to use ActionScript—mastering the Go To actions in the context of a Flash movie. You will find that you will use the Go To statements more than most other actions in your movies to provide control and structure to what the viewer ultimately sees. In Chapter 4, you will be introduced to far more powerful structures in conditional statements. However, the most important step in learning how to use ActionScript is mastering the Go To actions in the context of a Flash movie. You will also find that, more than most other actions, you will be using the Go To statements in most of your movies to provide control and structure to what the viewer ultimately sees.

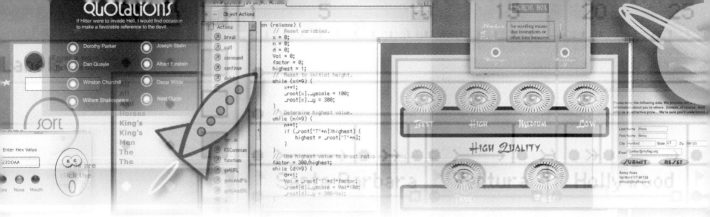

Chapter 4

Conditionals and Operators

This chapter explains how ActionScript "thinks" by making comparisons. Also discussed are the conditional statements and operators that make decision making in Flash possible. As a chapter bonus, a load-checking utility is included.

Making Comparisons

People make decisions by comparing two or more alternatives and then developing an action plan. If one condition exists, they'll follow Plan A; if another condition prevails, they'll follow Plan B. For example, if your vacation is in July, you might decide to go to the beach; if your vacation is in January, you might decide to go to the mountains.

Computer and scripting languages all have some kind of structure that allows for comparisons and alternative courses of actions. ActionScript is no exception. Conditional statements in ActionScript have three basic structures: IF..., IF...ELSE, and IF...ELSE IF. Each serves an important purpose and can be used in a number of different combinations. Following are explanations and examples of each.

IF...

The IF... structure waits until a single condition occurs and then takes a *single* course of action. For example, you may want to compare two variables. If the variables are equal, you may want the script to go to a particular frame. Another possibility may be that you want a script to compare values and go to a particular frame if the values are within a certain range. An actual script would look like the following:

```
If (input <=10) {
 gotoAndStop(10)
}
```

In this example, if the value of the variable "input" is less than or equal to 10, the script action commands the movie to jump to and stop at Frame 10. Assume that the variable called "input" is a text field in which a user enters a value. As long as the value is less than or equal to 10, everything works fine. But what happens if the value is greater than 10? In the current statement, nothing happens. If you want a unique event when a different condition occurs, however, you need to add an ELSE clause.

Like many languages using Object-Oriented Programming, Flash 5 ActionScript uses the curly braces ({ }) to enclose an action in response to a true condition. Throughout the book, you will see the curly braces replacing the older "End If" terminator found in Flash 4 ActionScript conditionals. The curly brace is also used as a container for sets of actions in several Flash 5 ActionScript script structures.

IF...ELSE

In addition to the If statement in the Action menu of the ActionScript Editor in the Action panel, you will see an Else statement. Double-click on the Else action only when you already have an If statement in your script. Figure 4.1

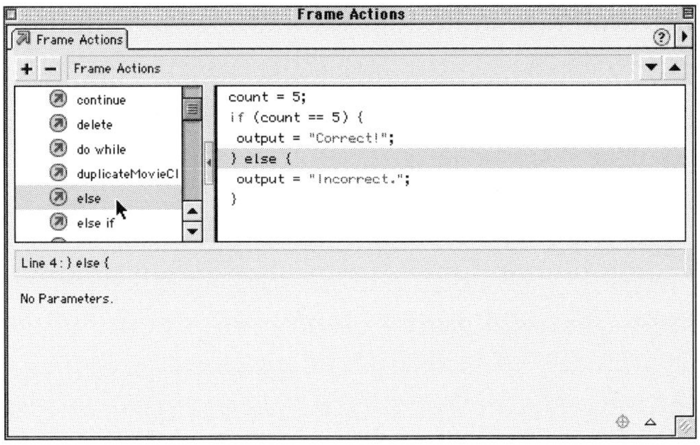

Figure 4.1
Inserting the Else statement adds another option for a false condition.

shows what happens when you add the Else action to the If statement in the Normal mode ActionScript Editor.

Another structure in ActionScript is the IF...ELSE structure. Using this second structure, you can have the script do one of two things. For example, the script determines IF a variable is equal to or greater than 10. If it is, an action commands a jump to Frame 10; or ELSE, if the variable is greater than 10, an action commands a jump to Frame 20. The following script shows this set of conditions:

```
if (input <=10) {
 gotoAndStop(10)
}
else {
 gotoAndStop(20)
}
```

The script directs the action according to one of two options—whether the value of the variable "input" is equal to or less than 10 or is greater than 10. The IF...ELSE structure has no condition on the Else clause. If you need a condition for ELSE, you need the third type of structure: IF...ELSE IF.

IF...ELSE IF

If an initial condition is *not* met, the ELSE condition that follows may also need an If statement. Consider the following statement:

"If it's sunny, we'll go to the park, but if it's rainy and 'The Slug from Outer Space' is playing, we'll go to the movies."

The script contains two If statements. IF the weather is sunny and IF a certain movie is playing set the conditions. If the first condition (IF) is true, however, the second condition (the ELSE IF) is never encountered because the script jumps over it. Let's examine that statement with a frame named "Park" and a frame named "Movies" along with variables named "Slug" and "weather." The "weather" variable is a text field where the user can put in the forecast.

```
Slug=new Boolean( );
Slug=true;
if (weather == "sunny") {
     gotoAndStop ("Park");
} else if (Slug == true) {
     gotoAndStop ("Movies");
}
```

First, create a Boolean object named "Slug" and assign the Boolean literal, "true." (Remember that Boolean literals can be "True" or "False," "1" or "0," or "Yes" or "No.") Next, the first If statement is encountered. In Flash 4, you would have to use a string operator (eq) instead of a numeric operator (=) because the word "sunny" is a string literal. In Flash 5, however, you can use the evaluation operator of double equals (==) for both strings and numbers. If the condition is true (it's sunny), the script goes to the "Park" frame and stops. If the weather is not sunny, however, the script first checks to see if the movie ("Slug" variable) in the ELSE IF statement is playing (True?). If it is true, the script directs the action to go to and stop at "Movies." Now try to create the movie using the following directions.

IF ELSE IF (IfElseIf.fla on CD-ROM)

This next movie shows the different conditionals at work using the following layers:

- Announce

- IF ELSE IF

- Input

Figure 4.2 shows the layers, as well as the layout of the initial frame and the script in the button. Each keyframe in the Announce layer has a different announcement. The conditional script is in the IF ELSE IF layer. The text field used for the input and a button are both placed in the Input layers. Set up the movie's stage to be 300 × 350 pixels by selecting Modify|Movie and changing the width and height dimensions.

Announce Layer

The Announce layer requires only that you put in different text at each keyframe. Insert keyframes at Frames 8 and 20 by selecting Insert|Keyframe from the menu bar or pressing the F6 key. It is important that you insert the keyframes prior to typing on the stage.

- *Frame 1*—Use the Text tool to type in the content. Be sure that Static Text is selected in the Text Options panel.

  Text on stage—Type in the word "sunny" or any other word. Then click on the button.

- *Frame 8*

  Text on stage—"It's Sunny! Let's have a picnic!"

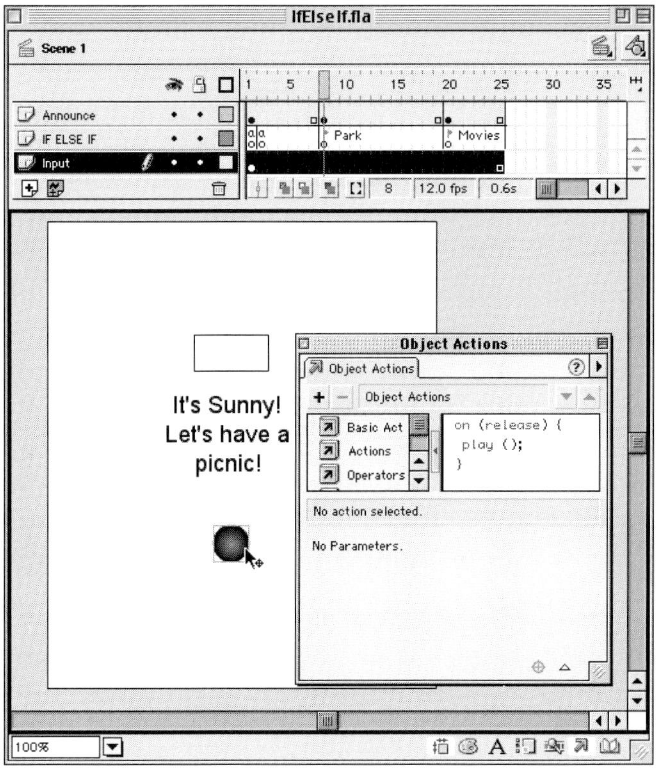

Figure 4.2
The initial page, layers, and frames. The only action outside the frames is the Button symbol with a play script seen in the Object Inspector.

* *Frame 20*

  Text on stage—"Look out! Here comes the slug!"

IF ELSE IF Layer

The IF ELSE IF layer contains all of the ActionScript that is placed in frames. The only other ActionScript in the movie is in the button.

* *Frame 1*—To give the user some time to type in the "weather," you use the following to make the movie stop at the first frame:

```
stop();
```

* *Frame 2*—This frame sends the action to either "Park" or "Movies." If the variable "Slug" were changed to "false," the movie would run through both "Park" and "Movies" and come to a halt at the beginning when it ran into the **stop();** action in Frame 1.

```
Slug=new Boolean( );
Slug=true;
if (weather == "sunny") {
    gotoAndStop ("Park");
} else if (Slug == true) {
    gotoAndStop ("Movies");
}
```

- *Frame 8: Park (label)*—This frame contains only the label.

- *Frame 20: Movies (label)*—This frame contains only the label.

Input Layer

The Input layer has two types of user input: the text field in which the user inserts the "weather," and the button used to play the movie after it has been stopped in one of the frames. Table 4.1 shows the text field properties used in our example.

To create a Go button, draw a button shape, select it, and choose Insert|Convert To Symbol from the menu bar or press F8. Select the button and enter the following script in the ActionScript Editor. When you select a button and begin adding script, the ActionScript Editor automatically adds an event handler.

```
on(release) {
play();
}
```

This movie is designed to illustrate the If and If...Else statements. After the user selects the "sunny" weather and "Park," if the user clicks on the Go button again, the script cycles through the rest of the movie until it stops at the first frame. How could you write your script so that, after the initial selection, the movie would always go back to the beginning without going through the frame labeled "Movies"? (Hint: Use Frame 11.)

Operators

To really understand and use conditionals to their full potential, you must learn to appreciate and use the operators in ActionScript. If you're familiar with other scripting or programming languages, most of the operators in ActionScript will be familiar. Programmers will notice that a separate set of operators for numbers and strings are used. You need to be concerned with the differences only if your script will be used in Flash 4 players, however. Table 4.2 shows a list of ActionScript operators.

The next two sets of operators can be skipped if you have no intention of using Flash 5 to create movies that can also be used for Flash 4 or if you are not going to be using binary math (see Table 4.3). You can be a great programmer and never have to deal with binary math; however, if you must, find a book on programming and binary numbers to appreciate and use the bitwise operators ActionScript has so generously provided.

Table 4.1 Text field properties and names.

Variable Name	Border/ Bg	Text Alignment
weather	Yes	Center

Table 4.2 ActionScript operators.

Type	Symbol	Use
Numeric		
	+	add (and concatenate)
	-	subtract
	*	multiply
	/	divide
	%	modulus
	++	increment
	—	decrement
Comparison		
	<	less than
	>	greater than
	<=	less than or equal to
	>=	greater than or equal to
Logical		
	&&	logical AND
	||	logical OR
	!	logical NOT
Equality and Assignment		
	==	equal
	!=	unequal
	=	assignment
	+=	add and assign
	-=	subtract and assign
	*=	multiply and assign
	%=	modulus and assign
	/=	divide and assign
Function, Dot, and Array access		
	()	function arguments
	.	structure member (called a dot)
	[ ]	array access

Table 4.3 String operators and bitwise operators needed for movies to be run in Flash 4.

String operators	
" "	string container
add	concatenation
eq	equal to
ne	not equal to
lt	less than
gt	greater than
le	less than or equal to
ge	greater than or equal to

(continued)

Table 4.3 String operators and bitwise operators needed for movies to be run in Flash 4 *(continued).*

Bitwise operators

&	bitwise AND
|	bitwise OR
^	bitwise XOR
~	bitwise NOT
<<	shift left
>>	shift right
>>>	shift right zero fill
<<=	bitwise shift left and assignment
>>=	bitwise shift right and assignment
>>>=	shift right zero fill and assignment
^	bitwise XOR and assignment
|=	bitwise OR and assignment
&=	bitwise AND and assignment

Precedence

For those new to scripting or programming languages, *precedence* is an important concept to understand when working with operators. Precedence refers to the order in which operators are executed in a program. For example, consider the following expression:

```
output = 2 + 2 *(2*4)
```

Depending on how the precedence works, you can get different answers. If you first add the 2s to equal 4 and then multiply by 8 (2 times 4), the result is 32. However, if you first multiply 2 times 4 to get 8, multiply the 8 by 2 to get 16, and then add 2, the result is 18. What would you get in Flash? The result would be 18.

As a rule of thumb, precedence first performs all of the math within parentheses, beginning in the innermost parentheses and working its way outward, then the multiplication and division, and finally the addition and subtraction. If two operations are on the same level of precedence, precedence goes from left to right. Before performing anything else, precedence evaluates whether a number is positive or negative and whether it is a number or string. Strings are in quotation marks (" "); numbers and operators are not.

Breaking down the example, precedence follows this sequence:

1. The math in parenthesis: (2*4) = 8

2. The multiplication and division: 2 * 8 = 16

3. The addition: 2 + 16 = 18

To reorder precedence, you just use the parentheses. For example, if you want the two 2s added before you multiply by 8, you would change the precedence to the following:

```
output = (2 + 2) *(2*4)
```

Instead of 18, your result is now 32.

Precedence Hierarchy

Table 4.4 shows the precedence hierarchy going from the highest to the lowest. The old Flash 4 string operators and Flash 5 binary operators are not included in the list. The associativity is summarized as LR (Left to Right) or RL (Right to Left).

Table 4.4   Precedence hierarchy.

Operator	Description	Associativity
+	pos. number	RL
-	neg. number	RL
!	logical NOT	RL
++	post-increment	LR
—	post-decrement	LR
( )	function argument	LR
[ ]	array access	LR
.	structure member	LR
++	pre-increment	RL
—	pre-decrement	RL
new	allocate object	RL
delete	deallocate object	RL
typeof	type of object	RL
*	multiply	LR
/	divide	LR
%	modulus	LR
+	add	LR
add	string concatenate	LR
-	subtract	LR
<	less than	LR
<=	less than or equal	LR
>	greater than	LR
>=	greater than or equal	LR
==	equal	LR
!=	not equal	LR
&&	logical AND	LR
||	logical OR	LR
?:	conditional	RL
=	assignment	RL
all	compound assignments	RL

Precedence Practice

The best way to find out more about precedence is to create a 1-frame script-tester and practice. Here's a short movie to practice with:

1. Open a new Flash scene or movie.

2. Select the Text tool from the Toolbox and click on the stage. Select Window|Text Options to open the Text Options panel. Select Dynamic Text from the top dropdown menu in the Text Options panel. Type in "output" in the Variable window in the Text Options panel.

3. Double-click on the first keyframe, type in the following scripts one at a time, and test them in your movie. See if you can guess what the result will be before you run the movie.

```
output = 3 * 8 / (4 + 2)
output = (3 / 2) * -4 /2
output = (2 * 3) / ((4 + 3) + (6 / 3))
output = (8 / (-4 -2) * (12 / 3))
output = (18 / 3) + -4 * (2 * 9 - 3)
```

Numeric Operators

Numeric operators are generally the easiest to use because they work the same as in math. Instead of writing 5×3, you write the expression 5 * 3. Otherwise, the only other thing you need to remember is how precedence works in ActionScript.

The comparative numeric operators, such as ">" and "<=," are probably new to nonprogrammers but they are also fairly straightforward. From the discussion of Boolean literals in Chapter 2, remember that Boolean expressions can have only one of two outcomes. When using the comparative numeric operators, the outcome is either "0" or "1" (True/False or Yes/No). Some confusion may arise when the comparison has a broad choice. For example, a statement such as

```
if (current>=7) {
    gotoAndStop ("FinishLine");
}
```

means that the variable named "current" is looking for a value that is either equal to or greater than the literal "7." Any value of 7 or greater qualifies.

String Operators

To help understand string operators, think of the alphabet as a hierarchy. If A = 1 and Z = 26, it's pretty easy to imagine that the letter "L" is greater than the letter "G." The statement

```
Higher = "Steeple";
Lower = "Basement";
if (Higher>Lower) {
    output = "That's right";
}
```

provides evidence that the word "Steeple" is greater than the word "Basement." Note that the variable names "Higher" and "Lower" were not considered in the comparison. After loading the variables with string literals, the If statement considered only the *value* of the variables, not the variable names. Note that the string literals are in quotation marks, but the variable names are not.

Logical Operators

I like to think of logical operators as "dessert choices." Would you like ice cream or cake? As a kid, my answer was, "I'd like ice cream AND cake." Mom would say, "You may have ice cream OR cake. You may NOT have both." Consider the following script:

```
IC = "ice cream";
C = "cake";
if ((IC == "ice cream") && (C=="pie")) {
    output = "Yahoo!";
} else if ((IC == "ice cream") || (C == "pie")) {
    output = "I'll take it!";
}
```

Two string variables are set at the beginning of the script. The first conditional asks if one variable equals one string literal and (&&) the other variable equals another string literal. You can see that "C" is defined as "cake" and not "pie," so even though the first part of the condition is true, the second part is not. Therefore, the script passes over the first conditional outcome, "Yahoo!" However, the second conditional, using Else If, just requires that one or (||) the other be true. Because one is true, the output is, "I'll take it!"

The format for the logical NOT operator (!) is a bit different. The following statement

```
else if (! ((IC == "ice cream") && (C == "pie")))
```

is true under the circumstances where the AND expression (&&) is NOT (!) true. Just like Mom who said, "You can't have both," the NOT (!) operator does the same thing. In a script where you do not want two or more different conditions occurring at the same time, the logical NOT (!) operator is handy.

Compound Assignments

Often a variable is incremented by itself plus an offset in a movie. For example, the expression

```
count=count +1
```

increments the variable "count" each time the expression is encountered in a movie. A shortcut operator, called "compound assignment," allows a single operator to perform an operation and make an assignment at the same time. The "count" variable expression above could be written as

```
count  += 1
```

using a compound assignment. The same may be done with subtraction, multiplication, division, and modulus (or modulo). For example, the following line of script subtracts 2 from the variable named "demote" each time it is encountered:

```
demote -= 2
```

and the variable "rabbit" multiplies by 4 each time the following line is encountered:

```
rabbit *= 4
```

> **Note:** You can enter compound assignments only using the Expert Mode in the Action-Script Editor.

Using compound assignments is a matter of taste instead of necessity in ActionScript. Use them or not at your own discretion.

Making a Preloader (preload.fla on CD-ROM)

A key consideration when creating a movie for the Internet is the time required for it to load. The loading time over a typical modem can be 20 to 100 times slower than over a T1 line or cable modem. Before the movie can be played, all—or a certain portion—of it must be loaded. Writing a script that checks to see when a movie is loaded is simply a matter of checking to see when the final frame is loaded (or the frame that you believe will run the movie until the last frame is loaded). To do this, you use a special conditional statement in Flash called **ifFrameLoaded()**. This next movie is divided into two layers:

- Scripts
- Heavy Load

The purpose of a preloader is twofold. First, it is used for loading "heavy" materials, such as music and graphics. Second, it tells the viewer that the movie is loading and there's nothing wrong with her computer, modem, or the Web. Figure 4.3 shows the beginning of the movie while the preloading is taking place, the layers, and the Library window; the latter displays everything that's been loaded.

Scripts Layer

All of the action scripts are on the Scripts (the first) layer. Two keyframes contain the scripts. Notice that the movie has only 10 frames, and the Library window shows that several graphics need to be loaded.

- *Loaded? (Label): Frame 1*—Frame 1 asks the question, "Are all of the frames loaded?" Because the movie has 10 frames, the script simply asks if Frame 10 is loaded yet. After the last frame is loaded, the movie jumps

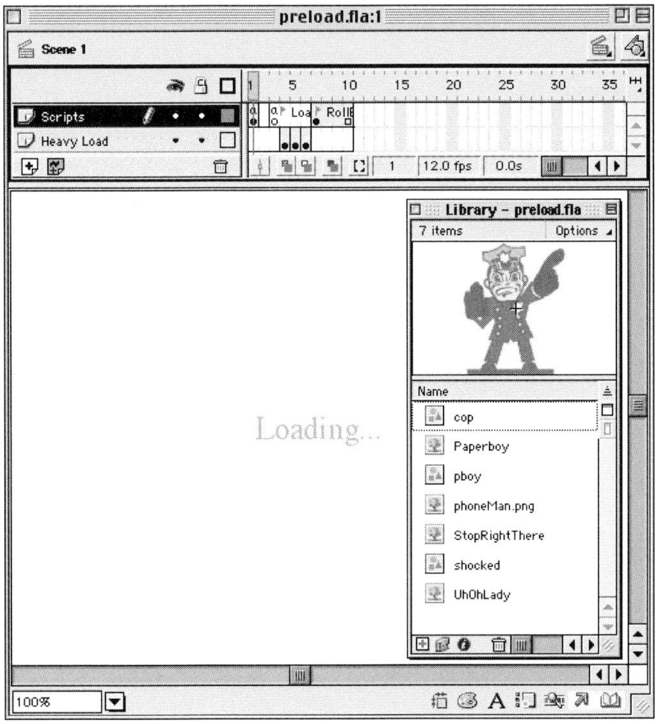

Figure 4.3
A preloader brings in those parts of the movie necessary for smooth play and informs the viewer that the movie is loading.

to the frame labeled "RollEm." Normally, I would go to the frame where the movie begins (RollEm) and have it play instead of stop; for this demonstration movie, however, I chose to have it stop.

```
ifFrameLoaded (10) {
      gotoAndStop ("RollEm");
}
```

- *Loading (Label): Frame 3*—Chances are that the first time the movie encounters Frame 2, the movie will not be entirely loaded. Therefore, you need an action in Frame 3 that keeps going back to Frame 1 until the action script detects that Frame 10 is loaded. At that point, the movie should jump to the frame labeled "RollEm."

```
gotoAndPlay ("Loaded?");
```

Also, I added the message "Loading..." in this frame by typing it in with the Text tool. For a longer movie, I may include a little movie clip or something more interesting for the viewer than just a one-word announcement.

- *RollEm (Label): Frame 7*—This frame is where the real body of the movie begins. It starts with a symbol instance of a woman who claims, "But I'm not ready!" (Well, I guess it was a fast preload.) Normally, I would put the graphic on another layer, but in this case I placed it on the Scripts layer to impress this point: The graphic itself was preloaded in the Heavy Load layer and was not visible until the beginning of the movie.

Heavy Load Layer

The Heavy Load (the second) layer of the movie is where all of your media goes that gobble up the most bandwidth and take the most time to load. The Library window in Figure 4.3 shows all of the graphics and symbols loaded in the movie. Frames 3, 4, and 5 contain the graphic symbols. All of them are preloaded and are ready for viewing when the movie begins. In Frame 6, I put in a blank keyframe so that the images prior to Frame 6 won't spill over into the movie.

In the Test Movie mode, everything loads so quickly that you cannot see what a person on the other end of a slow modem sees. To simulate different modem speeds, you need to select View|Bandwidth Profiler; View|Show Streaming; and View|Streaming Graph from the menu bar that appears when you run the test movie. In addition, select Debug|28.8 (2.3K/s) to simulate a relatively slow modem speed. Figure 4.4 shows what the movie looks like when you run it after the graphics are all loaded.

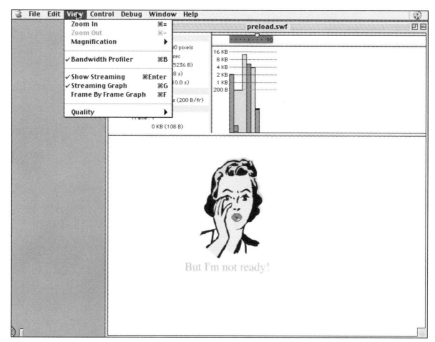

Figure 4.4

Using the modem speed simulation tools and Show Streaming, you will be able to see how long your movie takes to load.

PROJECT Learning Utility: Determining Multiple Responses (condQuiz.fla on CD-ROM)

With conditional statements, ActionScript can evaluate more than a single choice by the user and make more than a single response. In this learning utility, you will see how the scripts in four selection buttons are used to set a variable value. A fifth (answer) button evaluates the variable and makes one of four different responses. This is a very practical utility because it models how a single button script has several different responses. Use the following layers:

- Question

- Buttons

- Background

This particular project is set up primarily to show how multiple If...Else If statements are used in a Flash movie. The movie requires only a single frame because all of the scripts are in the five buttons. Figure 4.5 shows the initial stage and layer setup.

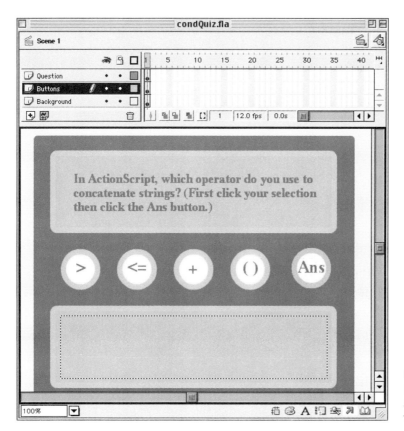

Figure 4.5
Four selection buttons and an answer button provide the stage for multiple feedback.

Background Layer

The Background layer is the foundation for the question and response windows and the buttons. The background is yellow and contains a red rectangle that establishes a platform for the question window at the top and an identical response window at the bottom. The buttons are inserted between these two windows.

Question Layer

The Question layer consists of text (not a text field) on top of the question window. Placing the question on its own layer makes it easier if you want to replace one question with another.

Buttons Layer

The Buttons layer is where all of the scripting is done. Each button contains a script that either sets or evaluates a variable and sends a message to a text field using the variable name "response." Each of the four buttons contains a response labeled on the button with simple text symbols. Each button has rollover behaviors created in the Symbol Editor by adding a different ring color for the Over and Down positions. The button labeled "Ans" is static to differentiate it from the four response buttons.

Each button in the response group contains a script to set an answer variable named (after much thought) "answer." Any unique value for the answer works; so I simply gave each one a value between one and four.

- *Button (>): Instance of Choice*

```
on (release) {
    answer = 1;
}
```

- *Button (<=): Instance of Choice*

```
on (release) {
    answer = 2;
}
```

- *Button (+): Instance of Choice*

```
on (release) {
    answer = 3;
}
```

- *Button(( )): Instance of Choice*

```
on (release) {
    answer = 4;
}
```

- *Button(Ans): Instance of Answer*—The Answer symbol is different from the other four in both appearance and script. The script looks at the value of the answer variable that is generated when the user clicks on any of the response buttons. The script sends an appropriate message to the text field using the variable name response. To understand this concept, read through the following script and the accompanying explanation.

```
on (release) {
    if (answer == 3) {
        response = "That's exactly right.";
    } else if (answer == 1) {
        response = "No,  >  compares 'greater than.'";
    } else if (answer == 2) {
        response = "No, the <= operator compares 'less than
```

```
and equal" +chr(13)+ "to' between values.";
      } else if (answer == 4) {
      response = "No,  parentheses are for re-ordering
precedence.";
      }
}
```

The correct answer is the plus sign (+). If the user clicks on the button with the plus on it, the answer variable is set to 3. The script sends a string to the text field using the variable name "response," and the user sees that his answer is correct. Because there are three other selections for incorrect answers, the IF...ELSE IF structure must be used. If the response is wrong, the script evaluates the answer variable to determine which message to send to "response."

Text Field: Response

Table 4.5 lists the properties for the text field used in this example.

Given the limited amount of space on top of each button, this particular design does not lend itself to longer responses. By making smaller buttons and having responses typed in below the response buttons, however, the quiz is very easy to change so that you can have a different set of multiple choice selections along with short explanatory responses. Figure 4.6 shows the running movie with an incorrect answer selected.

Table 4.5 Text field properties and names.

Variable Name	Border/Bg	Text Alignment
response	None	Center

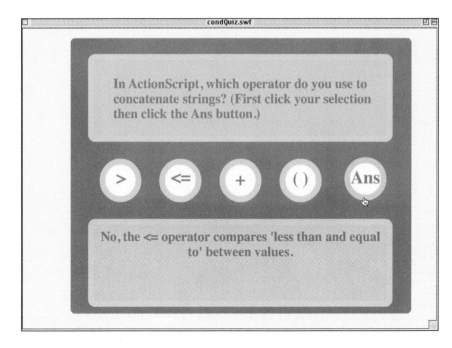

Figure 4.6

By clicking a selection and then the "Ans" button, the user gets immediate feedback.

A Tip on Script Organization

Different Flash designers have different strategies for organizing movie objects and scripts. Some designers like to put all of their scripts on the same layer. That's a good idea because it makes them easy to find when you need them. A close cousin to the all-scripts-on-one-layer strategy is to put all frame scripts on one layer and all buttons with scripts on another layer. I prefer this second strategy. Frames on the timeline are sequential unless an action tells the movie to jump around on the timeline. Having all of the frame scripts on the same layer makes it easier to debug a script because they have a sequential flow just as in a more conventional script or program listing. However, button scripts may not have the same sequential character as frame scripts do because they are fired when the user chooses to do so. Therefore, I find it more convenient to put the button scripts on their own layer separate from the frame scripts.

Who Said That? A Game of Famous Quotes

The preceding learning utility explained one method for responding to a user in several different ways. The purpose was to show how to use multiple layers of If...Else If in a script. This next movie project is a game of famous quotes. The viewer sees a quotation on the screen and clicks on the button next to the name of the person she thinks authored the quote. The movie uses a set of frames and buttons that communicate with one another through variables. Each frame sets an "answer" variable, and the button script compares whether its variable value is the same as the frame variable value. If the values are the same, the answer is correct. The script increments the score, sends a message telling the user that the answer is correct, and then stops the movie until the user clicks on the button for the next quote. Figure 4.7 shows the movie on the stage.

Figure 4.7

The buttons, their labels, and the text field are selected in this figure.

 Quotes Game (Quotes.fla on CD-ROM)

This game shows one way to organize a quiz with different choices. Use the following layers:

- Quotes

- Buttons

- Background

To create this script, follow these initial steps to put in a background layer and a header:

1. Create three layers with Quotes at the top followed by Buttons and Background.

2. Drag the cursor downward in Column 11 in the timeline, and press F5 to create 11 frames for each layer.

3. In the Background layer, use a black rectangle for the top drawing so that you will be able to see the white text in both the display window and the stage labels for the buttons. For the banner, I used a specialized font, which I turned into a symbol so that the banner will be displayed the same on all computers.

Next, you should get your symbols and instances on the stage as follows:

1. Create a Button symbol by selecting Insert|New Symbol or Ctrl+F8/ Cmd+F8.

2. In the Symbol Properties dialog box, click on the Button behavior option, and enter the name "Select" in the Name window.

3. Draw a button with the circle tool 30.5 pixels wide and high. Remember to use the Info panel to get the exact dimensions. Hold down the Shift key to constrain the circle so you don't get an oblong.

4. Create a second symbol the same size but a different color by repeating Steps 1 through 3. Name the second symbol "Next."

5. Create seven instances of the Select symbol and one instance of the Next symbol by dragging the Symbol Instance from the Library window to the stage.

6. Next to each Button Instance, type in a label corresponding to those in Figure 4.7.

Now the stage is set to put the scripts in the buttons.

Quotes Layer

The Quotes layer contains all of the frame scripts. Each script is identical except for two crucial values. One value is the quote that is displayed in the window. The other value is the "answer" variable value (I used the initials of the author of the quote).

Frame 1

The first frame sets the score to zero so that the user can restart the game.

```
score = 0
```

Frame 3

The next seven frames are all very similar except for a different quote. The longer quotes need a "line-feed." The plus sign (+) operator concatenates the code for a carriage return—**chr(13)**—followed by another plus sign (+) operator to link to the second part of the expression.

```
output = "It isn't pollution that's harming the environment." +
chr(13) + "It's the impurities in our air and water that are
doing it.";
answer = "dq";
stop ();
```

Frame 4

```
output = "As flies to wanton boys, are we to the gods; " +
 chr(13) + "They kill us for their sport.";
answer = "ws";
stop ();
```

Frame 5

```
output = "There is no sin except stupidity.";
answer = "ow";
stop ();
```

Frame 6

```
output = "If Hitler were to invade Hell, I would find occasion"
+ chr(13) + "to make a favorable reference to the devil.";
answer = "wc";
stop ();
```

Frame 7

```
output = "This is not a novel to be tossed aside lightly. " +
chr(13) + "It should be thrown with great force.";
answer = "dp";
stop ();
```

Frame 8

```
output = "The most beautiful thing we can experience is the " +
chr(13) + "mysterious. It is the source of all true art
and science.";
answer = "ae";
stop ();
```

Frame 9

```
output = "A single death is a tragedy." + chr(13) + "A million
deaths is a statistic.";
answer = "js";
stop ();
```

Score (Comment): Frame 11

In the scoring frame, the script takes the variable "score," divides it by the total number of questions (quotations), multiplies the results by 100, and turns the whole thing into an integer using the **int()** function. A plus sign (+) operator concatenates a percentage symbol (%) to the end of the score value.

```
output = "Your final score is " + int((score /7) *100) + "%.";
stop ();
```

Buttons Layer

The Buttons layer contains all of the buttons and button scripts.

Button: Instance of Select

```
on (release) {
    if (answer == "dp") {
        score +=1;
        output = "You got it!";
    } else {
        output = "Sorry, that was someone else's quotation.";
    }
}
```

Next Six Buttons: Instance of Select

For the other six buttons, repeat the identical script used for the first button, substituting the following abbreviations in the second line for "dp"—If (answer eq "dp"):

- Dan Quayle   dq
- Winston Churchill   wc
- William Shakespeare   ws
- Joseph Stalin   js
- Albert Einstein   ae
- Oscar Wilde   ow

Button: Instance of Next

This button sends the play to the next frame.

```
on (release) {
    play ();
}
```

Text Field: Output

Create a text field under the header measuring 355 pixels wide by 50 pixels high. (Use the Info panel to get the dimensions just right.) Select 14 point Arial (or Helvetica) font. The text field is used as a general display board for all of the quotes, feedback, and final scores. Table 4.6 shows the text field properties used for this example.

Table 4.6 Text field properties and names.

Variable Name	Border/Bg	Text Alignment
Output	None	Left

When you are finished, you should be able to run the program in either a Flash player or on the Web. Figure 4.8 shows how the screen appears in Microsoft Internet Explorer. Note that the quote blends into the design in the same font as the button stage labels.

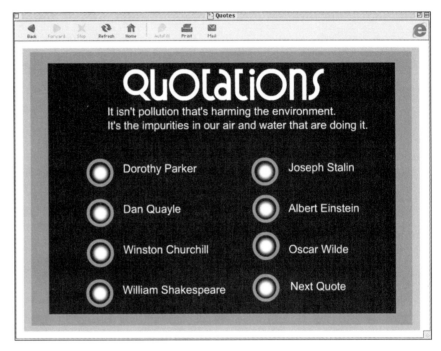

Figure 4.8
Shown in a Web browser, the Flash movie provides an interactive interface. All of the scripting is transparent to the user.

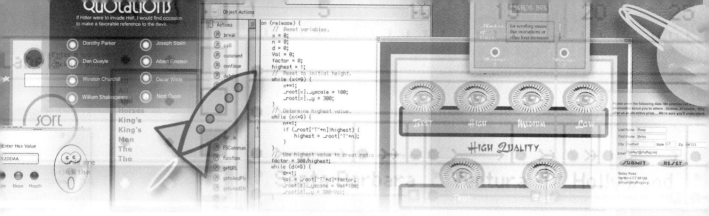

Chapter 5

Loops

Flash provides two basic types of looping actions. One loop uses the timeline and frames; the other uses a statement contained within a single script. This chapter explores using both types of looping actions.

Repeated Actions

In scripting, you often find that you need to do several very similar actions in a script. For example, in order to move an object across the screen, you may want a variable to have one value at one time and another value at another. Suppose you want to use all of the values between 1 and 10, but you want to use the values at different times. You can write

```
count = 1
count = 2
count = 3
count = 4
count = 5
count = 6
count = 7
count = 8
count = 9
count = 10
```

It is possible, however, that you may have to write a lot of other action scripts each time you change the variable. Your movie will work fine, but you'll have typing fatigue because you must write a whole script whenever the variable changes.

On the other hand, if you use either of the statements,

```
count = count + 1
```

or

```
count + = 1
```

10 times in a repeated script, the variable "count" will pass through all 10 values. When "count" reaches 10, a conditional statement stops the variable from incrementing further, and you'll save time and get the job done.

Programmers came to the same conclusion when programming languages were initially developed and thus created a structure called a *loop*. The loop simply repeats a process the number of times required to meet a given condition. In ActionScript and Flash, the looping process is achieved using either conditional statements or a loop statement. Flash 5 ActionScript has four different types of loop actions:

- **while**—In the **while** loop, a condition at the beginning of the loop specifies the conditions under which the loop terminates. All loop actions take place between the curly brackets ({}) and typically include an incremental or decremental counter variable.

Example:

```
count=20;
while (count >10) {
    Fungus[count]=count * 2;
    count -= 1 ;
}
```

- **do...while**—The **do...while** loop works like the **while** loop except the counter is at the bottom of the loop, allowing at least one pass through the loop before the termination conditions are met.

  Example:

```
do {
    Fungus[count]=count * 2
    count -= 1
} while (count >10)
```

- **for**—The **for** loop specifies a beginning value, a termination condition, and the counter (index) for the loop in a single line.

  Example:

```
for (count=100; count >10; count-) {
    Fungus[count]=count * 2
}
```

- **for...in**—This type applies only to properties of objects. Using a variable name to search the object ("feature" in the following example), the loop examines all of the object elements.

  Example:

```
auto = {make:'Rolls-Royce', model:'Silver Spur', year:'1983'};
for (feature in auto) {
    outtie+=("auto."+feature+"="+auto[feature])+newline;
}
```

The output from the preceding example where "outtie" is the name associated with a text field would be

- auto.make=Rolls-Royce

- auto.model=Silver Spur

- auto.year=1983

Loops using conditional statements typically rely on repeated passes through a frame or repeated clicks on a button or movie clip containing a variable that increments with each click. The former I call "repeater loops" because they involve some type of repeated action, and the latter, "structured loops" because they are a structure in the language.

Cut and Paste Scripts

When duplicating identical or similar scripts in different frames or buttons, select the completed script by clicking on the bottom line of the script, holding down the Shift key, and clicking on the top line of the script in the ActionScript Editor. Then select Edit|Copy from the menu bar. Open the ActionScript Editor window for the next frame or button, and select Edit|Paste to put the script right into the action list. (Using the keyboard shortcuts for copying—Ctrl+C [Windows]/ Cmd+C [Macintosh]—and pasting—Ctrl+V/Cmd+V— work just as well.) You can also right-click the mouse button on a Windows PC or Cmd+click on a Macintosh to open a contextual menu with cut and paste options.

Repeater Loops

In Chapter 4, you learned how conditional statements are able to evaluate data and make a decision. One decision format occurs when a movie runs back and forth between frames until a programmed condition is met. At the point where the condition is met, the movie quits looping between the frames and does something else. The "something else" can be anything from stopping the movie to jumping into another frame outside of the loop.

Creating Loops with Conditionals

Think of a frame loop in a movie as two frames. One frame increments (bumps) or decrements (demerits) a value, and the other looks at the value until a certain condition is met. If the condition is not met, the frame sends the movie back to the first frame. The basic model looks like this:

Frame A

```
varName = varName + 1
```

Frame B

```
if (varName=Condition) {
    gotoAndPlay ("OutOfLoop");
} else {
    gotoAndPlay ("Frame_A");
}
```

As you can see, the structure of frame loops is fairly simple. The next Flash movie example generates values seen on the screen. The movie is heavily labeled and has several comments to make it easier to visualize what each frame does. All of the work is done by the Bump and Evaluate frames, however. Figure 5.1 shows the initial setup and stage, along with the selected output text field and Text Options panel.

Frame Loop (FrameLoop.fla on CD-ROM)

This movie is a simple one that demonstrates a repeater loop using the following layers:

- Output

- Condition

- Comments

The following ActionScript movie is simplicity itself. Although only two frames were necessary, I added more than 25 frames so that the comments and labels are all visible and the loop nature of the movie is illustrated.

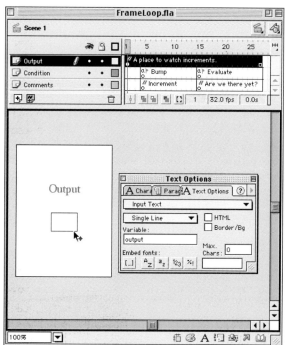

Figure 5.1
A simple frame loop movie.

Output Layer

The Output layer consists of a single text field (using 14 point, red, Times font to set up the dimensions of the output) and a green label named "Output." Table 5.1 shows the text field properties for this example.

Condition Layer

The Condition layer could have been named the "Loop" layer because it holds the frames that contain the action scripts for the essential loop.

Bump (Label): Frame 4

The Bump frame increments the value of a variable named "output" each time the movie passes through the frame. Because the variable name is assigned to the text field, the value appears on the screen.

```
output = output+1
```

Evaluate (Label): Frame 15

The Evaluate frame sets up a variable named "Beta" and gives it a value of 5. It then compares the value of "output" with "Beta" and sends the movie back to the Bump frame until "output" equals "Beta." It is possible—and much easier—to evaluate on the value 5 without introducing the variable "Beta." It

Table 5.1 Text field properties and names.

Variable Name	Border/Bg	Text Alignment
Response	None	Center

is important to get in the habit of using variables as conditional comparisons, however. As your scripts grow in complexity, you will be dealing with variables more than with literals.

```
Beta = 5;
if (output==Beta) {
    output = "End!";
    stop ();
}
```

Once the comparison variable's value and the incremented value are equal, the termination is announced with "End!" and the movie stops. Normally, the condition would jump out of the loop to some other part of the movie.

Frame loops are extremely useful in Flash. They are used to control the properties of Movie Clip objects and other repetitive actions requiring increments or decrements in an object's size, position, alpha level, or some other controllable property (discussed in more detail in Chapter 7).

Structured Loops

Structured loops are contained in a single frame, button, or movie clip script. Structured loops have similar conditional structures as the "IF" conditionals discussed in Chapter 4. For example, the following **while** and **for** loops look very much like the **if** conditional:

```
while (count < 3)

for (count=0; count < 3; count++)

if (count > 3)
```

The key difference between the preceding loop and conditional statements is this: The loop statement *keeps running* if the condition is not met; the **if** statement *drops through to the next statement* if the condition is not met.

In the **for** loop, the first parameter (count=0;) sets the value of the index variable; the next parameter (count < 3;) is the condition to continue the loop; and the third parameter (count++) is the assignment to change the index variable. In this case, it adds one to the value *after* each iteration.

Loops and Arrays

A common use of loops is to generate a set of values in an array or to get information from an array and make it available on the screen. Since arrays have multiple elements, and each element in the array can be identified by a number, beginning with 0, loops are often used to go through the array and either assign values or pull them out. For example,

```
Task = new Array();
for (count=0; count<10; count++) {
    Task[count] = count+1;
}
```

The alternative is to write each one out:

```
"Task1" = 1
"Task2" = 2
"Task3" = 3
.....
"Task10" = 10
```

Using a loop, you can set the loop counter to whatever value you want. Instead of rewriting simple statements several times to get something done, you just write it once inside a loop. In the learning utility later in this chapter, you will see an example using a pseudo-array and a loop.

Nested Loops (NestedLoop.fla on CD-ROM)

Loops can exist within other loops. They are called *nested loops*, and they deal with more than a single dimension in a script. For example, suppose you have two teams, and each team has 10 members. First, you want all 10 members of the first team to be entered into an array, then the next 10 members. The first loop counts to two, and the second, or inner loop, counts to 10. The following movie shows how nested loops appear in ActionScript. The frame script loop is simply establishing an array and "initializing" it by putting the index value plus 1 into each element of the array. The following exercise contains two layers:

- Build Array

- Button Out

Build Array Layer

This layer contains a single frame with a script that builds two arrays, and, using a nested loop, fills up the two arrays with numbers. If two teams with members were actually placed into the arrays, the team names and member names would be used instead of generated array element values.

Frame 1

In this frame, two global variables are initialized with values of 0. Because they are global, the two variables may have had their values changed in another script; therefore, to be on the safe side, they both are given zero values. The outside loop stops only after two loops, representing the two teams, and the inside loops 10 times for each of the team loops. The counter variables both use compound assignment operators to increment their values. At the end of the script, the counter variables are again assigned to zero.

```
t = 0;
m = 0;
Team = new Array();
Member = new Array();
while (t<2) {
    while (m<10) {
        Team[t] = t+1;
        Member[m+(t>0)*(m+11)] = m+1;
        m+=1;
    }
    t+=1;
    m = 0;
}
t = 0;
m = 0;
```

The only tricky part of the script is in defining the Member array element identifier. The value for the array element itself is simple, but specifying the particular array element takes some doing. The value of "t" in the outer loop is going to be either 0 or 1. The first time through the loops, you have 10 members, numbered from 1 to 10 for Team 1. When it comes to Team 2, however, the value of "m" has been reset to 0. So if you simply load up the array elements using the value of "m" from 0 to 9, the array elements are named twice without really differentiating the first and second team members with unique array names. Taking advantage of the fact that "t" is either 0 or 1, it is used as a multiplier in a Boolean expression. If "t" is not greater than 0, as is the case the first time through the loop, the multiplier is 0, and so nothing is added to the counter variable "m." On the second time through the outer loop, "t" is now worth 1, and so "m + 11" is multiplied by 1 and added to "m." The first value will be "m=0" + "1 times 0+11" or "11." The last array element for the Member array is "10" because 10 is the loop termination value. When the top of the loop reaches 9, the value is added to 11, totaling 20—the total number of team members.

Button Out Layer

The second layer consists of a single button and text field. The text field is associated with a variable name so that you can see what happens with the nested loop. The button script uses the array object defined in the frame script and does not need to redefine it. The script goes through the two arrays using a similar nested loop employed to generate the array and its elements' values. Note that after the outside (Team) array runs through once, the value of "m" is reset to zero so that when the loop goes through the members of the second team, it will begin with the first member of the second team. Using the same Boolean multiplier, it is possible to go through all 20 elements of the Member array. The text field properties of this example are shown in Table 5.2.

Table 5.2 Text field properties and names (Input).

Variable Name	Border/Bg	Text Alignment
arrayOut	None	Left

Button (Instance of Out)

Create a button by drawing a circle, selecting it, and pressing the F8 key. Select the Button behavior, name it "Out," and click on OK. The frame script loaded the array with values. To get those values out, all you have to do is to call up the array and put it into a variable that will accumulate all of the values entered with a script in the button. The accumulator variable ("cull") can then be placed into the variable associated with a visible text field on the screen ("arrayOut").

```
on (release) {
    while (t<2) {
        while (m<10) {
cull+="Team "+Team[t]+" member "+Member[m+(t>0)*(m+11)]+newline;
            m+=1;
        }
        t+=1;
        m = 0;
    }
    arrayOut = cull;
    t = 0;
    m = 0;
}
```

To help you understand how the nested loop works, I've broken down the process as follows:

1. At the beginning of the script, both loop counter variables—"t" and "m"—are given a value of 0.

2. The first loop goes through only twice because the loop counter ("t") reaches the limit (2) after the second time through the loop.

3. The second, or "nested," loop uses the loop counter ("m") and loops until the counter reaches 10. Therefore, the nested loop must loop 10 times before the first loop goes through a second time.

4. After the first time through the nested loop, the script increments the counter of the first loop ("Team") and resets the value of the nested loop counter ("Member") to 1. If the "Member" counter were not reset to 1, its value would be too high when it went through the loop the second time, and the inner loop would not execute a second time.

5. When the outer loop goes through its second and last time, it exits the loop. The nested loop is not executed again. Figure 5.2 shows the output when the button is clicked on.

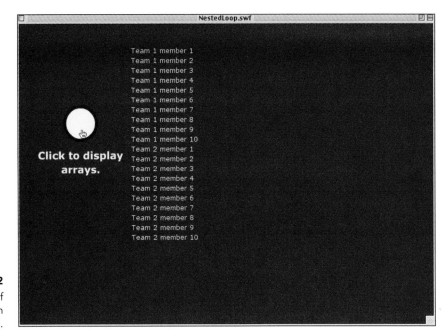

Figure 5.2
The arrays show the values of
their elements when the button
is clicked.

Using loops and nested loops in Flash is one way of orchestrating a multitude of objects on the stage. In Chapters 7, 8, and 9, you'll learn how to set properties and issue commands to objects anywhere in your movie. You'll find that using loops and nested loops enables you to set up different scenarios for interesting movement on your stage.

Learning Utility: Moving Data with a Loop (TransLoop.fla on CD-ROM)

This learning utility uses a single loop to move data from three input text fields to a single output text field using the following layers:

- ButtonActions

- Give

- Labels

- Show

- Background

Using array-like variable names in the three input text fields, the loop uses the **Eval( )** function with a loop counter to put the values from the text fields into an array. The loop reads in the data from the input fields, passes the input data into an array, and then formats the whole thing so that it can be placed into a single output text field.

Unfortunately, when data from multiple fields is placed in the same field, the data already in that field is removed. (The same thing happens with variables, and text fields act like variables in many ways.) For example, if you have 10 different items of data that you want to display in a text field and you use a loop to put them all into the same text field one at a time, only the tenth item remains in the field.

The way around that dilemma is to concatenate all of the data to be transferred and use the carriage return function—**newline**—to provide the line break between the separate data elements. Using a loop and an array makes the job easier. The trick lies in using numbered names in the input variables connected to the input text fields.

Setting up the movie requires only a single script, but the names of the text fields must be exactly as written. Each input text field associates with a numbered name: Name1, Name2, and Name3. In Figure 5.3, each input field has a text label over it that corresponds to the variable name you give it in the Text Field Properties dialog box.

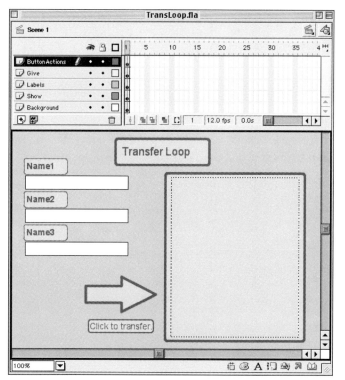

Figure 5.3

An arrow button contains the action script that uses a loop to transfer the user input data from the three text fields on the left to the larger one on the right.

ButtonActions Layer

In the ButtonActions layer, I used a button from the Flash Button Library. The large right-pointing arrow contains the action script that moves three separate fields of data to the text field on the right.

Button: Right Arrow (Instance)

The following script is short, but it does a great deal. To create it, follow these steps:

1. Enter the following script exactly as it appears. It is crucial to copy every parenthesis, operator, and space correctly.

2. Click on the arrow button to select it, and click the Object Actions button in the lower right corner to open the Action panel and Action-Script Editor.

3. Using either the Normal or Expert mode, add the following script.

```
on (release) {
    accum = "";
    show = "";
    tname = new Array();
    for (count=1; count<4; ++count) {
        tname[count] = eval("Name"+count);
        eval("Name"+count) = "";
        accum+=tname[count]+newline;
    }
    show = accum;
}
```

The key to the script is the eighth line, which sets the variable named "accum."

• The variable "accum" accumulates the data from the three input text fields. Note that "accum" adds itself to the new data each time through the loop using a compound assignment operator. In effect, it creates a big string that is sent to the "show" text field.

• The data in the three text fields shown in Figures 5.4 and 5.5 is transferred to the "accum" variable through the loop using an array—**tname[count]**—and pseudo-array—**(eval("Name"+count)**.

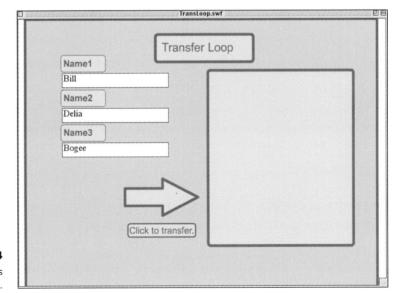

Figure 5.4

First, the user enters three names in the three left text fields.

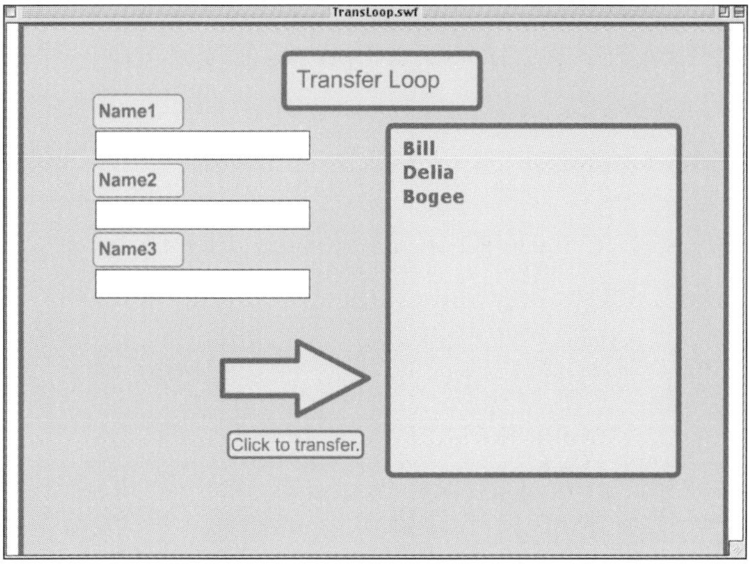

Figure 5.5
As soon as the user clicks on the button, the data in the left text fields is sent to the right, and the three text fields are cleared.

PROJECT Calendar Maker (Calendar.fla on CD-ROM)

Loops enable you to do multiple chores with short scripts. In this project, the movie allows the user to create a monthly calendar by clicking on a starting day and entering the number of days in the desired month. It uses the following layers:

- Start

- Dates

- Buttons and Actions

- Cells

The script immediately fills in the dates on the correct days. Buttons containing action scripts are used for the days of the week. A Clear button resets the calendar so that you can enter a different month whenever you want. All of the buttons use loops to generate the desired number of days in the right places and clear the calendar. Figure 5.6 shows the page in the ActionScript Editor with a button selected revealing the script. All of the button scripts are identical except that each has a different value for the "Begin" variable.

This particular project uses a lot of duplication and many symbols. All 38 cells for the individual dates are instances of a single symbol. Inside each cell is a text field duplicated from a single original. Because the action script in all of the buttons are similar, you can cut and paste the script from the first button into the other days-of-the-week buttons.

Cells Layer

On the foundation layer, I wanted to put in cells for the individual dates. A total of 38 cells were required because, if a month began on a Saturday and

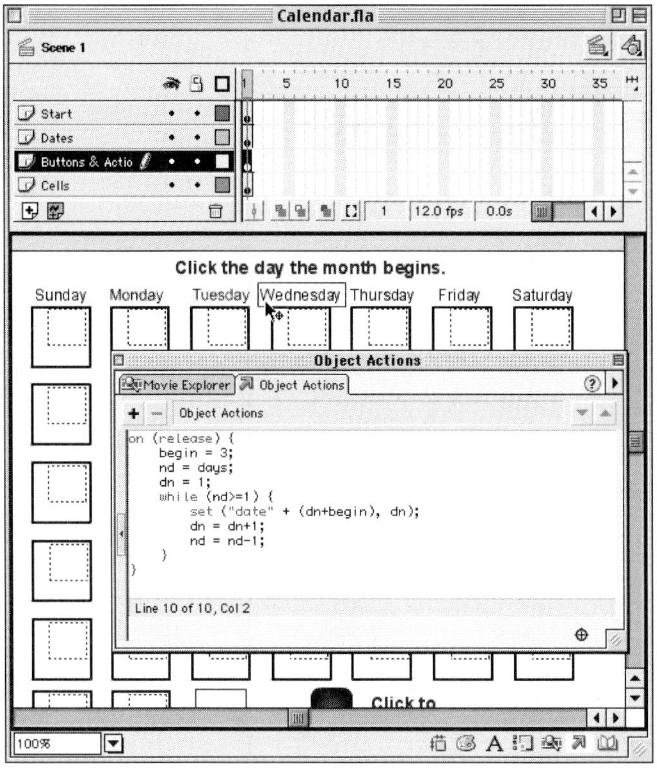

Figure 5.6
A Flash calendar generates the dates for a universal calendar using the power of loops.

was 31 days long (as was July 2000), the days would overflow beyond 31 days beginning on a Sunday. The following steps show how to create the basic layer:

1. Select Insert|New Symbol from the menu bar or use Ctrl+F8/Cmd+F8. In the Symbol Properties dialog box, select Graphic for the behavior, and type in the name "Cell" in the Name window.

2. In the Symbol Editor, draw a single square with the rectangle tool. Hold down the Shift key while drawing with the rectangle tool to maintain a square shape. Use a solid outside color in a 2-point width, no inside color, and a 45-pixel width and height. Use your Info and Stroke panels (they're in the same panel set) to ensure the right dimensions.

3. In the upper left corner of the Symbol Editor, click on the Scene 1 icon and label to return to the main stage.

4. Select Window|Library from the menu bar or use the Ctrl+L/Cmd+L shortcut to open the Symbol Library. Drag five instances of the Cell symbol onto the stage. Arrange the five cells vertically along the left side of the stage. (See Figures 5.6 and 5.7.) Don't worry about the additional cells at the bottom. They'll be added later.

5. Select Window|Panels|Align from the menu bar or use Ctrl+K/Cmd+K to open the Align panel. Use the Pointer tool from the toolbar to select all

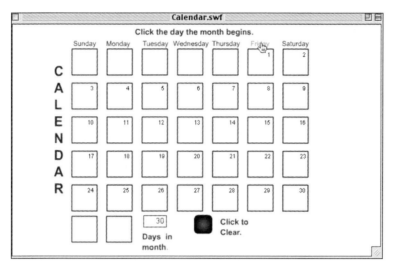

Figure 5.7
The completed calendar fills
up the dates automatically using
a loop.

five of the square symbol instances, click on the Left-Align icon and one of the Vertical Distribute icons, and click on OK. You should now have one vertical line of squares evenly distributed.

6. Select all five, and select Edit|Copy from the menu bar or use Ctrl+C/ Cmd+C to copy all five. Then select Edit|Paste, and paste six copies to give you a total of seven columns—one for each day of the week.

7. Use the Align tool to get all five columns aligned evenly, as shown in Figure 5.7. After you've lined them up, add two more instances of the Cell symbol to the lower left corner to complete the 38 cells needed for the calendar.

The Cells layer is a background layer. Using an instance of a single symbol cuts down on the weight (how long it takes to load) of the movie, and I find symbols a little easier than drawings to work with.

Dates Layer

The Dates layer consists of 38 text fields. The text fields are placed inside the cells in the upper right corner. Because they are text fields, they can be given variable names. In this case, the names will make up a pseudo-array. Here is how you create this layer:

1. Create a text field as a 29-by-27–pixel rectangle using the Text tool and selecting Input Text from the Text Options panel pulldown menu.

2. Select the text field with the Pointer tool. Using the Text Options panel, select each text field. In the Variable window, type in the variable names and other parameters shown in Table 5.3.

3. After you create the first text field, give it a variable name (date1 is the first name), set the options for it, and make 37 copies of it. Place all 38

Table 5.3 Text field properties and names.

Variable Name	Border/Bg	Text Alignment	Restrict Length
date1	None	right	2 characters
. . . .			
date38	None	right	2 characters

in the upper right corner of each cell. The first one (date1) is placed in the upper left cell.

4. Working from left to right and top to bottom (always begin in the far left cell of a new row), rename the 37 copies sequentially from date2 to date38. Leave the first one named date1. Because you set all of the parameters before you made your copies, all 37 copies have the correct settings. All you have to do is rename them ("date2" ... "date38").

Start Layer

The Start layer contains all of the text labels and a text field. You can place the labels wherever you think they look best. Table 5.4 shows the text field properties used in this example.

The role of the text field is to provide the upper limit of the days in the calendar. Because the field has a restricted length of two, any value larger than 99 will be rejected. After filling up all 38 text fields, however, the calendar runs out of room. No error occurs because the Button scripts keep churning out variable names ("date" and "dn") to the top limit of the entered value. In ActionScript, a variable name—even one associated with a text field—is just a variable name. The fact that 38 text fields use the variable name "dateN" does not mean that the text field *owns* the variable name. The text fields are simply associated with the variable name, and Flash makes it easy to display information on the screen by showing the contents of the variable in the text field. Think of a variable as a house and the text field as a window in the house that shows what's going on. However, remember that it is the house that's the variable, not the window.

Buttons and Actions Layer

The day-of-the-week buttons contain the primary code for this project. Each button has the same script except for a single value. The purpose of the code is to generate calendar values for the text fields exactly where they are supposed to go relative to the beginning day of the calendar and the number of days in the month. First, create the buttons as follows:

1. Type in the day of the week using the Text tool.

Table 5.4 Text field properties and names.

Variable Name	Border/Bg	Text Alignment	Max. Char.
days	None	right	2 characters

2. Select the text, and press F8 to turn the text into a symbol. Select Button for the behavior, and type in the day of the week for the name beginning with Sunday. Leave the new symbol selected.

3. Press Ctrl+E/Cmd+E to enter the Symbol Editor.

4. Right above the Layer window, you will see the Up, Over, Down, and Hit options. Click the Over tab, and press F6 to insert a keyframe.

5. Select the symbol, and select Modify|Break Apart from the menu bar or use Ctrl+B/Cmd+B with the Over tab selected.

6. Using the Bucket tool, select red from the color swatches, and click on the text. The entire word should turn red.

7. Select the Down tab, insert a keyframe by pressing the F6 key, and repeat steps 5 and 6 using the color yellow.

8. Repeat steps 1 through 7 for the remaining days of the week.

The next step is to add the action scripts to the buttons, but you first need to understand the overall concept of what this calendar is doing. In the following Sunday button action script, all of the text fields in the cells are targets for data. The loop allows you to start the process of sequentially entering dates without having to write 38 separate scripts to do so.

Button: Sunday...Saturday (Instance)
The action script for the buttons is similar for all seven. The only difference is the value of the variable "begin," which is an offset for the beginning day of the month. Following is the Button action script for Sunday:

```
on (release) {
    begin = 0;
    nd = days;
    dn = 1;
    while (nd>=1) {
        set ("date"+(dn+begin), dn);
        dn = dn+1;
        nd = nd-1;
    }
}
```

The "begin" variable is an offset. Because Sunday is the very first day, it needs no offset; its value is 0. Even though Sunday needs no offset variable, I added one anyway so that I could use the same script for all seven buttons.

The variable "nd" represents the number of days in the month. The value for "nd" is derived from the variable "days" that are associated with the text field in which the user enters the number of days in the month. The value should be between 28 and 31. (If you want to improve the movie, create a script to act as an error checker to make sure that only values from 28 to 31 are allowed. *Hint:* Use the If...Else statement.)

The "dn" variable represents the first day's value, which is always 1. It is used to insert the days of the months sequentially in the calendar as it is incremented in the loop.

The loop condition is that the "nd" variable must be equal to or greater than 1. No matter what value is placed in "nd" (via the text field days), the loop can match it.

The heart of the script lies in placing the right value in the calendar cells. Because each text field is named "dateN" where N is a value from 1 to 38, the job of the script line is to find the right text field to place the number generated in the "dn" variable. Because a real calendar can start on any day of the week, you cannot rely on the sequential numbers in the text fields. Therefore, by adding an offset from the "begin" variable to the string date, you can create a script that concatenates the date with the correct number. For example, if a month begins on a Wednesday, the offset in the variable "begin" is 3. If the first value of "dn" is 1 and is added to the offset of 3, the concatenated value of the date is "date4." Looking at the position of Wednesday on the calendar, you can see it is the fourth from the left; therefore, the text field in that cell would be "date4." By maintaining the offset, the entire calendar can be accurately labeled.

The next two lines of script change the values of "dn" and "nd." The loop increments the "dn" value as the dates are sequentially added to the calendar. At the same time, the loop must decrement the value of "nd" as it uses up the number of days that the calendar can have.

After you type in the script, do the following:

1. Select the script in the Actions list by clicking on the bottom line, holding down the Shift key, and clicking on the top line.

2. Choose Edit|Copy from the menu bar or use Ctrl+C/Cmd+C to copy the script.

3. Click on the next day-of-the-week button, and click in the right window of the Object Actions panel—the ActionScript editor.

4. Select Edit|Paste or use Ctrl+C/Cmd+C.

Voilà! Your script is all ready to go except for one item. Change the "begin" value to the correct day of the week. Use the values shown in Table 5.5.

Button: Clear (Instance)
The Clear button resides at the bottom of the calendar. To look at different months, the user selects the Clear button to clear the calendar for each new month.

Table 5.5 Sunday...Saturday variable values.

Day	Variable Value
Sunday	begin = 0
Monday	begin = 1
Tuesday	begin = 2
Wednesday	begin = 3
Thursday	begin = 4
Friday	begin = 5
Saturday	begin = 6

Test Drive Before You Paste

Before you paste in the code from the Sunday button, finish up the rest of the movie and test to make sure the Sunday button works right. If it has a typo in it, you don't want to duplicate the bug.

```
on (release) {
    clear = 1;
    while (clear<=37) {
        set ("date"+clear, "");
        clear = clear+1;
    }
}
```

The loop simply goes through all 38 text fields and places a null value in each. Because the text field is named like an array, very little script is required to change every single text field.

Using Loops and Arrays for Sort (loopSort.fla on CD-ROM)

Another project using sorts and arrays shows how data entered into a text field and put into an array can be easily sorted for output. The movie uses the following layers:

- Text Fields

- Buttons

- Background

Figure 5.8 shows the initial stage, buttons, labels, and text fields for the movie. The user presses the small button each time she enters a word; after all the words are entered, she presses the large button to sort the words and display them in a second text field.

Text Fields Layer

The first layer contains the text fields for both entering the data and displaying it on the screen. In the "signIn" text field, the user enters data that is then placed into an array when the button above the text field is clicked on. The second text field shows the sorted words. Table 5.6 provides the information to enter into the Text Options panel.

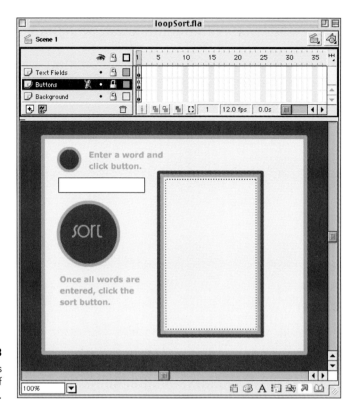

Figure 5.8
Two buttons and two text fields make up the key elements of the movie.

Table 5.6 Text field properties and names.

Variable Name	Border/Bg	Text Alignment	Lines
signIn	Yes	Left	Single line
sortOut	No	Left	Multiline

Buttons Layer

The Buttons layer contains two buttons, each with a script, and the first frame of the layer contains a small script as well.

1. Draw a circle using the circle tool. I used a stroke of 4 with complementary colors for the inside and outside circles with W=24 and H=34. Use the Info panel to get the size correct.

2. Select the drawing, and press the F8 key to open the Symbol Properties dialog box. Select Button as the behavior, and type in the name, "SortIt." Click on OK. Press Scene 1 to exit the Symbol Editor.

3. Draw a second circle with W=94.5 and H=94.5. Select the drawing, and press the F8 key to open the Symbol Properties dialog box. Select Button as the behavior, and type in the name, "sortMe." Click on OK to enter the Symbol Editor.

4. In the Symbol Editor, select the Text tool, and type "Sort" in the center of the button. Use the Align panel to ensure that the label is centered in the middle of the new button.

5. After your second button is labeled, click on the Scene 1 icon to exit the Symbol Editor.

Frame 1

The script in the first frame initializes an array so that both buttons can use the same array without re-initializing it with every click.

```
lword = new Array();
w=0;
```

The array—named "lword"—is globally defined, and any script can reference it. In this movie, both button scripts do so.

Button : SortIt

The first button's script links it to the top text field. As the user enters each value, the script enters it into the array created in Frame 1 and increments the index variable, "w." Then it clears the text field for the next word to be entered.

```
on (release) {
    lword[w] = signIn;
    w+=1;
    signIn = "";
}
```

Button: sortMe

The second button's script is a little more involved, but the sorting routine is very simple. As each word is entered, it is placed in the array named "lword." The single line in the script

```
lword.sort();
```

did all of the sorting. (Figure 5.9 shows what happens when the Sort button is pressed.) Now all you have to do is to use a loop to go from the beginning to the end of the array and put the data into an accumulating variable. This variable can then be placed into the text field used for the output window associated with the variable name "sortOut."

```
on (release) {
    accum = "";
    la = lword.length;
    lword.sort();
    for (x=0; x<la; x++) {
        accum+=lword[x]+newline;
    }
```

Break Apart Fonts

When you use nonstandard fonts, select them and break them apart so that they become drawings using Modify| Break Apart from the menu bar. In that way, you'll be assured of getting the right look of the font.

```
sortOut = accum;
// Clear out the array for another sort.
for (x=0; x<la; x++) {
    lword[x] = "";
}
w = 0;
lword.length = 0;
}
```

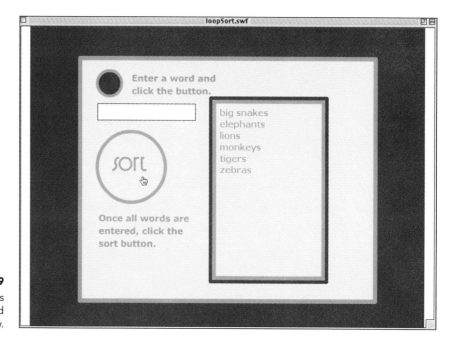

Figure 5.9
As soon as the Sort button is pressed, all of the words entered are sorted alphabetically.

If the movie is to be used more than once, you need a script to clear out the array and get it ready for the next one. So, a second loop goes through the array and places a null ("") into the array. Then, the script resets the index variable ("w") and the length of the array to 0. If a second set of words is placed into the movie with a different number of array elements, the next one will use the previous array length unless you clear the first one.

Background Layer

The Background layer in this movie contains the background patterns. A frame is placed around the output text field to better define it. If you use a border in defining a text field in the Text Options panel, the default is always white. However, I wanted a text field background the same color as the stage. In order to highlight the output text field, I drew a rectangle around it with no inside color, using the Rectangle tool. After drawing it, I selected it, copied it using Edit|Copy, and then pasted it into place, using Edit|Paste In Place from the menu bar. Then, in the Info panel, I enlarged it and selected a different outline color for the rectangle so that it would conform to the general color scheme and design.

The rest of the background is made up of different-colored panels. I've been using background panels for better control over the background when the movie runs in a Web page. Sometimes the background color of the movie is not transferred because I forget to make the necessary adjustments in the export or the HTML, so it's easier to put in all the colors you want in the background to avoid getting stuck with a background color you don't want.

Room for Improvement

If you want a better understanding of how sorts work with ASCII values, try entering a mix of words beginning with upper- and lowercase values. You will find that all of the uppercase words are sorted and placed before the lowercase words. This is because uppercase characters have a lower ASCII value than lowercase words do. Uppercase letters have an ASCII range from 65 (A) to 90 (Z), and lowercase letters range from 97 (a) to 122 (z). As a result, when a sort places words in ascending order, all of the uppercase letters are placed before the lowercase ones.

What if you want to sort words that are a mix of upper- and lowercase words? The quick and dirty way of doing it is to create a string object (see Chapter 7) and use the method

```
stringObj.toUpperCase
```

or

```
stringObj.toLowerCase
```

All of your output would be either in all upper- or lowercase depending on the method you selected. What if you wanted to sort a combination of words beginning with upper- and lowercase letters and you wanted them sorted with the correct letter case? That would be a little trickier, but using string objects, quite possible. See if you can figure it out, but read Chapter 7 first. (Hint: Flag uppercase characters before making them all upper- or lowercase. The magic number is 32—the offset between all upper- and lowercase characters. [For example, 65 + 32 = 97.] Several possible ways can be used to solve this interesting problem.)

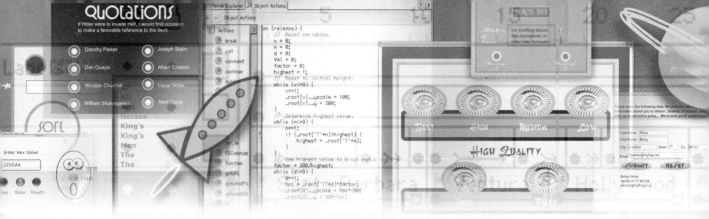

Chapter 6

Handling Events

This chapter shows how to detect mouse and keystroke events and how to handle those events. In addition, the chapter explains how to drag movie clips across the screen.

Understanding Mouse Actions

Did you know that your computer constantly records what your mouse is doing? It keeps track of where the mouse pointer is positioned, whether the mouse button is pressed, and when the button is released. In ActionScript, the detection of a mouse event is handled by the On Mouse Event script action. Figure 6.1 shows the different Mouse Event options that are available in the ActionScript Editor.

Figure 6.1
Mouse Event options in
ActionScript Editor.

Each Mouse Event option can be put to a unique use or combined with another to create more than one mouse event simultaneously. Following are brief descriptions of the various mouse events and when they are recorded:

- *Press*—When the mouse button is pressed to its full limit. The Press option is typically selected to initiate the drag when dragging a movie clip (MC), as explained later in this chapter, but it can also be a "click."

- *Release*—When the mouse button is released. The Release option works like the opposite of Press, but it also can be treated as a mouse click that is typically used for both clicking and releasing a drag operation.

- *ReleaseOutside*—The mouse button must be released when the cursor is not touching any part of the button. The ReleaseOutside event is triggered by placing the mouse pointer on the button and pressing it. With the button still pressed, you drag the mouse cursor off the button and release it.

- *RollOver*—When the mouse pointer is over the button. In the Button editor, the Over frame detects when the mouse pointer is over the button and works in the same way. However, using the action to detect a RollOver event, you can affect any other object as well or fire an action in a selected frame.

- *RollOut*—When the mouse is moved off a button.

- *DragOver*—When the mouse pointer is dragged over the button. The DragOver event handler can be a little tricky and sometimes requires a finer touch than the other mouse events. To fire an event, you may have to scoot it around to just the right places.

- *DragOut*—When the drag is off the button after it has been on the object. This event seems much easier to detect than the DragOver mouse event.

The On Mouse Event action in Basic Actions or the **on()action** is available only when you are providing actions to a button. Also, in Flash 5 ActionScript, the **onClipEvent( )** statement has another set of button event actions discussed later in this chapter. The **on()action**, though, is never available when you are working on a Frame action script. The following example shows how the different buttons react to the mouse in a movie script.

Mouse Event (mouseEvent.fla on CD-ROM)

Focusing on the mouse event-handling elements associated with button symbols, this next script contains three layers:

- Action Button
- Sound
- Tomato Blaster

This minimalist, arcade-type movie is centered around a deadly "Tomato Blaster" (patent pending), which is made up of a tweened splattering of a tomato. It even includes sound effects, representing a typical arcade application of a mouse event. Figure 6.2 shows the layers and initial view of the movie layout.

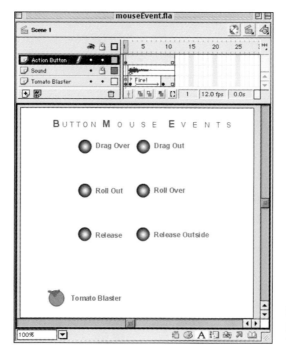

Figure 6.2

Different event handlers used in a "Tomato Blaster" movie.

Tomato Blaster Layer

To make the Tomato Blaster, you use a simple drawing of a tomato tweened into a splatter, as follows:

1. Select Frame 12 by clicking on it, and press the F5 key to insert a row of 12 frames.

2. Use the circle tool to draw the tomato's body in the lower left corner of the stage. Add a couple of green vine remnants on the tomato with the brush tool.

3. Insert a keyframe in Frame 2 by selecting the frame and pressing the F6 key. Open the Frame panel using Ctrl+F (Windows)/Cmd+F (Macintosh), and with the keyframe still selected, name the keyframe "Fire!" in the Label window. In Frame 9, insert another keyframe using the same technique. (You don't need a name for Frame 9.)

4. In the keyframe in Frame 9, draw a "splattered tomato" like the one in Figure 6.3.

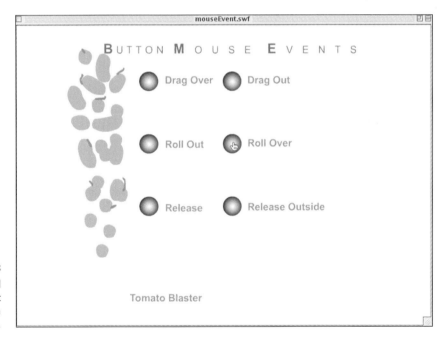

Figure 6.3
The blast effect is morphed into place by the different event handlers in the buttons on the stage.

5. In the Frame panel, select the Tweening pulldown menu, and choose Shape.

6. Double-click on Frame 1 to open the Frame Actions window and ActionScript Editor. Enter the script indicated for Frame 1. (It's just a single stop action.)

Frame 1

```
stop();
```

The Tomato Blaster is a generic concept for any action on the stage. The mouse events trigger the action in the movie.

Sound Layer

You now need to create a Sound layer. On this layer, do the following:

1. Add a keyframe in Frame 2 by selecting the frame and pressing the F6 key.

2. Select Window|Common Libraries|Sounds from the menu bar. From the Sounds Library, choose "Metal Klank" because it is similar to the sound of a tomato blaster.

3. Double-click on the keyframe in Frame 2 to open the Sound panel. In the Sound pulldown menu, select "Metal Klank." You can leave the rest of the parameters as the default, but make sure that Loops are set to 0 in the Sound panel. (You don't want more than one "Klank" sound.)

Action Button Layer

On the Action Button layer, create six buttons. Each will be used to demonstrate different mouse events. After the buttons are created, lay them out on the stage as shown in Figures 6.2 and 6.3. Use the Align window to arrange all of the buttons. Provide labels to the right of each button. Add the following action script to each button. (Begin with the top pair of buttons and work downward, beginning with the left button in each pair.)

```
on (dragOver) {
    gotoAndPlay ("Fire!");
}

----------

on (dragOut) {
    gotoAndPlay ("Fire!");
}

----------

on (rollOut) {
    gotoAndPlay ("Fire!");
}

----------
```

```
on (rollOver) {
    gotoAndPlay ("Fire!");
}

- - - - - - - - - -

on (release) {
    gotoAndPlay ("Fire!");
}

- - - - - - - - - -

on (releaseOutside) {
    gotoAndPlay ("Fire!");
}

- - - - - - - - - -
```

Note: Be careful not to select more than one checkbox initially. If you do, you will see two or more events in the same line of script.

The event conditions are selected from the checkboxes in the bottom portion of the ActionScript Editor.

After you have finished, try out the different buttons. Figure 6.3 shows the movie firing the Tomato Blaster when the mouse cursor is passed over the RollOver selection. Also notice what happens when you "rapid fire" one of the buttons.

When you have the movie working as expected, try putting multiple events in a single button. You will get no error messages, but you may be surprised by what you do find.

The On Mouse Event handlers in ActionScript are vitally important to different kinds of actions. Unlike the limited Up, Over, Down, and Hit functions built into buttons, the On Mouse Event action allows a far wider range of events to influence different parts of your movie. In Chapter 7, when you begin using scripts that change properties, you can control how the properties use different mouse events.

When a Key Is Pressed

One of the more unusual implementations in Flash ActionScript is the use of key presses to influence a movie. As discussed in the previous section, only buttons can generate the On Mouse Event actions. One of the options for an On Mouse Event (in Basic Actions) is a key press, even though a key press is *not* a mouse event. After you get past that paradox, detecting a key press is quite simple to implement with ActionScript.

Key presses are *case sensitive*; variables and labels are *case insensitive*. For example, if you label a frame "Q," invoking the action of Go to and Stop ("Q") or Go to and Stop ("q") takes the movie to the frame named "Q." If you designate a key press as "Q" and then press the lower case "q," however, you won't fire the event. Just think of the keyboard as being "sensitive" to the touch of your fingertips and remember that the key presses are (case) sensitive as well. Labels and variables are (case) insensitive brutes.

Where's the Button?

The big question for me when I first started using key presses in my scripts was "How do you see the buttons for key presses?" If I want a key press to fire an event, do I have to put a button on the stage? The answer is that you don't need to see a button, but you do need at least one button to enter the script for all of the key presses that you want. To work effectively with invisible buttons on the stage, I found that creating a separate layer for the invisible key press button allowed me to edit the button by selecting the layer and then choosing Edit|Symbols from the menu bar. In the Symbol Editor, all that is visible is a plus sign (+). By selecting it and pressing the Scene icon to return to the main timeline, the invisible button is selected. Then in the ActionScript Editor, any script that I write is in the invisible button until I deselect it by clicking on the stage or some other layer. The next movie shows how key presses work.

Keyboard (Keyboard.fla on CD-ROM)

Three layers make up the movie:

- Invisible Button

- Letters

- Background

This movie uses four different key presses consisting of upper- and lowercase instances of the letters "R" and "L." (In a movie, you may want to use those letters to move an object "Right" and "Left.") A single layer houses the invisible button, a second layer shows the different letters that are pressed in a static text message linked to the labeled frames, and a third layer uses a graphic to frame the static text messages (see Figure 6.4). At each keyframe, a little man holding an announcement shows the letter, including case, that the user selected. Notice that each key press button layer uses single upper- and lowercase letter characters, but the labels on the keyframes spell out the "capL" and "capR" to distinguish the frames from the lowercase "l" and "r."

In the Library window on the right side of the stage in Figure 6.4, note the button icon labeled "invisible." Also note in the Library preview window that only the crosshair icon is visible, which means that the button cannot be seen. Because the buttons are used to detect key presses, they are supposed to be invisible; however, the button must be placed on the stage. Creating an invisible button with a script to fire an event when a key is pressed does no good unless the button is placed on the stage. (It doesn't matter that the button is invisible to the user because there is no visible button target—only a key on the keyboard.)

Figure 6.4
The invisible key press button appears as a plus (+) sign in the Library preview window and in the Symbol Editor.

Letters Layer

Click on Frame 21, and press the F5 key to bring the movie out 21 frames. The Background layer has four keyframes beyond the first one. Each one has a slightly different message on the stage, representing the key press used. Figure 6.4 shows the frame labeled "capL." Each of the other keyframes use the identical text and image except that each has a different letter—L, l, R, and r—corresponding to the key pressed.

Frame 1

Double-click on the frame to open the Actions panel and insert a stop action in the ActionScript Editor.

```
stop();
```

l (Label): Frame 4

Use the Text tool to create the text, "You chose l, an excellent choice if I do say so." (For example, see Figure 6.5.) In the Text Options panel, be sure that the text type is Static text. All of the other keyframes use the same text, changing only the letter.

capL (Label): Frame 8

Modify the text from Frame 4 to substitute the lowercase "l" for an uppercase "L."

r (Label): Frame 13

Modify the text from Frame 8 to substitute the uppercase "L" for a lowercase "r."

Figure 6.5
In the Shockwave (SWF) file, you can see the message for each of the keyframes when the corresponding key is pressed.

capR (Label): Frame 16

Modify the text from Frame 13 to substitute the lowercase "r" for an upper-case "R."

Each of the key presses jumps to the frame with the corresponding character. Be sure to name the frames as shown so that the program will not confuse the "r" and "R" or "l" and "L" labels. The labels are *case insensitive*.

Invisible Button Layer

The Invisible Button layer contains most of the ActionScript for the movie. Follow these steps:

1. Select the Invisible Button layer.

2. From the menu bar, select Insert|New Symbol. The Symbol Properties dialog box appears.

3. Select Button for the behavior, and name it "invisible."

4. Click on the Scene 1 icon to return to the main timeline.

5. Select Window|Library from the menu bar. In the Library window, select the button icon labeled "invisible," and drag it onto the stage. Because it is invisible, all you will see as you drag the icon is a square made of broken lines. Put it in the corner, out of the way.

6. Keep the Invisible Button selected by not selecting any other layer or clicking on any object on the stage. Open the ActionScript Editor by clicking on the Show Object Actions arrow icon in the Launcher Bar.

7. In the ActionScript Editor, double-click on the "on" action in the Action submenu. At the bottom of the editor, select Key Press, and type in a lowercase "l," as shown in Figure 6.6.

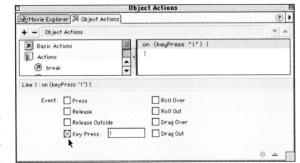

Figure 6.6
In the ActionScript Editor, the "on" action provides a Key Press option.

8. Next, double click on the "goto" action, deselect the Go To And Play checkbox at the bottom of the editor, and type in "l" for the label name.

9. Complete the button script so that it looks like the following:

Invisible Button

```
on (keyPress "l") {
    gotoAndStop ("l");
}
on (keyPress "r") {
    gotoAndStop ("r");
}
on (keyPress "L") {
    gotoAndStop ("capL");
}
on (keyPress "R") {
    gotoAndStop ("capR");
}
```

Note: Key press assignments are case sensitive. Frame labels and variable names are case insensitive. (Don't say I didn't remind you.)

Key Objects

In addition to using a button for getting a key press, you can also do it with the new Key object and the methods and constants associated with the object. Also, it's about time to start using the Expert Mode in the ActionScript Editor. When you enter the script for these next examples, use the Expert Mode by selecting the pulldown menu on the upper right corner of the Actions panel.

The Key object has 4 methods and 18 constants. Before getting into some script, review the following lists of the Key methods and Key constants.

Key Methods

The four Key methods are all associated to the Key object using the dot (.) association operator.

- **Key.getAscii();**—Gets the ASCII code for the last pressed key.

- **Key.getCode();**—Gets the virtual keycode for the last pressed key.

- **Key.isDown(n);**—Boolean true if the key of keycode value (n) is pressed.

- **Key.isToggled();**—Boolean true if either the Caps Lock or Num Lock is on.

Using **Key.getAscii()** in combination with the **chr()** function, you can identify any of the standard keys. For example, the following script returns the last key pressed as a string in a text field associated with the variable name "write." This can be entered into a frame script as well as a script in either a button or MC.

```
x=Key.getAscii();
write=chr(x);
```

This script is simplicity itself, especially compared to using a separate script for every single key. The value of the last key pressed is put into a variable, and the **chr()** function returns the string of the ASCII value. The Key object does not use a constructor; therefore, the data returned by the Key methods and constants can be placed right into a variable, just as the preceding script does.

Key Constants

Note that all of the Key constants are in all uppercase letters. Use the following Key constants with one of the Key methods listed earlier:

- **Key.BACKSPACE**—Returns the keycode value (8) for the Backspace key.

- **Key.CAPSLOCK**—Returns the keycode value (20) for the Caps Lock key.

- **Key.CONTROL**—Returns the keycode value (17) for the Control key.

- **Key.DELETEKEY**—Returns the keycode value (46) for the Delete key.

- **Key.DOWN**—Returns the keycode value (40) for the down arrow key.

- **Key.END**—Returns the keycode value (35) for the End key.

- **Key.ENTER**—Returns the keycode value (13) for the Enter/Return key.

- **Key.ESCAPE**—Returns the keycode value (27) for the Esc key.

- **Key.HOME**—Returns the keycode value (36) for the Home key.

- **Key.INSERT**—Returns the keycode value (45) for the Insert key.

- **Key.LEFT**—Returns the keycode value (37) for the left arrow key.

- **Key.PGDN**—Returns the keycode value (34) for the Page Down key.

- **Key.PGUP**—Returns the keycode value (33) for the Page Up key.

- **Key.RIGHT**—Returns the keycode value (39) for the right arrow key.

- **Key.SHIFT**—Returns the keycode value (16) for the Shift key.

- **Key.SPACE**—Returns the keycode value (32) for the spacebar.

- **Key.TAB**—Returns the keycode value (9) for the Tab key.

- **Key.UP**—Returns the keycode value (38) for the up arrow key.

These keys are often used in arcade-style games. The following script shows how a conditional statement used with the Key object is used to go to a frame that simulates firing a space blaster or triggering a cloaking device.

```
if (Key.isDown(Key.SPACE)) {
    gotoAndPlay("Fire")
}
if (Key.isDown(Key.TAB)) {
    gotoAndPlay("Cloak")
}
```

Several conditionals using the same frame, button, or MC can be used to program as many keys as you want. In Chapter 7, you will see how the keys can be used to change MC properties as well.

Mouse Objects

One of the new Flash 5 objects is Mouse. It has only two methods: **hide()** and **show()**. You can use these two methods to create custom cursors. You can either hide the mouse cursor or show it. The statements

```
Mouse.hide();
Mouse.show();
```

will hide and show the mouse arrow, respectively. The movie in the next section shows how to hide the arrow cursor and replace it with an MC standing in for the standard cursor.

Two properties related to the mouse are **_xmouse** and **_ymouse**. Both are read-only functions that return the position of the mouse on the screen. They can be used with an MC to make their positions that of the MC.

Clip Events

One of the major changes in ActionScript is the use of MCs as a home for scripts and the new **onClipEvent** action. The **onClipEvent** action is similar to the **on(MouseEvent)** actions, except that it lives on the MC as a whole and not inside it in a frame or button action. The following events serve to trigger the scripts:

- *load*—The script is executed as soon as the MC is loaded.

- *unload*—When the Unload MC event occurs, the associated script runs.

- *enterFrame*—Runs the script as each frame is entered.

- *mouseMove*—As soon as the mouse moves, the script initiates.

- *mouseDown*—This is the equivalent to the **on(press)** statement in buttons. The script is launched by the mouse button being in the down position.

- *mouseUp*—This is the equivalent to the **on(release)** statement in buttons. When the mouse button is up, the script plays.

- *keyDown*—Using the Key object, **Key.getCode()**, the script launches when a key is pressed.

- *keyUp*—Using the Key object, **Key.getCode()**, the script launches when a key is pressed.

- *data*—The script plays when data from a loadVariables or loadMovie is detected.

Using clip events makes creating interactive movies relatively simple. The following movie shows how to use MC events and the Mouse object.

Drag and Drop a Cursor MC (newCursor.fla on CD-ROM)

This movie shows how to use a clip event in conjunction with a Mouse object and an MC to create an alternate cursor using three layers:

- Cursor

- Release

- Background

Figure 6.7 shows the stage with the layers and objects laid out and the Library window displaying an enlarged preview of the MC used as a cursor.

Cursor Layer

On the Cursor layer, create an MC to be used as a cursor. In this example, I used a "thumbs up" icon I borrowed from a font set (Kobalt Kartoon— **www.flashfonts.com**). Font sets are a good place for such items as specialized cursors. The following steps show how create an MC with a font. (Instead of using a font, you can also use a drawing.)

1. Type a character to be used as a cursor using the Text tool from the toolbox. Open the Text Objects panel, and select Static Text as the type of text.

2. With the text selected, choose Modify|Break Apart or Ctrl+B/Cmd+B. Now the text is a graphic image instead of a font.

3. With the graphic from the broken text still selected, press the F8 key to open the Symbol Properties dialog box.

Figure 6.7
A replacement cursor is made up of a movie clip that is dragged on the stage.

Note: The name you type in is the instance name and is used in the script to reference the MC.

4. In the Symbol Properties dialog box, select Movie Clip for the behavior, and type in "Cursor" for the MC label. Click on OK to enter the Symbol Editor, and then click on the Scene icon to return to the main timeline.

5. Select the new MC, and open the Instance panel using Ctrl+I/Cmd+I. Type in "thumb" in the Name window.

6. Select the MC, and enter one of the following two scripts.

MC: Instance Name "thumb"

These two scripts are identical in what they accomplish. The second uses the MovieClip object. When using the object method, using the **_root** path for the MC on the top level specifies exactly where the MC is located. If you use clips that are not on the top level, you can create an absolute path beginning with **_root** and then name all of the objects in the MC's hierarchy. It's a good habit to maintain consistent form when using Object-Oriented Programming. The load event is used to launch the script in both scripts. The Mouse object using the **hide**() method makes the arrow pointer disappear.

```
onClipEvent (load) {
    Mouse.hide();
    startDrag (thumb, true);
}
```

or

```
onClipEvent (load) {
    Mouse.hide();
    _root.thumb.startDrag(true);
}
```

You will find that the substitute cursor acts like a regular cursor in terms of clicking on buttons and other objects. You need to place the cursor on the top layer, however, to make sure that it does not pass beneath the object it is being used to click on.

Release Layer

After you have created your new cursor, you may want to get the old mouse cursor back and release the cursor made from an MC. The Release layer provides two ways to release the MC. One release script is in Frame 1 of this layer, and one is in a button.

Frame 1

This script uses the Esc (escape) key to release the MC with the **stopDrag()** action and to show the mouse. Using the Key object method, the conditional statement simply asks whether the last key down was the Esc key. If it was, then it stops the drag (i.e., it releases the cursor), and the original cursor appears the first time the mouse is clicked.

```
if (Key.isDown(Key.ESCAPE)) {
stopDrag();
}
```

MC Release

Create an MC by drawing an oval with a black center and an outer ring with a 6-point stroke. To demonstrate that an MC cursor works like a regular cursor for activating button scripts, a second script in the release MC provides an almost identical script to that in Frame 1. Note that in both scripts the **stopDrag()** contains no arguments. Because only a single object can be dragged at one time with the mouse, whatever is being currently dragged is released with no need to specify the instance name.

```
onClipEvent (mouseDown) {
    Mouse.show();
    stopDrag ();
}
```

Background Layer

The background is made up of a single large rectangle covering the stage and concentric circles ending with the button in the middle. The message, "Click anywhere on the stage to get your cursor back," is another specialized font. (I used RocketGothic from **www.flashfonts.com**.) Because it is probably not on most computers, I broke it apart using Ctrl+B/Cmd+B, colored it using the Paint Bucket tool, and turned it into a symbol for easy maintenance and preservation. Figure 6.8 shows the movie as it appears in the Flash player.

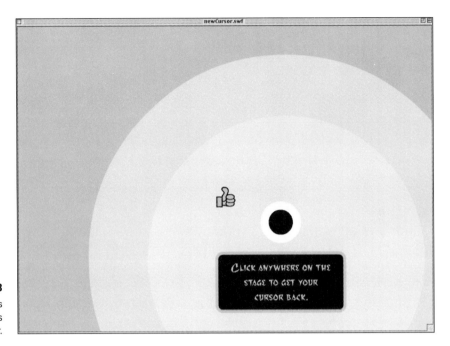

Figure 6.8
The mouse arrow cursor has been replaced by the "thumbs up" movie clip as the cursor.

MovieClip Objects

The MovieClip object allows you to attach many of the actions found in the ActionScript Editor as well as some that are not. Using the MovieClip object and the attached method takes less code and is usually clearer than using some of the other methods. No constructor object is required, but an instance name for the MC is. All MovieClip object names are instance names.

MovieClip Methods

Many of the following methods are discussed in later chapters; therefore, the following list simply shows which methods can be associated with a MovieClip object without defining them. Most of the methods covered in the book so far are fairly clear [for example, **gotoAndPlay()**]; others are defined later on.

- **MCInstanceName.attachMovie()**

- **MCInstanceName.duplicateMovieClip()**

- **MCInstanceName.getBounds()**

- **MCInstanceName.getBytesLoaded()**

- **MCInstanceName.getBytesTotal()**

- **MCInstanceName.getURL()**

- **MCInstanceName.globalToLocal()**

- MCInstanceName.gotoAndPlay()

- MCInstanceName.gotoAndStop()

- MCInstanceName.hitTest()

- MCInstanceName.loadMovie()

- MCInstanceName.loadVariables

- MCInstanceName.localToGlobal

- MCInstanceName.nextFrame()

- MCInstanceName.play()

- MCInstanceName.prevFrame()

- MCInstanceName.removeMovieclip()

- MCInstanceName.startDrag()

- MCInstanceName.stop()

- MCInstanceName.stopDrag()

- MCInstanceName.swapDepth()

- MCInstanceName.unloadMovie()

Formatting the MovieClip Object Action

The format of a MovieClip object statement uses the dot operator and clearly lays out the clip and its method. For example, to stop all actions in an MC with the instance name "Fred," use the following script for the correct format:

```
_root.Fred.stop();
```

Chapter 9 explains how to use the **tellTarget()** action to do what this script does. As you will see in Chapter 9, however, substituting a MovieClip object and format for **tellTarget()** is actually easier and more consistent with Object-Oriented Programming.

Collision Detection

One important method in the MovieClip object is **hitTest()**, the collision detection method for MCs. This method is not available as an action, and so it must be used as a method with a MovieClip object. For creating games and interactive Web sites, and for engaging e-commerce sites, the **hitTest()** method has many applications.

Two different sets of arguments may accompany **hitTest()**. The simpler of the two specifies the target. For example, the following conditional script looks to see if an MC has collided with another MC with the instance name "fatCat."

```
if (this.hitTest(_root.fatCat)) {
      _root.gotoAndPlay("whiskers");
   }
```

Note that the **_root** property is used in identifying both the target MC and the timeline for the frame target named "whiskers." Where "/" is used in Flash 4 to identify the root level, "**_root**" is now used in Flash 5.

A second set of arguments associated with **hitTest()** are the actual coordinates. The coordinates can be entered as variables or constants in global coordinate space. For example, the following script will test any object for a hit at X=228 and Y=114 by an MC:

```
if (this.hitTest (228, 114, false)) {
}
```

Using the second **hitTest()** method, you rely on whatever is at a given coordinate instead of a specific MC instance name.

Colliding Objects (planetCollide.fla on CD-ROM)

This next movie shows how to use **hitTest()** with an unguided missile crashed into a planet. The movie uses four layers:

- Rocket
- Planet
- Stars
- Background

Figure 6.9 shows the initial stage and graphics. Both the rocket and planet images are MCs.

When you get started on a movie, first create the layers in the order shown. Then select Frame 35, and drag the cursor downward from the Rocket to the Background layer. Press the F5 key to bring all active frames to Frame 35.

Rocket Layer

The rocket MC is one side of the collision equation. Its job is to run into the planet MC containing the ActionScript that detects the collision. It then bounces off the planet MC once the detection is made. The rocket flame out the back is an animated movie on the MC's timeline.

MC: Instance Name "zoom"

When you make the rocket and transform it into an MC by pressing F8 and selecting Movie Clip as the behavior, remember to give it an instance name in the Instance Panel. The instance name for the rocket is "zoom." You want it to "fly" straight to the planet. Here's how:

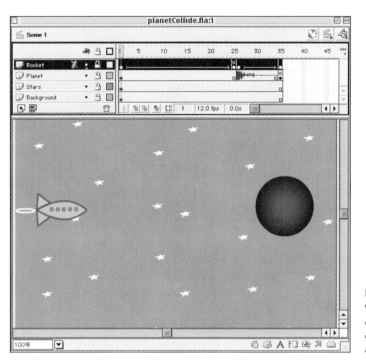

Figure 6.9
When two movie clips collide, a test for collision can be used in establishing a conditional outcome.

1. Once you have the rocket MC created and named with an instance name, drag it to the far left side of the screen, as shown in Figure 6.9.

2. Click on Frame 25, and insert a keyframe by pressing F6. Drag the rocket so that its nose will overlap the side of the planet MC. (See "Frame 25," below.)

3. Click on Frame 1, and select Window|Panels|Frame or Ctrl+F/Cmd+F to open the Frame panel. In the Tweening pulldown menu, select Motion. You will now see a tweening arrow between Frames 1 and 25.

4. Insert a keyframe in Frames 26 and 35. Move the playhead to Frame 35, and drag the rocket to the upper left corner of the stage.

5. Click on Frame 26, and select Motion in the Tweening pulldown menu of the Frame panel. In the Rotate pulldown menu, select CW, and type in "8" for the number of times.

Frame 25

To demonstrate that the rocket's reaction is to the collision condition, you need to enter a script in the frame to stop the movie. Just select Frame 25, and enter the following in the ActionScript Editor. If there is no collision detection, the rocket just stops when it hits the planet.

```
Stop();
```

Planet Layer

The planet is a big circle with a radial fill. Just draw the circle, select it, and press F8 to turn it into an MC. Give it the instance name "stone" in the Instance Panel. Also on this layer is the frame to begin a bounce off the planet. Follow these steps:

1. Click on Frame 26, and press the F6 key to insert a keyframe. Name the frame "bang" in the Frame panel Label window.

2. Select Window|Common Libraries|Sounds to open the Sounds library. Select Frame 26, and drag the sound "Bucket Hit" to the stage. In the Sound pulldown menu in the Sound panel, you should see "Bucket Hit"; select Frame 26, and you should see the sound wave icon in the frame. In this case, the sound wave icon gets in the way of seeing the label, "bang."

MC: Instance Name "stone"

The heart and soul of the movie is in this MC. It sets a variable in the main timeline called "collide." If the variable is not set to 1, the script in Frame 25 on the Rocket layer stops the movie. Only by hitting the planet with the instance name "stone" can the movie proceed to its logical condition.

```
onClipEvent (enterFrame) {
    if (this.hitTest(_root.zoom)) {
        _root.gotoAndPlay("bang");
    }
}
```

Stars Layer

Draw a white star. Select it, press the Alt/Option key, and drag several copies scattered around the stage. You can also use the copy and paste method.

Background Layer

Reduce the zoom to 50 or 25 percent. Select the Rectangle tool, and draw a solid blue background over the whole stage. If you're not sure whether you have it completely covered, use the Info panel to make adjustments.

Figure 6.10 shows the rocket bouncing off the planet after the collision detection sends the movie to the "bang" frame and the bounce sequence.

Selection and Text Fields

Selection objects belong to the realm of text fields. Most of the methods associated with the Selection object are read-only and deal with the span within a text field. No constructor object is required, and so the methods are all linked to Selection with a dot operator. The following is a brief description of the methods in the Selection syntax:

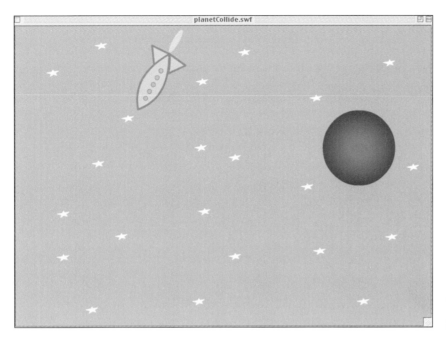

Figure 6.10
After the collision detection, the rocket appears to bounce off the planet movie clip.

- **Selection.getBeginIndex**();—Beginning with 0, the method returns the index at the beginning of the current field.

- **Selection.getCaretIndex**();—The blinking cursor's position is returned by the methods with 0 as the first.

- **Selection.getEndIndex**();—Index at the end of the selection span.

- **Selection.getFocus**();—Variable name with **_levelN** returned.

- **Selection.setFocus**();—Sets the focus to the variable name associated with the text field.

- **Selection.setSelection**();—Both the beginning index and ending index of the selection span is set.

Because text fields in Flash 5 can be used for data entry, the Selection object and methods have a number of applications. The movie in this next section shows one.

Forms and Selection (SelectForms.fla on CD-ROM)

Rather than using up screen space with several labels, the next movie uses the information in the text fields to tell the user which field she is in and what information to put in it. It uses two layers:

- Forms

- Background

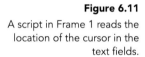

Figure 6.11

A script in Frame 1 reads the location of the cursor in the text fields.

Figure 6.11 shows the initial layout. Five input text fields and a dynamic text field make up the bulk of the movie.

The concept behind the movie is to determine the message the viewer sees when she is in the different text fields. Using **Selection.getFocus()**; a script in the first frame keeps looking to see which text field the cursor is currently in. If it is in no field, a **null** is returned, which is ignored by the script. Add a layer, label both the script and the layer, and add a frame in Frame 2 to prepare the movie for production.

Background Layer

The Background layer is made up of different colored rectangles to provide a base for the forms that are added. First put in the background so that the input text fields show up more clearly.

Forms Layer

The Forms layer is made up of five text fields set to Input Text and one text field set to Dynamic Text. Table 6.1 shows the variable names and characteristics of the fields.

The text fields for input are numbered from 1 to 5 for ordering them on the basis of how they will be encountered sequentially. Although I usually do not recommend using nondescriptive variable names, in this case the emphasis should be on the order of the fields instead of on the descriptive labels for

Table 6.1 Text field properties and names.

Variable Name	Border/Bg	Text Alignment	Format
1	Yes	Left	Text Input
2	Yes	Left	Text Input
3	Yes	Left	Text Input
4	Yes	Left	Text Input
5	Yes	Left	Text Input
instruct	No	Center	Dynamic Text (non-select)

them. When you create the Input Text field, use a 12-point Verdana font. The Dynamic Text field instructs the user as to what to place in the other five text fields and uses a 36-point Verdana font.

Frame 1

The script finds the focus (which text field the cursor is in) by using **Selection.getFocus()** placed into a variable "a." The **Selection.getFocus()** object and method return the variable name connected to a **_level0** path. As the user tabs through the text fields, new information is returned to the variable and passed through a conditional statement that sends a different message to the text field associated with the variable name, "instruct."

```
a = Selection.getFocus();
if (a == "_level0.1") {
    instruct = "Name Please";
} else if (a == "_level0.2") {
    instruct = "Address Please";
} else if (a == "_level0.3") {
    instruct = "City Please";
} else if (a == "_level0.4") {
    instruct = "State Please";
} else if (a == "_level0.5") {
    instruct = "Zip Code Please";
}
```

Although the movie script is fairly small, it represents a different way of employing screen space and an object that deals exclusively with text fields. Figure 6.12 shows the movie with a completed form and the cursor in the last form field.

Drag and Drop with Buttons inside Movie Clips

Flash provides actions that allow you to create MCs that the user can drag across the screen and drop in different locations on the screen. Everything from product selection to the creation of learning games can be done with drag and drop. For example, geography lessons can be designed around the

Figure 6.12
The user is given instructions
from a single source based on
the field the cursor is currently in.

outlines of states or countries that are dropped into place by students. User interfaces can offer Web site visitors the option of dragging service or product icons into shopping baskets.

Button Script Drag (Duster.fla on CD-ROM)

This is a very simple movie using one layer on the main timeline and a single layer on the MC's timeline.

- MainTimeLine

- MC: dragMe

  - Button

Preparation

To create the drag-and-drop effect in your movie, you need an MC with an instance of a Button symbol inside it. Inside the button, you place an action that allows the user to press the mouse button while over the MC's button and then to drag the entire MC around the screen, releasing the clip when the button is released. The following movie example shows the basics of a drag-and-drop operation in a movie. (With it, you can dust your screen and keep it nice and clean. Amaze your friends, especially the more gullible ones.) Figure 6.13 shows the MC being created in the Symbol Editor. On the screen, the viewer sees just the MC because it is the only object with visible features in the movie.

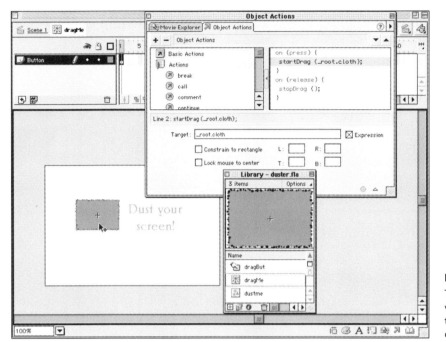

Figure 6.13
The movie clip contains the
visible portions of the movie, and
the button in the movie clip
contains the ActionScript.

MainTimeLine Layer

Duster is a simple movie that shows how drag and drop works. The stage holds
a rectangle "dusting cloth" and a graphic admonition to "Dust your screen!"

1. On a new page, select Insert|New Symbol... to open the Symbol Proper-
   ties dialog box.

2. Select Movie Clip for the behavior, and name it "dragMe." Click on OK.
   You are now in the Symbol Editor.

3. Draw a rectangle with a broken, ragged border. Select it, and press the
   F8 key to turn it into a symbol. (To achieve a ragged border effect, use
   the Stroke panel, and select a ragged line.)

4. In the Symbol Properties dialog box, select Button for the behavior,
   and name the symbol "dragBut." Click on OK. (You are still in the Symbol Editor.)

5. Select the button you just created, and open the Expert Mode of the
   ActionScript Editor. Enter one of the following scripts—they both do the
   same thing:

MC: dragMe Button Script, Button Layer

In the Expert Mode, you have to watch carefully that you put in all of the
necessary symbols. If you are still more comfortable in the Normal Mode,
use it. Figure 6.13 shows the script in the Normal Mode with the options
for starting a drag operation.

```
on (press) {
    startDrag (_root.cloth);
}
on (release) {
    stopDrag ();
}
```

or substitute in the second line

```
startDrag (this);
```

6. Click on the Scene 1 icon to exit the Symbol Editor and return to the main timeline. Type in the message "Dust your Screen!" with the Text tool next to the button, but not *on* the button.

7. Select the text, and press the F8 key to turn it into a symbol. Select Graphic for the behavior in the Symbol Properties dialog box, and name it "dustme." (You may also leave the text as is without turning it into a symbol.) Because a nonstandard font is used, I turned the font into a symbol so that users who don't have that font on their computers can still view it.

8. You are now finished with the objects and script for the MC. Use the keyboard shortcut Ctrl+L/Cmd+L to open the Library where you will see three symbols.

Note: You must type in an instance name. Without one, you cannot address an MC with any script.

9. Drag the MC from the Library window to the stage in the main timeline. Select the MC, and press Ctrl+I/Cmd+I to open the Instance panel. Click on the Name window in the Instance panel, and type in "cloth" for the MC's instance name.

Save the program, and take it for a test drive. Place the mouse pointer over the button image, and drag the MC around the screen. (Now, get busy and dust off your screen.) Figure 6.14 shows the cloth busily cleaning a screen.

PROJECT Learning Utility: Viewing the X, Y Values of the Mouse Pointer on the Screen (DragXY.fla on CD-ROM)

By placing the X (horizontal) and Y (vertical) coordinates on the stage, you can get a clearer idea of exactly where the pointer is. This next movie uses mouse pointer information and sends the X/Y coordinates to a text field so you can see where the mouse currently is located, using the following layers:

- Position
  - MC: Text
- Show X Y

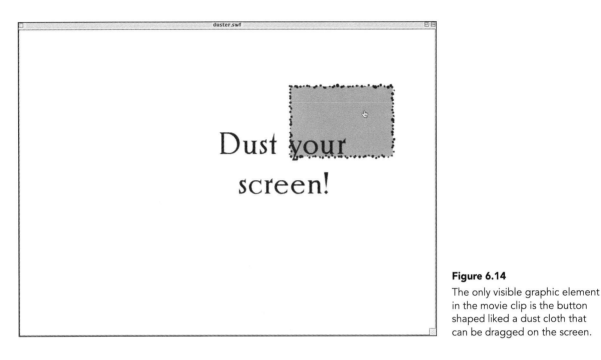

- DragClip
  - MC: Track
  - Bug

The following example explains how to put scripts for dragging into a frame. (Although I prefer scripts for dragging in a button, some applications require a script for dragging in a frame.) Also explained here is how to constrain a dragging area for a movie. Instead of dragging the mouse anywhere on the screen, you can keep the MC drag area in a defined rectangle. The initial screen for the movie and its objects are shown in Figure 6.15.

Position Layer
The Position layer contains the MC that holds the location data for the mouse position on the screen.

MC: Text (Show XY Layer)
Your first task is to create the MC, as follows:

1. Create a new MC, and name it "Text" in the Symbol Properties dialog box. Click on OK to enter the Symbol Editor.

2. In the Symbol Editor, place two text fields on the stage, and select Dynamic Text from the Text Options panel. Use the specifications in Table 6.2, and note the variable names carefully.

3. Open the Library window, and drag an instance of the "Text" MC onto the stage.

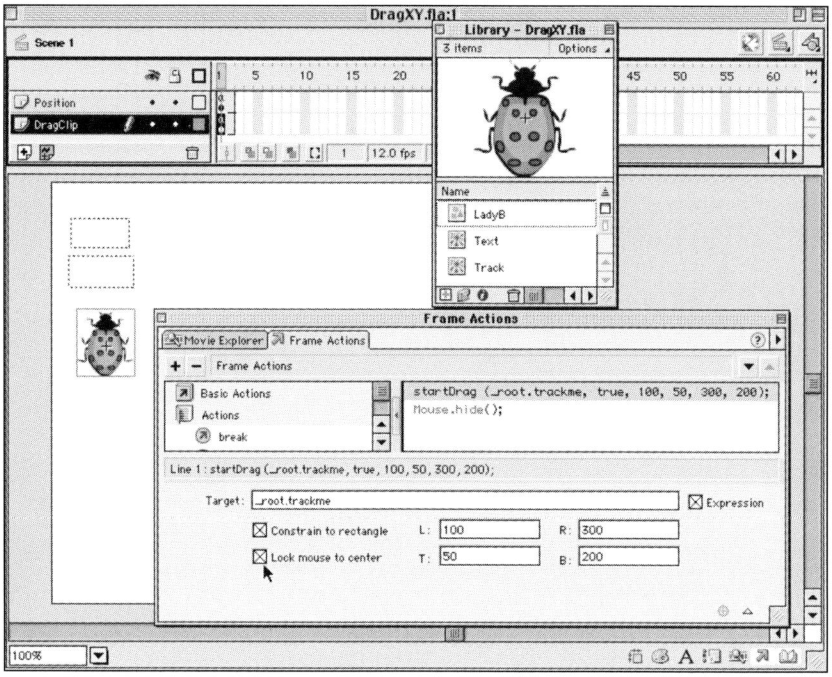

Figure 6.15
Two movie clips, a graphic instance, and two text fields make up the objects in the movie.

Table 6.2 Text field properties and names.

Variable Name	Border/Bg	Text Alignment	Single Layer	Selectable
hor	No	Right	Yes	No
vert	No	Right	Yes	No

4. With the MC selected, type Ctrl+I/Cmd I to open the Instance Panel. Type in the name "pos" for the MC. You will be referencing this name in the script in Frame 1.

Frame 1
Put the following script in the first frame of the Position layer. Note how the objects of the main timeline (**_root**), the MC (pos), and the variable name in the MC (hor and vert) are connected by the dot operator.

```
_root.pos.hor = "X: "+_xmouse;
_root.pos.vert = "Y: "+_ymouse;
```

The script uses the **_xmouse** and **_ymouse** properties to get the position of the cursor, which is located by the Lady Bug. It passes the value of the position of the Lady Bug to the two text fields.

DragClip Layer
Both the draggable MC and the script for dragging the object are in the Drag-Clip layer.

MC: Track (Bug Layer)

To create the Track MC Bug layer, do the following:

1. Select Insert|New symbol in the menu bar. Select Movie Clip for the behavior and "Track" for the label name.

2. In the Symbol Editor, draw a ladybug, and select it.

3. Press the F8 key to change the drawing into a symbol. In the Symbol Properties dialog box, select Graphic as the behavior, and name the symbol "LadyB."

4. Press the Scene 1 icon to return to the main timeline.

5. From the Library window, drag an instance of the Lady Bug MC onto the stage.

6. In the Instance Panel, type in "trackme" in the Name window.

Frame 1

Put the following script in the first frame of the DragClip layer:

```
startDrag (_root.trackme, true, 100, 50, 300, 200);
Mouse.hide();
```

The script names the MC to be dragged ("trackme") and then sets up four parameters. The parameters in Figure 6.15 clearly show where the boundaries for dragging the MC are located relative to the left, right, top, and bottom of the screen. The zero point is the top left corner of the screen. In addition, the Lock Mouse To Center option is selected so that the center of the MC is in the middle of the object instead of the coordinates where the pointer is located when the drag action begins. Figure 6.15 shows the four "Constrain to rectangle" parameters that keep the ladybug pointer in a confined area.

Drag to Shopping Cart (shoppingCart.fla on CD-ROM)

This next project shows how to create a very simple e-commerce site using drag and drop. Creating a more complex, front-end "checkout" requires more functions, actions, and properties. You'll be able to do this after you learn the material in Chapters 7 and 8. You can then return to the shopping cart and supercharge it. To begin, the movie has the following layers and MCs:

- Shopping Cart
- Fruits
  - MC: apple
    - Apple

- MC: apple
  - Pear
- MC: apple
  - Banana
- MC: apple
  - Orange
- Cash Register
- Background

Figure 6.16 shows the layers and basic setup for the shopping cart. It contains five MCs—one for each of the four fruits and one for the shopping cart. (The shopping cart movie is not used now but is set up as an MC so that you can add more property functions and statements to the movie later if you want.) So, for this movie, you will be dealing with only four MCs. Each MC contains a single button instance, which contains the scripts. A single text field is used as a "register" to tally up purchases as the user drags each fruit into the shopping cart.

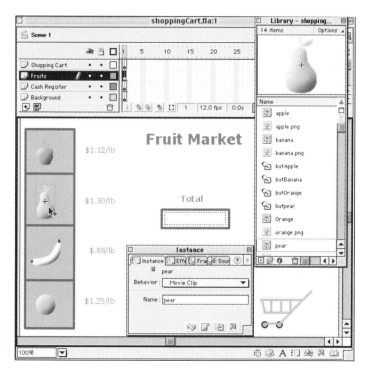

Figure 6.16
Initial setup of the shopping cart movie.

This particular project is designed to show how drag and drop can be used as an interesting user interface. Each click of the mouse adds the cost of the product to the total bill because an accumulator is in the drag-and-drop portion of the script where press and release events are recorded. After the initial drag and drop, clicking on the item in the shopping cart adds another bunch of bananas or pound of apples to your total.

Background Layer

First, you need to set up the Background layer. No action scripts are involved. You can probably draw everything you need by looking at Figures 6.16 and 6.17. The fruits and the grocery cart are added on other layers.

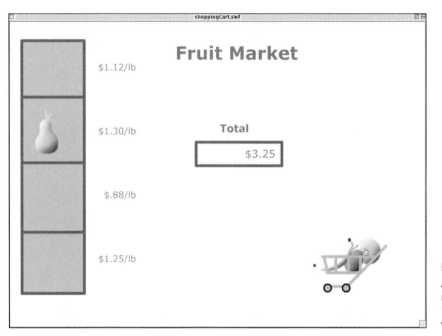

Figure 6.17
After each drag and drop, a running total is placed in the "register" variable associated with the text field on the screen.

1. Select Modify|Movie, and click on the Background window to bring up the color swatches. Select a light yellow from the swatch table.

2. Using the rectangle tool, draw a dark brown rectangle with a light brown center. With the line tool, draw a dark brown line across the larger rectangle to make "racks" for the fruit.

3. After drawing the lines, use the keyboard shortcut Ctrl+K/Cmd+K to open the Align panel. Select all of the rack lines, and distribute them evenly with the Distribution tools in the Align panel.

4. Draw one more dark brown rectangle in the center of the screen to outline the Cash Register window (to be placed later).

5. Finally, type in these labels: a "Fruit Market" title, prices of the fruit, and the "Total" label above the cash register outline.

Cash Register Layer

To see a running total of purchases, insert a text field on the screen in the Cash Register layer. Use the parameters in Table 6.3 for the Dynamic Text field.

Table 6.3 Text field properties and names.

Variable Name	Border/Bg	Text Alignment	Single Line	Selectable
register	None	Right	Yes	No

Place the text field inside the brown rectangle under the "Total" label on the stage. If you want, you can draw an elaborate cash register around the text field.

Fruits Layer

The heart of the program—and all of the ActionScript—is in the Fruits layer. Each fruit is an MC, and each MC contains a fruit-shaped button that contains the ActionScript. The script is very simple. After each drag and drop, an "accumulator" variable is incremented. A running total is kept and is placed in the "register" variable used by the text field. Thus, each time a fruit is dragged and dropped, the register shows the current total. Figure 6.17 shows what the screen looks like after three fruits have been dragged and dropped.

For each of the four fruits, use the following steps, and enter the scripts for each of the buttons within the MC.

1. Select Insert|New Symbol from the menu bar. The Symbol Properties dialog box opens.

2. Select Movie Clip for the behavior, and name the MCs "apple," "pear," "banana," and "orange."

3. You're now in the Symbol Editor. Create or import a fruit image of the fruit associated with the MC. You can use a graphics program and import the image or use the drawing tools in the Toolbox.

4. After you have completed or imported your drawing, select it, and press the F8 key to turn it into a symbol. In the Symbol Properties dialog box, select Button for the behavior, and use "butApple," "butPear," and so on, for the names of the buttons.

Note: When you set the values for the variables, be certain to use expressions. Click on the expression checkbox if the value is an expression.

5. Still in the Symbol Editor, select your fruit symbol, and open the Action-Script Editor by selecting Window|Actions or Ctrl+Alt+A/Cmd+Option+A. Use the following action scripts for the respective fruit buttons:

MC: apple (Apple)—butApple Button

```
on (press) {
    startDrag (_root.apple);
}
on (release) {
    stopDrag ();
    _root.accum+=1.12;
    _root.register = "$"+_root.accum;
}
```

MC: pear (Pear)—butPear Button

```
on (press) {
    startDrag (_root.pear);
}
on (release) {
    stopDrag ();
    _root.accum+=1.30;
    _root.register = "$"+_root.accum;
}
```

MC: banana (Banana)—butBanana Button

```
on (press) {
    startDrag (_root.banana);
}
on (release) {
    stopDrag ();
    _root.accum+=.88;
    _root.register = "$"+_root.accum;
}
```

MC: orange (Orange)—butOrange Button

```
on (press) {
    startDrag (_root.orange);
}
on (release) {
    stopDrag ();
    _root.accum+=1.25;
    _root.register = "$"+_root.accum;
}
```

6. After finishing the MCs, select Window|Library from the menu bar, or use the keyboard shortcut Ctrl+L/Cmd+L to open the Library window.

7. Drag an instance of each *fruit MC* from the Library window to the "fruit bins" on the screen. *Do not drag instances of the fruit buttons.* The buttons are inside the MCs, and they are dragged to the screen when you drag the MC containing the button.

8. Choose Window|Panels|Instance or Ctrl+I/Cmd+I to open the Instance panel. Select each MC, and type in an instance name for each MC in the Name window of the Instance panel. Use these instance names: "apple," "pear," "banana," and "orange."

Note: If you forget or put in the wrong instance name, the movie will not work.

Test run your movie to make sure everything is working correctly. The best strategy is to get one of the MCs working correctly. Then, using copy and paste, copy the action script into the other three, and edit them to insert the right names and values. You can use either the Normal or Expert Mode.

Shopping Cart Layer

The Shopping Cart layer for this movie can contain only a drawing of a shopping cart and nothing else. Use the drawing tools to create any kind of cart you want. If you use an MC for the shopping cart, you can come back and improve on this movie after you learn more functions and actions for dealing with properties. You can also make the shopping cart a button symbol so you can add ActionScript to it later. I suggest using the instance name "cart" for the MC, also.

Whether you use an abstract drawing of a shopping cart in a button inside an MC or a drawing on the stage, it's important to consider alternative images for a cart. The one used in this example is an icon of a grocery store cart. Although some groceries are sold on the Web, other images for a cart may be more appropriate and fun, such as a flower basket for a flower shop or a clothes rack for clothing.

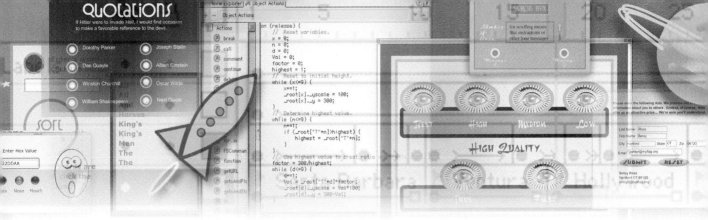

Chapter 7

Working with Properties and Functions

This chapter introduces the properties and functions in Flash. The key to dynamic movies is the ability to change properties and pass information about the state of different objects' properties. Additionally, this chapter examines the many functions in Flash and how they are used in conjunction with objects and properties.

Properties in Flash

Chapter 1 introduced the concept of Object-Oriented Programming (OOP). The key to OOP lies in addressing the properties in objects. In Flash, the movie clip (MC) is the main object where ActionScript realizes OOP. Scripts can determine the state of a property in an MC and set an MC's property. Until now, the main focus of this book has been on using and changing variables. This chapter shows how to use and change properties.

What Is a Property?

A property is an element, state, or condition of an object. Just as people have characteristics—or properties—so do objects in a Flash movie. For example, a person can be described by name, height, weight, appearance, address, accomplishments, and relationship. You can describe Fred as being 6 feet tall, 200 pounds, ruddy, living in St. Louis, a college graduate, and married. Fred may change. He may move from St. Louis to Chicago, lose or gain weight, and change his marital status. Certain conditions or properties will remain the same, however. He will continue to be a male, a college graduate, ruddy in appearance, and the same height (at least until he is very old).

Flash operates the same way. Some objects can be changed, and others remain constant. Although you can find out what an object's properties are, you may not always be able to change them.

Setting Properties

Of all the Flash properties, only certain ones can be set. We'll learn about the *general* properties that can be set first. Other properties associated with unique objects and object constructors, such as Color and Sound, are discussed in Chapter 8. Previous chapters covered other object properties, such as Array and Mouse objects. Table 7.1 provides a brief description of the various MC properties that can be set and their ActionScript codes.

Table 7.1 Movie clip properties that can be set.

Property	Code	Description
Horizontal Position	_x	Location of movie relative to the center position of the object and the parent position on horizontal plane (X-axis). The positions are measured in pixels. The default position is from the upper left corner (or center) of the object to the upper left corner of the movie. When the parent of the instance changes, the center may also change. This is especially challenging when the parent rotates from the original position.
Vertical Position	_y	Location of the movie relative to the center position of the object and the parent position on a vertical plane (Y-axis). Same position measurement as "_x."
Width (relative)	_xscale	Relative scale on the horizontal plane (X-axis) measured as a percentage with 100 percent as the default. Scale changes the object to greater or less than 100 percent.

(continued)

Table 7.1   Movie clip properties that can be set *(continued)*.

Property	Code	Description
Height(relative)	_yscale	Relative scale on vertical plane (Y-axis) measured as a percentage with 100 percent as default. Scale changes the object to greater or less than 100 percent.
Transparency	_alpha	The alpha level is on a sliding scale from 0 (fully transparent) to 100 (fully opaque) measured as a percent. Alpha is still interactive when zero.
Hidden/Visible	_visible	Boolean visibility (True/False, 1/0).
Rotate	_rotation	Like a compass, rotation has values from 0 to 360. Use negative degrees for counterclockwise rotation. (360 and 0 are equivalent rotation positions.)
Dynamic Name	_name	Provision for naming or renaming an MC from a script.

The example that follows uses a single movie and MC to illustrate which properties can be set. The movie is very simple and shows what happens when you change a property. The property-setting movie contains an MC with a button consisting of a 50 × 200 pixel rectangle with a green radial gradient fill on a 400 × 400 pixel stage. Rather than using numerous buttons to make the changes, however, you will insert different scripts for the same green bar button (the rectangle). This provides you with practice in changing the scripts and seeing the results. To set up the movie, follow these steps:

1. Open a new movie and select Insert|New Symbol. In the Symbol Properties dialog box, select the Movie Clip behavior, and name it "Property Test." Click on OK, and you will be in the Symbol Editor.

2. Select the Info panel from the Launcher Bar to open the Info panel. Keep it handy, as this is where you can set some of the properties.

3. Using the Rectangle tool and the green gradient radial fill from the Color palette, create a rectangle roughly 50 × 200 pixels. After the drawing is changed into a symbol, you can more easily insert the exact dimensions right in the Object window.

4. Select the rectangle, and press the F8 key to open the Symbol Properties dialog box. Select Button as the behavior, and use "Stick" as the name. Click on OK.

> **Note:** The position and size of the rectangle symbol is relative to the MC it is in—not to the main timeline.

5. While still in the Symbol Editor, select the green rectangle. In the Object window, type in "50" for width (W) and "200" for height (H). Type in "0,0" for the "x" and "y" values, and click on the center point of the position box in the Info panel.

6. Click on the Scene 1 icon to get to the main timeline. Drag an instance of the MC "Property Test" onto the stage. In the Info panel, enter "200" for "x" and "100" for "y." Click on the Apply button in the Object window. The position for the MC on the main timeline is 200 pixels from the left of the stage and 100 pixels from the top. The center point is the upper left corner.

Note: This is a crucial step and provides the object with a name.

7. Press Ctrl+I (Windows)/Cmd+I (Macintosh) to open the Instance panel. With the MC selected, type in "greenbar" as the instance name.

8. Select the MC, and use the keyboard shortcut Ctrl+E/Cmd+E to open the Symbol Editor.

9. Select the green rectangle instance, and click on the Show Object Actions button on the Launcher Bar to open the ActionScript Editor. You can now enter the following scripts. To test the movie, do not exit the Symbol Editor. Because you'll be changing the different scripts, you save a step by selecting Control|Test Movie from the menu bar or by using the keyboard shortcut Ctrl+Enter/Cmd+Return. Remember in the following scripts that "Stick" refers to the Stick button inside the MC. Figure 7.1 shows the initial setup in the Symbol Editor.

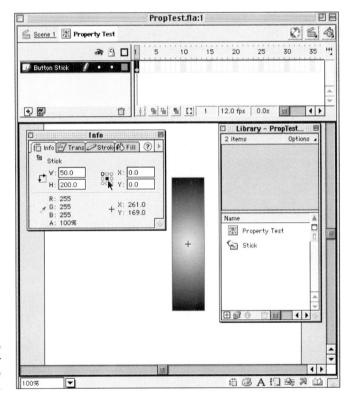

Figure 7.1

The position of an object inside an MC may be the same or different from the position of the object on the main timeline.

Setting "Set Property" in the ActionScript Editor

Before entering the script to test the properties, take a quick look at how the ActionScript Editor deals with the Set Property action. Figure 7.2 shows the first script you will be entering in the following examples. In the Normal Mode, the actions are treated just like variables. The major difference is that instead of having a variable, you have an object with properties.

Instead of selecting **set Property** in the Actions list, select the Properties category or submenu. Then in the Properties list, select the property you want, as follows:

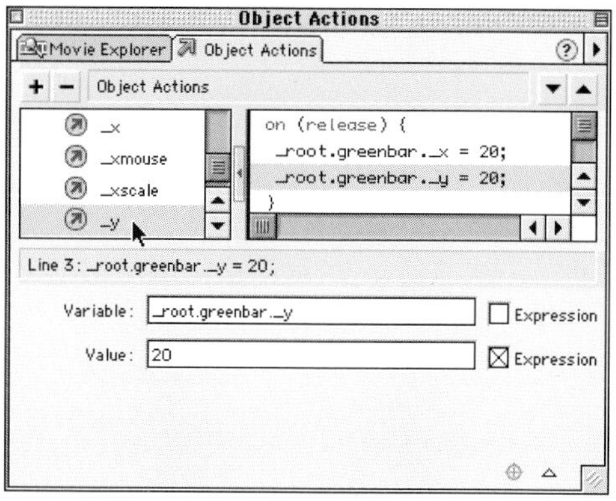

Figure 7.2

Using Set Property requires three elements: the property to be set (**_x** and **_y**), the target MC instance name (**_root.greenbar**), and the value (20).

- The property from the Properties submenu in the action list.

- The instance name of the MC, and its path.

- The value for the property (which may be a calculated expression using information from other parts of the movie) or a literal.

Property Tests

Each of the following scripts shows how to set different properties. Instead of using the **setProperty()** action, the properties are linked using the dot (.) operator. The crucial element in setting properties is the instance name, or a reference to that name indirectly in the affected MC. In the previous section, the Property Test MC was given the instance name of "greenbar," which is used in all of the examples. In Flash 4, the leading slash "/" denotes that the MC is on the top level; in Flash 5, however, the top or root level is indicated by **_root**. Although the button with the action script is *inside* the MC, addressing the MC from the top level—an absolute address—eliminates the problem of wondering where the MC is relative to the button. To run all of the scripts, just click on the green bar.

Button: Stick in Property Test MC (X and Y Position)

This script shows how to change an object's position on the stage using both the older notation in Flash 4 and the newer OOP designation. You can see that the OOP format is simpler. The MC—not the button inside the MC—is the reference point. Try changing the position values until you can place the stick anywhere on the screen.

```
on (release) {
    setProperty ("/greenbar", _x, 20);
    setProperty ("/greenbar", _y, 20);
}
```

—

```
on (release) {
    _root.greenbar._x = 20;
    _root.greenbar._y = 20;
}
```

Results: When you click on the Stick button, the bar jumps up to the left.

Button: Stick in Property Test MC (X and Y Scale)

By changing the X and Y scales, you can resize any object on the stage. In this example, the dimensions are dramatically altered from the original 50 × 200 rectangle.

```
on (release) {
    _root.greenbar._xscale = 225;
    _root.greenbar._yscale = 5;
}
```

Results: When you click on the Stick button, a small wide bar replaces the original.

Button: Stick in Property Test MC (Alpha)

In this example, two mouse events are used to set and reset a property. The Alpha level affects the transparency (opaqueness) of an object, ranging between 0 to 100 percent. In this next script, pressing the mouse button sets the Alpha level to 0 percent. Releasing the button sets the Alpha level to 100 percent. Now, change the first Alpha value to 25 percent and the second to 50 percent.

```
on (press) {
    _root.greenbar._alpha = 0;
}
on (release) {
    _root.greenbar._alpha = 100;
}
```

Results: When you press the Stick button, the object disappears. When you release the button, it reappears.

Button: Stick in Property Test MC (Visibility)

In Flash, Visibility is a Boolean condition that is set to either True or False. It does not work like the Alpha property, however. After the script sets the Visibility to False, the same script changes the Visibility back to True.

```
on (press) {
    _root.greenbar._visible = false;
}
on (release) {
    _root.greenbar._visible = true;
}
```

Results: When you press the Stick button, the object disappears. When you release the button, the button reappears as it did with the Alpha settings.

Button: Stick in Property Test MC (Rotation)

Rotation is on a scale from 0 to 360. Numbers greater than 360 or less than 0 are treated as continuations over 360 or under 360. For example, a setting of 365 is the same rotation angle as 5, and –10 is the same as 350. The following script provides both a positive and a negative value.

Note: Pay attention to where you put your pointer. If the object moves away from the pointer when you press the key, nothing happens when you release the key. That's because the pointer is off the button object that responds to the mouse event.

```
on (press) {
    _root.greenbar._rotation = 270;
}
on (release) {
    _root.greenbar._rotation = -10;
}
```

Results: When you press the mouse key down, the object turns sideways. When you release the key, it moves left to an angle of 350 (–10) degrees.

Button: Stick in Property Test MC (Name)

You can change the instance name of an MC on the fly. You can both change the name and use the new name in a single script. The following script changes the instance name "greenbar" to "sidebar" when the mouse button is pressed. When the button is released, the new name is used to rotate the object 80 degrees.

```
on (press) {
    _root.greenbar._name = "sidebar";
}
on (release) {
    _root.sidebar._rotation = 80;
}
```

Results: When the mouse button is released, the bar rotates 80 degrees.

Variation: On the main timeline, add a new round button to the movie and the following script. (Leave the preceding original script, button, and MC as is.)

```
on (release) {
    _root.greenbar._rotation = 120;
}
```

Test run the movie, and press the new round button. It rotates the green rectangle 120 degrees. Now press the green bar button, and the green bar button rotates to 80 degrees. Finally, press the new round button again. *Nothing happens!* The first time you pressed the round button, the instance name of the MC was "greenbar." After you pressed the green bar button, however, the instance name of the MC was changed to "sidebar." As a result, when you pressed the round button a second time, it was looking for "greenbar," but "greenbar" no longer existed because its instance name had been changed to "sidebar."

Global Properties (Globalquality.fla on CD-ROM)

In the previous section, you saw how to set properties in a movie script. This section looks at some specialized properties that affect the entire movie and all the MCs. Because global properties change all movie properties, there is no target specification. Everything in the movie is the target by default. Three layers make up this example:

- Buttons

- Labels

- Background

The movie demonstrates all six settings for the two quality properties controlled by ActionScript. To set the quality of anti-aliasing (aliasing is the jagged edges around some graphics and text), use the **_highquality** and **_quality** properties. The **_highquality** property has Boolean values of **true** or **false**. The new Flash 5 property has string values of **LOW**, **MEDIUM**, **HIGH**, and **BEST** to adjust the quality of the images on the screen. Table 7.2 shows the values for each **_quality** setting.

The **_highquality** property is either the equivalent of the **HIGH** or **LOW** settings for **_quality**. When specifying the value of **_quality**, the values *must* be written as strings and in all caps. For example,

```
_quality="MEDIUM"
```

is correct. However,

```
_quality="Medium"
```

and

```
_quality=MEDIUM
```

are both incorrect.

Figure 7.3 shows the movie's stage and initial setup.

Table 7.2 Quality values.

Value	Anti-aliasing 2x2	Anti-aliasing 4x4	Bitmapped Smooth
LOW	No	No	No
MEDIUM	Yes	No	No
HIGH	—	Yes	Yes (Static only)
BEST	—	Yes	Yes

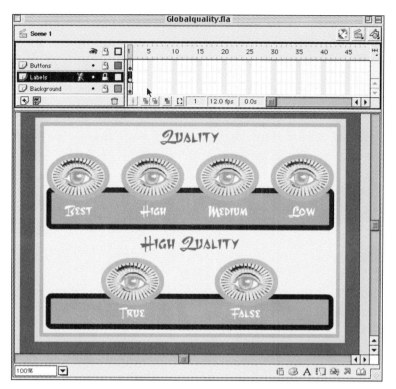

Figure 7.3
Six buttons control the global qualities.

Background Layer

The Background layer is a series of colored rectangles made with the Rectangle tool. Initially, I laid out each rectangle on a separate layer to align them without having them get tangled up. Once everything is in place, select the second-to-lowest layer, cut it using Ctrl+X/Cmd+X, and then paste it in place on the bottom (Background) layer. To paste a graphic into place, select Edit|Paste In Place from the menu bar. Then cut and paste into place the other layers on the Background layer. Finally, remove the empty layers and lock the Background layer.

Labels Layer

After all of the background materials are in, select a font with lots of edges to demonstrate the effect of anti-aliasing and bitmap smoothing. I used Rocket Gothic (**www.flashfonts.com**) and then broke it apart to have lots of bit-mapped images to smooth and unsmooth when changing the **_quality** property value. Lock the Labels layer so you don't corrupt the graphics when placing the buttons.

Buttons Layer

All of the buttons are instances of a single button. Here are the steps used to create them and their scripts.

1. Draw or import a graphic with lots of lines with different radials. The example uses clip art of an eye (from **www.flashfonts.com**).

2. Use the Oval tool to draw an oval with a 6-point stroke around the graphic. Select both the oval and graphic, and press the F8 key.

3. Select the drawing and text for each, and press the F8 key to open the Symbol Properties window. Select Button as the behavior, and the button "eye."

4. Drag an instance of the button over the six labels on the stage. Enter the ActionScript as follows:

Button: Best

```
on (release) {
    _quality="BEST";
}
```

Button: High

```
on (release) {
    _quality="HIGH";
}
```

Button: Medium

```
on (release) {
    _quality="MEDIUM";
}
```

Button: Low

```
on (release) {
    _quality="LOW";
}
```

Button: True

```
on (release) {
    _highquality=true;
}
```

Button: False

```
on (release) {
    _highquality=false;
}
```

Then save the program, and test it.

When you run the program, you can easily see the difference in quality. Figure 7.4 shows the figure when a "LOW" value is placed into the **_quality** property, and Figure 7.5 shows **_highquality** set to "TRUE." The low anti-aliasing images have jagged edges on the graphics, whereas the images with anti-aliasing have smooth edges.

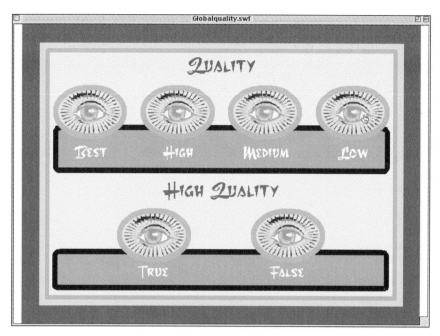

Figure 7.4
The Low Quality button selection makes the graphics appear ragged.

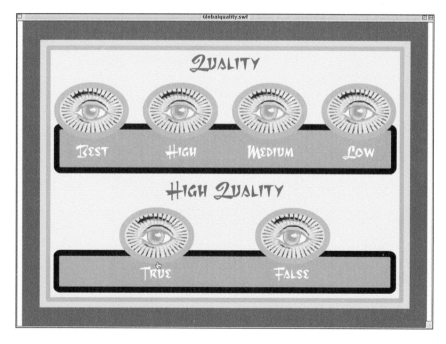

Figure 7.5
With High Quality set to "TRUE," the graphics are smooth and clear.

Tab Rectangle (TabOutline.fla on CD-ROM)

The **_focusrect** property is another Boolean condition using true/false (or 0/1) for displaying a yellow rectangle that surrounds buttons when the user presses the Tab key to go from one button to another. A **true** value displays the yellow rectangle; a **false** value makes the rectangle invisible. The default for Flash movies is **true**. Like other global properties, no target is specified because all elements of the movie are affected. The movie has two layers:

Figure 7.6

Initial layout of the movie requires four button instances and a text field.

- Buttons
- Background

For a simple demonstration, create a movie made up of four buttons, as shown in Figure 7.6.

Background Layer

Before you put in the background, select Modify|Movie, and change the dimensions of the stage to 250×250 pixels. Select the Rectangle tool, and draw a black background over the entire stage.

Buttons Layer

Create a button symbol, and then drag four instances of the button from the Library to the stage. Place labels on top of the four buttons, and use the Align panel to organize the buttons and their labels as shown in Figure 7.7. Of the four buttons, only Buttons 1 and 2 have scripts. One turns the rectangle on, and one turns it off. To give you a starting place, use the Text tool to select an Input Text field from the Text Options panel. Finally, using Static Text, type in a "Start Here >" label next to the Input Text field.

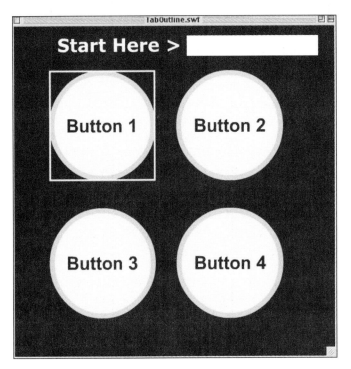

Figure 7.7

When the **_focusrect** is set to **true**, a rectangle appears around the button when the Tab key is used to select the button.

Button: Button 1

```
on (release) {
    _focusrect = false;
}
```

Button: Button 2

```
on (release) {
    _focusrect = true;
}
```

Save and test the movie. When the movie first appears, click in the text field, and press the Tab key to navigate through the four buttons. Around each button, you see a yellow rectangle. Click on Button 1 to turn off the focus rectangle. Begin again in the text field, and press the Tab key again. On the second try, no rectangle appears. Click on Button 2, press the Tab key, and the focus rectangle reappears.

Setting Sound Buffering

The final global property is **_soundbuftime**. The default preload time, before streaming sound is played during download, is five seconds. For faster or slower delays, however, adjust the buffer time. For example, in a Frame script,

```
_soundbuftime=15;
```

sets the time delay to 15 seconds. In streaming audio, the slower connections need higher buffer times. Otherwise, the music stops while more of the movie, including the sound, is loaded. Pre-buffering allows the sound to be in place and ready to play.

Getting Properties

Flash uses slightly different codes in getting information about properties than it does in setting them. All of the properties that can be set in MCs can also be read. You can get more properties in Flash than you can set, however. Table 7.3 shows both the codes for the information that ActionScript can get and what the **getProperty** function or a variable receives.

Table 7.3   Movie clip properties.

Code	Description
_alpha	The percent of opaqueness in an object (Alpha). A value of 100 percent is totally opaque; 0 percent is totally transparent.
_currentframe	Frame number of an MC's current frame.
_droptarget	The value of the path of the MC on which another MC is dropped.
_framesloaded	Current number of frames loaded thus far in an MC.
_height	Height of an MC measured in pixels.
_name	The instance name of an MC.
_rotation	Rotation angle (0 to 360).
_target	Full target path of an MC.
_totalframes	Number of frames in an MC.

(continued)

Table 7.3 Movie clip properties *(continued)*.

Code	Description
_url	URL of SWF file containing an MC.
_visible	Boolean of visibility (true/false, 1/0).
_width	Width of an MC measured in pixels.
_x	The number of pixels from left boundary of the stage to the center point of an MC.
_xmouse	The current x position of the mouse pointer.
_xscale	Percent scale of an object's horizontal (X) axis.
_y	The number of pixels from top boundary of the stage to the center point of an MC. If the clips are nested, the _x and _y are relative to the clips in which they're nested.
_ymouse	The current y position of the mouse pointer.
_yscale	Percent scale of an object's vertical (Y) axis.

To find out something about a target MC, you can still use the **getProperty (target, property)** function similar to the Flash 4 script. The target is the absolute or relative path to the target, and the property is one of the properties listed in the preceding section. For example, the following script places the number of frames loaded into the variable "howMany":

```
howMany = getProperty ( _root.purpleHaze, _framesloaded );
```

Using the dot (.) operator, however, the script is much easier and, I believe, clearer. Use the following format to accomplish the same goal:

```
howMany = _root.purpleHaze._framesloaded;
```

This next movie uses all of the properties and shows how they are passed to a variable.

Passing Property Values (callingAllProps.fla on CD-ROM)

This movie uses all of the properties and demonstrates what type of information they contain. The movie has four layers and two MCs:

- Show
- Property Buttons
- MCs
  - MC: Cop
  - Seven Frames
  - MC: Cop2
  - Nothing Here
- Background

This movie contains 18 buttons, each with an action script that places the value of the 18 different properties on the screen. Two MCs on the stage contain the properties returned by the buttons. One of the MCs is draggable so that you can see what value **_droptarget** returns when one MC is dropped on another. A text field named "show" displays the values that the properties contain. Figure 7.8 shows the initial stage in the main timeline. (Not all layers are visible.)

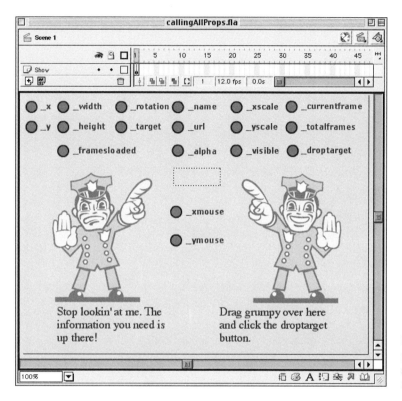

Figure 7.8
Each property is shown on the screen with action scripts in the movie buttons.

Show Layer

In the center of the stage, place a text field between the two police drawings. Select the text field and Modify|Text Field from the menu bar. Enter the variable name "show" in the Text Field Property window using the properties in Table 7.4.

Property Buttons Layer

On the Property Buttons layer, create a button on the main timeline level as follows:

1. Use the Drawing tool to make a button 17 pixels wide and high. Use a 2-point border. Select powder blue for the inner color and black for the outer color.

Table 7.4 Text field properties and names.

Variable Name	Border/Bg	Text Alignment	Disable Editing	Disable Selection
show	None	Center	Yes	Yes

2. Select the drawing, and press the F8 key to open the Symbol Properties window. Use the name "PropButton," and select Button as the behavior.

3. In the Symbol Editor, select the Over frame, and press the F6 key to insert a keyframe. Select yellow from the swatch palette, and use the Bucket tool to color the center circle yellow. Click on the Scene 1 icon to get back to the main timeline.

4. Use the keyboard shortcut Ctrl+L/Cmd+L to open the Library window. Drag 16 instances of the button from the Library onto the main stage.

The 18 buttons are instances of the same button. Each one has an identical script but with different properties. The text next to each button identifies the property it gets from the MC. The graphic image on the left is a draggable MC with the instance name "cop," and all of the properties reference it as the target. The following script should be used in all buttons replacing **_width** with the property name label to the right of each button.

Button: All Instances of PropButton

```
on (release) {
    show = _root.cop._width;
}
```

MCs Layer

On the MCs layer, two MCs provide the source of the properties. One MC is the primary source, and the other demonstrates how the **_droptarget** property works. The MC that is to be underneath the draggable MC is created first with the instance name "Cop2."

1. From the main timeline, select Insert|New Symbol. In the Symbol Properties dialog box, choose Movie Clip as the behavior, and use the name "Police1." (Yes, the instance name will be "Cop2," but the name of the MC is "Police1" because it is the first MC to be created.)

2. Draw or import an image to help identify the MC. (I used clip art from **www.flashfonts.com.** I named the one layer in the MC "Nothing here" to indicate that no scripts are in the MC.)

3. Press the Scene 1 icon in the upper left corner to return to the main timeline. Drag an instance of the MC on the right side of the stage as shown in Figures 7.8 and 7.9.

Note: This is a crucial step and provides the object with a name.

4. Press Ctrl+I/Cmd+I to open the Instance panel, and type in the instance name "Cop2."

After you've completed the first MC, create the second one. Name the second MC "Police2," and give it the instance name "Cop."

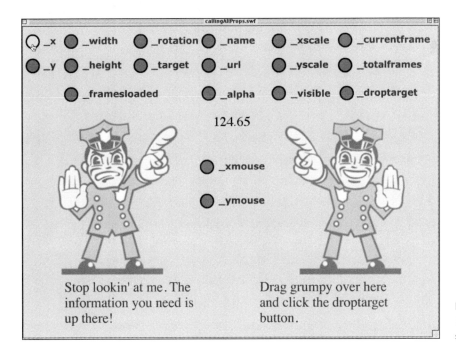

124.65

Figure 7.9
If the figure on the left is dragged, several of its properties change.

1. From the main timeline, select Insert|New Symbol. In the Symbol Properties box, choose Movie Clip as the behavior, and use the name "Police2." Click on OK to enter the Symbol Editor.

2. Draw or import an image to help identify the MC.

3. Select the drawing, and press the F8 key to turn the drawing into a symbol. In the Symbol Properties dialog box, type in "CopA" for the name, and select Button for the behavior. Click on OK.

4. Double-click on the new button symbol to open the Instances Properties window, and select the Actions tab to open the ActionScript Editor. Enter the following action script in the CopA button.

Button: Instance of CopA

```
on (press) {
    startDrag (_root.cop);
}
on (release) {
    stopDrag ();
}
```

5. While still in the Symbol Editor, select Frame 7, and press the F5 key to make the MC seven frames long. The purpose is to show how the different frame properties work—the frames are not used for anything.

6. Press the Scene 1 icon in the upper left corner to return to the main timeline. Drag an instance of the MC on the left side of the stage as shown in Figures 7.8 and 7.9.

7. Press Ctrl+I/Cmd+I to open the Instance Panel, and type in the instance name "Cop."

8. Click on OK to complete the second MC.

Your movie is now complete. The most important feature of the movie is that it illustrates the nature of the information that returns when a variable contains property data. In your scripts, you can "ask" what any movie script is doing and receive an appropriate response for the condition in the rest of your script.

Now, try dragging the figure from the left onto the figure on the right. Click on the **_droptarget** button. You should see "/cop2" in the output window. In Chapter 6, the Shopping Cart project dropped MCs into a "basket" MC. With each hit returned by the **_droptarget** property, you can add more information into the movie for calculating what the shopper wants. Also, when you drag the MC, notice how the **_xmouse** and **_ymouse** respond. Because the two properties are tied to the MC's initial position—not the global position of the stage—when the MC moves below or to the right of the buttons, the script returns a negative value.

Functions in Flash

Twenty-five functions make up the ways that ActionScript can take in arguments and return a value. Eight additional string functions are also included. Some functions—such as **eval**, **init**, **true**, **false**, **chr**, and **getProperty**—have been discussed elsewhere in the book. Following is a list of these functions with a short description of each. A number of these functions in Flash act very much (or exactly) like properties, methods, and arguments.

- **Boolean**—Converts arguments to Boolean string or primitive value type.

- **escape**—Converts string to URL encoded format.

- **eval**—Evaluates an expression and returns the calculated results.

- **false**—Boolean expression of false or 0.

- **getProperty(target, property)**—Generates the immediate state of the target's property.

- **getTimer**—Milliseconds since SWF (Shockwave Flash) file began playing.

- **getVersion**—Returns the version of the Flash player that is playing the movie.

- **globalToLocal**—Converts global coordinate system into local coordinates.

- **int(number)**—Rounds off decimals from a number to make an integer. (See Chapter 2.)

- **isFinite**—Boolean value for finite (true) or non-finite number (false).

- **isNaN()**—Evaluates argument to be a number (false) or not (true).

- **keycode**—Argument for code for keyboard (not ASCII).

- **localToGlobal**—Converts local MC coordinate system into global coordinates.

- **maxscroll**—A read-only property that determines maximum value for scroll in a text field.

- **newline**—Functional carriage return. Works the same as chr(13).

- **Number**—Number converts Flash 4 variables using nonfunctional operators into numbers.

- **parseFloat(string)**—Takes string argument and converts it into floating point number.

- **parseInt()**—Converts expression into integer.

- **random(number)**—Generates a random number from 0 to (number-1).

- **scroll**—A property that establishes the topmost line in a text field.

- **String()**—Converts expression into a string. (This is different from the String object.)

- **targetPath**—Converts the target path to a string that can be used with the dot operator to issue commands. (An alternative to tellTarget.)

- **true**—Boolean expression of true or 1.

- **unescape**—Decodes string from URL format. Reverses escape function.

- **updateAfterEvent**—Updates screen after clip event (only) without regard to FPS setting with any mouse or key action but not with frame, data, or load.

In addition to the general set of functions, Flash 5 has a separate set of string functions. The separation is a categorical rather than functional one.

- **chr(integer)**—Generates the ASCII character represented by the number (integer) code.

- **length(string)**—Generates an integer the length of the string.

- **ord(character)**—Generates the ASCII value for the character.

- **substring(string, start, length)**—Generates a portion of string (substring) of the "string," beginning at "start" (index) in range of "length."

All of the string functions have multibyte versions as well—**mbchr()**, **mblength**, and **mbord()**.

String Functions

Taking the last first, string functions are the text formatters and manipulators of ActionScript. They perform a number of important functions and, as in most other programming languages, are very useful when working with strings. In e-commerce sites, you can use Flash string functions to put together different types of information for server-side applications.

To illustrate how string functions work and what they return, I developed the following movie that uses string functions based on user input. You can manipulate the different parameters in the movie and see what the functions generate in several text fields. A single button contains the script.

Using Substrings (substrings.fla on CD-ROM)

This movie contains a single button, several text fields to show off results, and appropriate labels in four layers.

- Button

- Text Fields

- Labels

- Background

This movie is another example to help you better understand what's going on under the hood where the ActionScript lives. By experimenting with different strings, you can clearly see what you get. Figure 7.10 shows all of the parts on the stage with the Text Fields layer selected.

Background Layer

Select orange from the Swatch panel or mix the color FF8000 in the Mixer panel for both fill and stroke colors. Then select the Rectangle tool from the

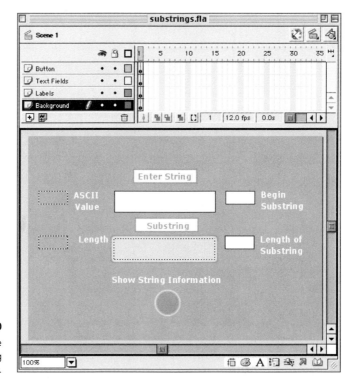

Figure 7.10

Several text fields are used to show what string functions generate.

Toolbox and draw a rectangle that covers the entire stage. Lock the layer when you are finished.

Button Layer

All of the script goes into the button on the Button layer. The script looks at the string and the substring data entered by the user and places the different functional outcomes into the appropriate text fields. When the user clicks on the button, it fires several Set Variable commands with values that are expressions made up of string functions. To create the button, follow these steps:

1. Draw an image at the bottom of the stage using the Oval tool from the toolbar. Select the circle, and press the F8 key to open the Symbol Properties dialog box. Select Button as the behavior, and type in "doit" as the name. Click on OK.

2. On the stage in the main timeline, select the button you just created and press Ctrl+I/Cmd+I to open the Instance panel. Click on the arrow icon on the Launcher Bar to open the ActionScript Editor.

Button: doit

The following script addresses variables associated with text fields. Be sure to use the variables names exactly as they are listed, and check to make sure that the text fields have the correct variable label. The variable named "entry" is a string, and the script uses the string functions to extract the ASCII value, length, and a portion of the string (substring).

```
on (release) {
    ascii = ord(entry);
    stLength = length(entry);
    partString = substring(entry, index, subLength);
}
```

In looking at the script, remember that the variable names and attributes in the functions are text fields. The data is sent to or gathered from these text fields. Examine each Set Variable statement, the variables, and the data:

- The **ord()** function looks at the first character in a string and returns an ASCII value for that character. If you place a space before the first alphanumeric character in the string entry box, the function returns the value of the space (32) instead of the first visible character's ASCII value.

- The **length()** function reads the full string rather than just the first character. Often the **length()** function is used to keep string entries limited to a given number—for example, limiting the abbreviations for states to two characters. An error routine can generate a message advising the user to reenter the data according to the required number of characters.

- Substrings are handy functions for slicing and dicing strings. In the preceding script, the "entry" variable is whatever string the user enters, "index" is the point in the string where the substring begins, and "sub-Length" is how long the substring will be. Notice the parameters used in Figure 7.11 to generate the word "kim" as a substring.

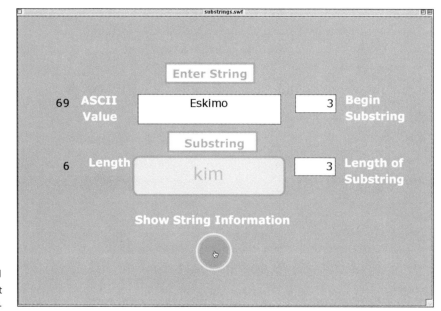

Figure 7.11
Output of different string functions.

Text Fields Layer

All of the input and output goes on the Text Fields layer. Text fields are used for both. Table 7.5 shows the text field properties and names for each, and Figure 7.10 (shown earlier) shows where they go. When placing the text fields, remember to select the Input Text or Dynamic Text menu selection in the Text Options panel.

Labels Layer

The Labels layer provides labels and locations for entering the string and substring information. Table 7.6 lists the labels to be attached to the text fields and their locations.

The final step is to place a label under the button "Show String Information."

Table 7.5 Text field properties and names.

Variable Name	Border/Bg	Text Alignment	Disable Editing	Disable Selection
entry	Yes	center	No	No
ascii	No	right	Yes	Yes
stLength	No	right	Yes	Yes
index	Yes	right	No	No
subLength	Yes	right	No	No
partString	No	center	Yes	Yes

Table 7.6 Text field labels.

Text Field Name	Label	Location
entry	Enter String	Above
ascii	ASCII Value	Right
stLength	Length	Right
index	Begin substring	Right
subLength	Length of Substring	Right
substring	Substring	Above

Why Substrings?

When I first encountered substrings, I wondered why a programming language would need them. The following example provides an answer. This example shows how an e-commerce site can incorporate substrings to determine whether a client had entered a correct email address by searching for the "@" character in the string.

Using a loop for an index value and a length of one (1), you can examine an entire string one character at a time. The following script uses a loop to examine a string to determine whether the user inserted an "@" character—**chr(64)**—in his email address:

```
on (release) {
    n = length(string);
    i = 0;
    flag = 0;
    while (Number(n)>=1) {
        n-=1;
        i+=1;
        if (substring(string, i, 1) == chr(64)) {
            flag = 1;
        }
    }
    if (flag == 1) {
        error = "Correct";
    } else {
        error = "You forgot to include the '@' sign in the email
address.";
    }
}
```

Both "flag" and "error" are variable names. The "flag" variable is set to 1 if the "@" sign—**chr(64)**—is encountered in the string during the **while** loop that examines each character in the string. If the flag variable is "set"—that is, it equals 1—the program knows that the "@" sign has been found in the string. The error variable sends the "Correct" message. Otherwise, the user gets a short lecture about the importance of including the "@" character in his email address. Figure 7.12 shows how the output would look in a movie where the user forgot to enter his "@" sign. (See Find@.fla on CD-ROM.)

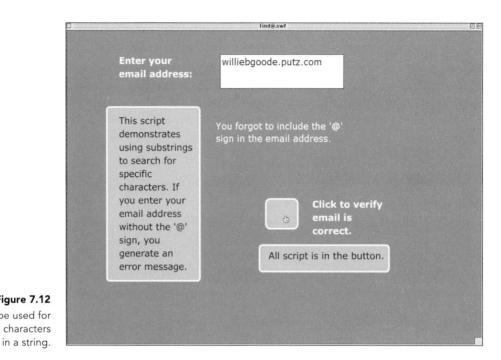

Figure 7.12

Substrings can be used for checking for special characters in a string.

String Objects

Like some of the other objects in ActionScript, the String object contains a "wrapper" to create an object that can be linked to the methods and property using the dot (.) operator. The string functions discussed in the previous section perform a number of the same operations as string objects, but they cannot be used to call their own methods and properties.

The constructor object, String, works like other objects requiring a constructor. For example, the following definition creates a string object named "Sam" with the string, "Web page designer."

```
Sam= new String("Web page designer");
```

The "Sam" object can now call up any of the String methods or its properties using the dot (.) operator. For example,

```
Job=Sam.slice(9,17);
```

places the substring "designer" into the variable named "Job." When dealing with sophisticated movies requiring more elaborate string-handling, using the String object instead of string functions can simplify the job. The following are the 12 methods and the single property associated with the String object. ("StringName" refers to any string name used in conjunction with the method.)

- **StringName.charAt ();**—Retrieves the character at a specified location in the string.

- **StringName.charCodeAt();**—Gets the value of the character at the indexed position and returns an integer between 0 and 65535 (0-FFFF).

- **StringName.concat();**—Concatenates two strings and returns a new one made up of the previous two.

- **StringName.fromCharCode();**—Returns a string from the specified code.

- **StringName.indexOf();**—Retrieves the character at a specified location in the string.

- **StringName.lastIndexOf();**—Returns the last occurrence of a substring within a string.

- **StringName.slice (s,e);**—Extracts a substring from a string with starting and ending points specified relative to the beginning of the string.

- **StringName.split();**—Looks for a specified delimiter and places substrings between delimiters into an array.

- **StringName.substr(s,l);**—Extracts a substring from a string with the starting point and length specified.

- **StringName.substring(f,t);**—Extracts a substring between specified points.

- **StringName. toLowerCase();**—Changes all characters to lowercase.

- **StringName.toUpperCase();**—Changes all characters to uppercase.

- **StringName.length**—Property that returns the string length.

Random Number Generator

The random number generator in Flash is one of the best I've seen in scripting, because it's so easy to specify the number range for random numbers. For example, the line

```
fortuitous = random(25)
```

generated values between 0 and 24. The **random()** function is a specialized one but very useful when random distribution is important. For example, you may want a movie in which an MC moves in random locations by generating random X and Y values for it. (I don't use the function often, but when I need it, I *really* need it.) For example, if you want a bug flittering around the stage, try the following script to generate random movement within a square 200 pixels wide and high. The word "fly" is the instance name of an MC:

```
bugX=random(200);
bugY=random(200);
fly._x=bugX;
fly._y=bugY;
```

Games often require random number generators to give them interest and excitement. Even the designer doesn't know what the next event will be in the movie.

User-Defined Functions

Functions add additional ways to reform, change, and use data in a script. The built-in functions in Flash were originally written by programmers for their own use. An infinite number of functions would be necessary to cover all the different possible routines designers and programmers would want. Therefore, ActionScript in Flash 5 provides user-defined functions so you can write your own. The basic script for a function is

```
function titleOfFunction (arguments) {
    actions go here
}
```

The argument simply means some kind of data. The data can be a literal, string, number, or Boolean. For example, an e-business may need to reuse a function that enters an item's price and then calculates the sales tax and adds shipping charges. Shipping charges are a constant ($6.99), and the tax is eight percent (.08). The price is variable, so price can be used as an argument. Also, a little fancy footwork by strings will make it look pretty. The following function has a single argument, price:

```
function ringUp (price) {
    goFigure = price*1.08+6.99;
    sayFig = new String("bogus");
    sayFig = String(goFigure);
    for (i=0; i<=sayFig.length; i++) {
        if (sayFig.charAt(i) == ".") {
            x = i+3;
        }
    }
    sayFig = sayFig.substr(0, x);
    total = "$"+sayFig;
    showCus = total;
}
```

Chapter 8 discusses the Math object and performs the same function given above with much less code, as can be seen in the following script:

```
function ringUp (price) {
    goFigure = price*1.08+6.99;
    sayFig = Math.floor(goFigure*100)/100;
    total = "$"+sayFig;
    showCus = total;
}
```

The script first uses the argument (price) to figure out what the combined price is going to be in the variable "goFigure." Next, using the **String** object constructor, it creates a string object, **savFig**. Initially, it provides it with a string literal— "bogus"—because the initial constructor is less likely to have problems with a string literal than with a variable. In the next step, however, the **String** function (not the object constructor) converts the value of "goFigure" into a string and places the value in the string object, **savFig**. So now the calculated price is in a string object.

Next, the function uses a loop to search the string object for a decimal point ("."). Once the decimal point is located, the loop index value is placed in the variable "x," and 3 is added. The value "3" is to extend the length to two characters beyond the decimal point. Then the **savFig** object is given a value of the portion of the calculated value from the beginning to two characters beyond the decimal point. Finally, a variable named "total" combines a dollar sign ($) with the value of **savFig**, and the whole thing is passed to the variable "showCus" that will be used in association with a text field.

The function's script is intentionally a bit cumbersome to elaborate the script inside the function, but using the function is quite simple. Suppose that the function definition is in the first keyframe of a layer. You want a button to take a price from an input text field and output it to another text field. Because the function uses the variable name "showCus," that name can also be used for a text field for output. So, all you have to do is to use a variable name for the input in the argument where the price will go and name the output text field "showCus." The following script is all that is needed for a button used to call up the function:

```
on (release) {
    ringUp(itemCost);
}
```

In fact, you could put that function (or any other function) on any frame, button, and MC scripts without ever writing the set of statements that make up the function—only the data for the argument. The following movie shows how this function works. The script is in the first frame, and the function is in the button. The top Input text field has the variable name "itemCost," and the bottom Input text field (with no border or background) has the variable name "showCus." Figure 7.13 shows the layers and setup, and Figure 7.14 shows how it looks when run. (See ownFunction.fla on the CD-ROM.)

Chapter 9 shows how the old **call** action (in Flash 4) has been replaced by user-defined functions. Addressing MCs and writing functions that can be used in several different MCs are also addressed in Chapter 9.

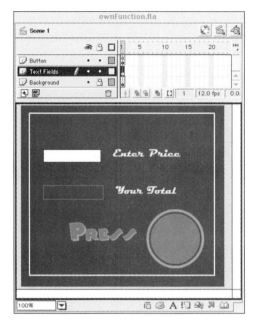

Figure 7.13
The function is in the button, and the script for the function is in the frame.

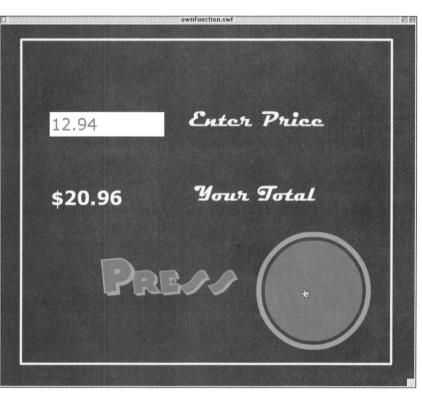

Figure 7.14
When run, the function in the button executes when the button is pressed.

PROJECT Learning Utility: Slide Bar to Change Directions on a Compass (SlideRotation.fla on CD-ROM)

This learning utility shows how to use a slide bar to issue a property action command. The movie requires two MCs. One MC is a draggable slide bar constrained to a narrow horizontal "groove" to simulate an adjustable sliding control. The other uses the built-in Black Cat graphic to serve as an apparently unwilling compass pointer. By moving the bar right and left, the compass rotates clockwise and counterclockwise. Four layers make up the movie.

- Slide Handle MC

- Whirly MC

- Labels and Groove

- Background

The key to this movie is precision. The slide bar moves within a constrained drag rectangle, making it appear to slide. Coordinating the beginning position of the slide handle MC and groove line requires using the Info panel to set the positions and the length of the line. Because there are 360 degrees in a circle, the line is 360 pixels in length to simplify calculating the degrees. To get started, select Modify|Movie and create a stage 450 × 300 pixels using a light green background in the Movie Properties dialog box.

Background Layer

Draw two rectangles. The first is solid black and covers the stage, and the second has a light tan fill and a 6-point stroke in a reddish brown. Select the layer, and choose Modify|Group to join all three. Lock the layer.

Slide Handle MC Layer

Because the slide handle must be dragged to simulate the handle on a slider bar, you must use an MC. (Remember that only MCs can be dragged.) Follow these steps:

1. From the main timeline, select Insert|New Symbol. In the Symbol Properties box, choose Movie Clip as the behavior, and type in the name "Slide Handle." Click on OK. You are now in the Symbol Editor.

2. Draw a slider bar handle or lever by using the Rectangle drawing tool with 6-point corners, green for the interior color, and a reddish brown stroke. Use the Info panel to make the rectangle 49 pixels high and 12 pixels wide. (See Figure 7.15.)

3. Select the slider bar image, and press the F8 key to open the Symbol Properties box. Choose Button as the behavior, and type in the name "handle." Click on OK.

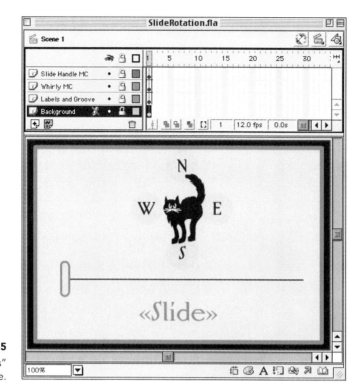

Figure 7.15
Slider bar and "Cat Compass" movie clips on the main stage.

4. Select the newly created button and click on the Action panel icon on the Launcher Bar. Enter the following script in the button while still in the Symbol Editor:

    MC: Slide Handle. Button: Handle
    In this script, the slider effect is created by constraining the drag within a Top and Bottom value of 200. Using a left (L=) constrain of 50 and a right (R=) constrain of 410 creates exactly 360 pixels in the drag area.

    ```
    on (press) {
        _root.lever.startDrag(false, 50, 200, 410, 200);
    }
    on (release) {
        stopDrag ();
    }
    ```

5. Still in the Symbol Editor, click on Frame 2, and press the F5 key to insert a frame. Rename Layer 1, "Activate Slider." Put the following script in Frame 1:

    MC: Slide Handle. Layer Activate Slider: Frame 1
    Note that this script has references to two different MCs—"Whirlygig" and "lever." The information from the lever MC is used to change the property of the WhirlyGig MC. The subtraction of 50 at the end of the line reflects the beginning point of 50 on the left where the lever MC begins its

drag movement. Because the beginning –x value of 50 should be 0, you must subtract 50. Using –50 as an offset, the rotation value stays between 0 and 360.

```
_root.Whirlygig._rotation = (_root.lever._x)-50;
```

6. Click on the Scene 1 icon in the upper left corner to exit the Symbol Editor and go to the main timeline stage. Drag an instance of the Slide Handle MC (not the button) to the main stage. Using the Info panel, place the MC at x = 50, y = 175.

7. Select the Slide Handle MC, and press Ctrl+I/Cmd+I to open the Instance Panel. In the Name window, type in "lever."

Note: This is a crucial step and provides the object with a name.

Whirly MC Layer

The Whirly MC layer uses a rotating cat MC as a compass pointer. (If you don't like the cat, you can substitute an arrow or some other favored pointer.)

1. From the main timeline, select Insert|New Symbol from the menu bar. In the Symbol Properties dialog box, choose Movie Clip as the behavior, and type in the name "WhirlClip." You are now in the Symbol Editor again.

2. Draw or import the image you want to use for a pointer. The black cat I used was borrowed from the Flash 4 library, but use any graphic you want. (If you really want to use the cat, select Window| Library in the SlideRotation.fla file on the CD-ROM—that cat is waiting for you there.)

3. Click on the Scene 1 icon in the upper left corner to exit the Symbol Editor and go to the main timeline stage. Drag an instance of the WhirlClip MC to the stage. (See Figure 7.15 to see the approximate location of the black cat.)

4. Click on the WhirlClip MC to open the Instance Panel, and type in the instance name, "WhirlyGig."

Note: This is a crucial step and provides the object with a name.

Labels and Groove Layer

Draw a straight black line with the Line tool, typing in "3" for the stroke in the Stroke panel. Using the Info panel to make any final adjustments, adjust the line to 360 pixels long with h = 0, beginning at x = 50, y = 200. (It's easier to draw a horizontal straight line and then enter the exact values in the Info panel.)

The Labels layer consists of the cardinal values of the compass—N, E, S, and W. Place the labels around the cat MC so that N is directly above, S is directly below, and E and W are directly to the right and left, respectively. Figure 7.16 shows how the cat will look at an angle when the slider moves.

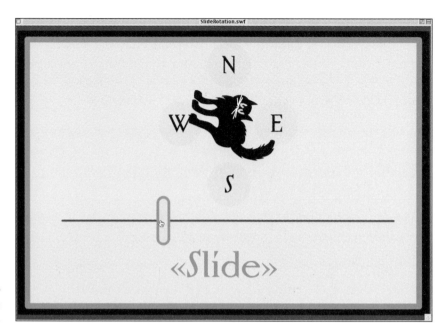

Figure 7.16
As the slider moves, the rotation of the cat MC changes as well.

 A Dynamic Bar Chart for Displaying Proportional Data (barChart.fla on CD-ROM)

A bar chart is a useful tool for presenting data visually. Using Flash and ActionScript, you can create a bar chart that takes any data and charts it dynamically. In this project, only 10 cases are used to keep the project relatively simple in terms of getting the images on the screen and explaining what the action script is doing. The following four layers are used:

- Bars

- Text Fields

- Button

- Background

The key challenges for making a good bar chart are to create proportional bars for the data entered and to deal with values beyond the vertical pixels on the screen. To create proportional sizes, all data must be multiplied by the same factor. In this project, the factor is derived by finding the maximum value in the data set and dividing the maximum number of pixels used by the data set's highest value. Because 300 vertical pixels are to be used, all values must be converted to fit proportionally between 1 and 300. Therefore, data values greater than 300 must be proportionately reduced, along with all of the other data in the set. For example, if the highest value in a data set is 500, the factor will be 300 divided by 500, or 0.6. If all of the values are multiplied by 0.6 in the script, all of the other bars are proportionate to the highest one.

Each layer provides the three key elements of the movie. The bars expand to become bars in a bar chart. The text fields are data entry windows, and the button contains the script to generate the chart using the data in the text fields and changing the properties of the bars. Figure 7.17 shows the initial stage with 10 MCs (the bars), 10 text fields, and the button with the script.

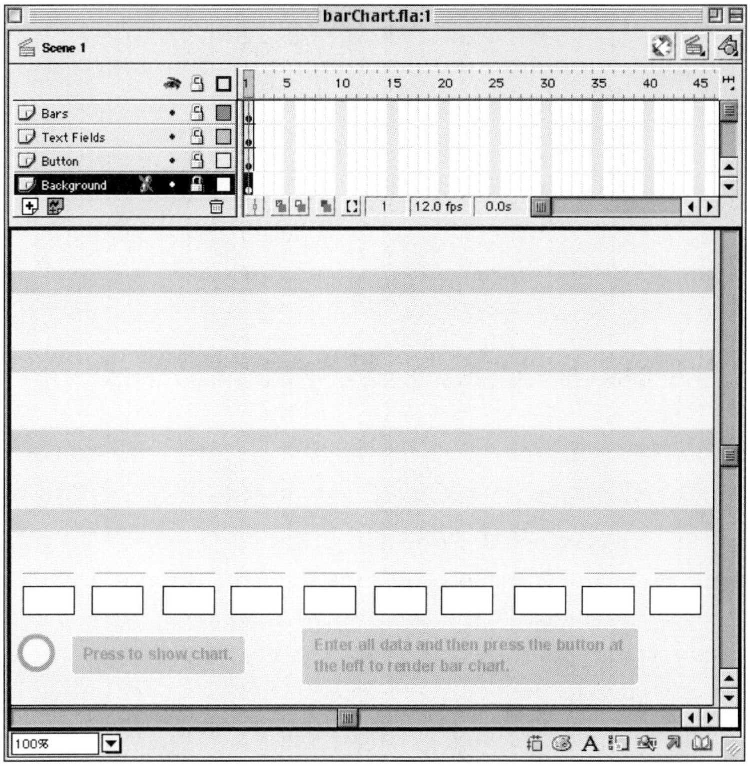

Figure 7.17
All of the lines above the text fields are movie clips to be altered by a script in the button.

Background Layer
Draw a light tan background and overlay it with bars of a slightly darker tan, as shown in Figure 7.17.

Bars Layer
Creating expandable bars for the chart requires an MC with a narrow rectangle that looks like a straight line. You can create this as follows:

1. From the main timeline, select Insert|New Symbol from the menu bar. In the Symbol Properties dialog box, choose Movie Clip as the behavior, and type in the name "bar." Click on OK. You are now in the Symbol Editor.

2. Using the Rectangle tool from the toolbar, draw a rectangle with W = 40 and H = 1. You will need to use the Info panel to get the values correct.

3. Click on the Scene 1 icon in the upper left corner to exit the Symbol Editor and go to the main timeline stage. Drag 10 instances of the bar MC to the stage.

4. Using the Info panel, make sure that each MC has Y = 300. Use the Align tool (Ctrl+K/Cmd+K) to distribute the 10 MCs evenly as shown in Figure 7.17.

5. Name each MC with instance names of "1" to "10." Just select each MC, and type in the numbers from 1 to 10 in the Instance Panel Name window.

Text Fields Layer

In the Text Fields layer, the 10 text fields must be placed directly under the instances of the bar MC, as shown in Figure 7.17. The common values are Y = 310, W = 40, and H = 21. The X (horizontal) value should be the same as the bar MC that they are positioned below. Use the text field properties shown in Table 7.7.

Use the Align tool (Ctrl+K/Cmd+K) to help you get the text fields aligned with the bar MCs. It is very important that the numbers on the bar correspond with the numbers in the variable names. For example, the text field "T7" should be aligned with the bar MC with the instance name "7."

Button Layer

The Button layer has a single button containing all of the script. As mentioned earlier, the script has a lot of work to do because so many different elements have to be considered and coordinated. The following script takes the values in the text fields, finds the highest value in the data set, and creates a common factor. It then takes the converted data and generates 10 proportional bars, as shown in Figure 7.18. An explanation of how the script works follows the script. Also, the script contains several comments identified by double slashes (//).

Table 7.7 Text field properties and names.

Variable Name	Border/Bg	Text Alignment
T1	Yes	right
T2	Yes	right
T3	Yes	right
T4	Yes	right
T5	Yes	right
T6	Yes	right
T7	Yes	right
T8	Yes	right
T9	Yes	right
T10	Yes	right

```
on (release) {
    //  Reset variables.
    x = 0;
    n = 0;
    d = 0;
    Val = 0;
    factor = 0;
    highest = 1;
    //  Reset to initial height.
    while (x<=9) {
        x+=1;
        _root[x]._yscale = 100;
        _root[x]._y = 300;
    }
    //  Determine highest value.
    while (n<=9) {
        n+=1;
        if (_root["T"+n]>highest) {
            highest = _root["T"+n];
        }
    }
    //  Use highest value to create ratio for bar values.
    factor = 300/highest;
    while (d<=9) {
        d+=1;
        Val = _root["T"+d]*factor;
        _root[d]._yscale = Val*100;
        _root[d]._y = 300-Val;
    }
}
```

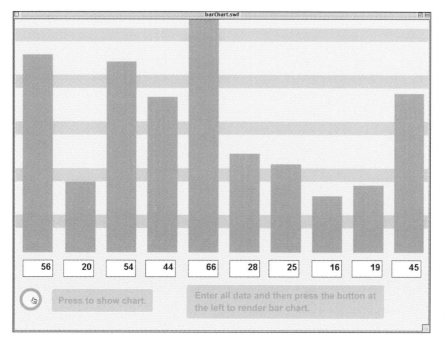

Figure 7.18

Any data entered into the bar chart generates a proportional bar for the data in the text fields.

- First, the script establishes and resets some key variables ("x," "n," "d," "Val," "factor," and "highest") used in the script. Resetting the variables at the beginning allows the user to enter different sets of values during the same session to explore different charts.

- The first loop resets the size of the bar MCs to their original size. Because a scale property is used, "100" represents 100 percent of its size.

- The second loop examines each of the 10 text fields to determine the highest value. Because the text fields are part of a pseudo-array numbered from T1 to T10, the loop can step through the same steps using the loop value and concatenating "T" to the loop variable. The statement, **_root["T" + d]** replaces the Flash 4 script, **eval("/:T" & d).**

- Because 300 vertical pixel positions are to be used in the bars, the script creates a "factor" variable by dividing the 300 by the variable named "highest," which is the value of the highest value entered by the user.

- Next, the script adjusts all of the values by multiplying the text field values (data entered by the user) by the common factor in a loop that again takes advantage of the pseudo-array in the text field names. The value for each bar is placed in the variable "Var."

- Because the Y Scale property of each of the bar MCs is a percentage, "Var" is multiplied by 100. Remember, 100 percent of the bar MC is only 1 pixel high. With 300 pixels, the program must be able to generate values up to 30,000 percent to take advantage of all 300 pixels.

- Finally, the adjusted data value in the variable "Val" is subtracted from the maximum pixels—300—so that the bar maintains its anchor _y position at 300.

For nonprogrammers, the script may look a bit forbidding. When you break it down into its component parts, however, you can see that it simply uses calculated ways to use the MC properties and the data from the text fields.

You can change the bar MCs to generate a different color for each bar, use bar rectangles with rounded corners, or create many variations using the same basic script.

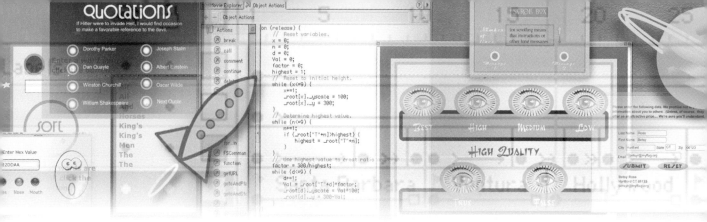

Chapter 8

Using Specialized Objects

This chapter covers a number of specialized objects—color, date, math, number, and sound objects—not yet reviewed in previous chapters. The chapter also discusses each object's construction, methods, and properties.

Built-In Objects

Throughout the book, you have seen what can be done with Flash 5's new ActionScript objects. From the powerful array objects discussed in Chapter 2 to the specialized mouse objects in Chapter 6, ActionScript objects with built-in methods enable you to create interesting effects and change properties. This chapter describes each of the objects—Color, Date, Math, and Number—and the description of each object is accompanied by a learning utility. At the end of the chapter, a Sound project explains how to set sound levels in two pulsating on-screen and computer speakers.

Many of the objects in this chapter cover materials that are highly specialized and technical. If you find some of the objects, their methods, or properties difficult to comprehend, that is due to the micro-tuning of elements in color, math, date, and sound that is out of the everyday use of most people. For those of you who need specialized applications for the objects presented, however, they are included for your use. In most cases, the learning utilities attempt to show how each of the methods can be applied and what information is returned to the user.

Color

The Color object has two general ways to transform the color of an object—namely, a movie clip (MC). The first method uses a hexadecimal value and RGB (Red, Green, Blue) code. (The second method for transforming color is discussed in a learning utility a bit later in this section.) For those unfamiliar with RGB and hexadecimal code from HTML, you will find it relatively simple. The RGB values in decimal are from 0 to 255, which translates to 0 to FF in hexadecimal. A six-character, alphanumeric value in hexadecimal is broken down into R, G, and B values individually, as shown in Table 8.1.

For example, pure red is FF0000. To increase or decrease the mix of a color, you must increase or decrease the hexadecimal value of the R, G, or B. Hexadecimal is like decimal except the base is 16 (0–F) instead of 10 (0–9). As in decimal, you count 0, 1, 2, 3, 4, 5, 6, 7, 8, 9, A, B, C, D, E, and F to get the base-16 characters. Hexadecimal values just add A, B, C, D, E, and F to the base 10. For example, if F = 16, 10 would equal 17, 11 would equal 18, and so on. You only need to understand that F is the highest and 0 is the lowest. To increase a value, you just make it larger as you would in decimal. In other words, if you want to add more green to a G value that is C5, you would change that G value to D6, E9, FC, or anything up to FF.

Table 8.1 Conversion of hexadecimal values to RGB values.

Decimal Value	Color	Hexadecimal Value
0–255	Red	0–FF
0–255	Blue	0–FF
0–255	Green	0–FF

Defining a Color for an Object

To define a color for an MC, define a color variable using the "new" Color statement. For example, to set the Color object for an MC with the instance name "dress," you would first define the color variable and then set the color as follows (blue is the example color):

```
gownColor= new Color(dress)
gownColor.setRGB(0x0000FF)
```

The color code is preceded by "0x" (zero x), which is the escape code for hexadecimal values. To input colors as straight hexadecimal values, you need to transform the input text into a number. Instead of using Number, however, you use the **parseInt** () function with a base of 16. For example, the following code takes the value from a text field and changes it into a base-16 (hexadecimal value).

```
hexV=parseInt(txtFldInput,16)
```

When hexadecimal values are placed into the text field (txtFldInput), they are interpreted as base-16 numbers with no need to use the "0x" escape sequence. The movie in the learning utility that follows shows how to set colors in different MCs.

PROJECT Learning Utility: Setting and Changing Colors (setColors.fla on CD-ROM)

This next movie uses the following layers:

* Input

* Buttons

* Movie Clips

This movie is a simple learning utility that helps you see how to enter hexadecimal values and get some practice in generating different colors in MCs. Figure 8.1 shows a face created from an oval and three MCs—"eyes," "nose," and "mouth." The movie lets you change their colors using three buttons. Each button targets a single MC and thus each can have a different color.

Input Layer

The Input layer consists of a single Input text field with a six-character limitation. A label and a frame (drawn) make it stand out. Table 8.2 shows its characteristics.

By specifying "6" in the Max. Chars. window in the Text Options panel, you help remind the user that she can use only six hexadecimal characters to enter the color. (That's FFFFFF or 16,777,215 color combinations.)

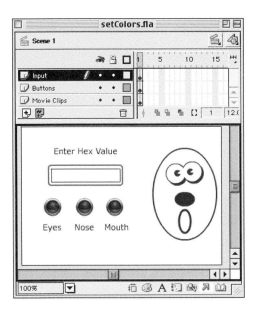

Figure 8.1
Three buttons change the color
of the three movie clips made up
of the eyes, nose, and mouth of
the figure.

Table 8.2 Text field properties and names.

Variable Name	Border/Bg	Text Alignment	Maximum Characters
colorIn	Yes	Left	6

Buttons Layer

In the Buttons layer, the three buttons take the hexadecimal (hex) value from the "colorIn" variable (the text field) and translates the value into a base-16 value that is placed into the MC. I used the Push Button Red from the (circle) LED Button Set in the Common Libraries Buttons.fla, but you can use whatever button you want. The references in the script color definition are the instance names of the MCs.

Button: Eyes

```
on (release) {
        hexV = parseInt(colorIn,16);
        eyeColor=new Color(eyes);
        eyeColor.setRGB(hexV);
}
```

Button: Nose

```
on (release) {
        hexV = parseInt(colorIn, 16);
        noseColor = new Color(nose);
        noseColor.setRGB(hexV);
}
```

Button: Mouth

```
on (release) {
    hexV = parseInt(colorIn, 16);
    mouthColor = new Color(mouth);
    mouthColor.setRGB(hexV);
}
```

Movie Clips Layer

In the Movie Clips layer, you first create three MCs—one each for the eyes, mouth, and nose—as follows:

1. Draw the image, and select it. Use any of the drawing tools, or import a file created in another application such as Freehand or Illustrator.

2. Press the F8 key, and select Movie Clip as the behavior in the Symbol Properties dialog box.

3. Draw an oval on the stage large enough to contain the three MCs.

4. Drag the eyes, nose, and mouth MCs into the oval as shown in Figure 8.2.

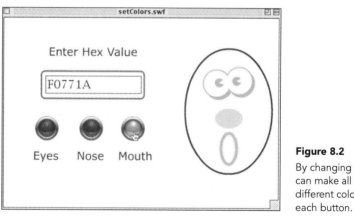

Figure 8.2
By changing the color value, you can make all three movie clips a different color just by clicking on each button.

5. Complete each MC, place it on the face, and then select it. In the Instance panel, type in the Instance Names "eyes," "nose," and "mouth" (with no quotation marks).

Transforming Color (transColor.fla on CD-ROM)

Use the following layers for this next movie:

- Swatch MC

- Button

- Input

In addition to the **setRGB()** method for changing object colors with MCs, ActionScript also has a **setTransform** method. This second method uses four color values: R, G, B, and A. The "A" stands for the Alpha level (transparency) in an object. Each color value has two values: the percentage of color and the offset for the color component. Percentages range from −100 to 100 and offsets from −255 to 255. All values are in decimal. Working with transforming color requires some organization because you have to set eight values for each color. The following steps show you how to set up a movie that uses all eight parameters and allows you to change a swatch to see how the values affect the colors. Figure 8.3 shows the initial stage and layers with all of the components in place.

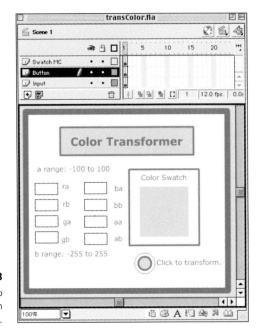

Figure 8.3

Eight text fields, a movie clip (color swatch), and a button make up the movie's objects.

In Figure 8.3, the eight text fields are labeled "ra" to "ab." These labels are the actual parameter names used in the **setTransform()** method. Before starting, each parameter must be defined as follows:

- **ra**—Red percentage from −100 to 100

- **rb**—Red offset from −255 to 255

- **ga**—Green percentage from −100 to 100

- **gb**—Green offset from −255 to 255

- **ba**—Blue percentage from −100 to 100

- **bb**—Blue offset from −255 to 255

- **aa**—Alpha percentage from −100 to 100

- **ab**—Alpha offset from −255 to 255

Swatch MC Layer

In the Swatch MC layer, you create a simple square to use as a color swatch and turn it into an MC. The color swatch's role is to be a target for changing the color. Follow these steps:

1. Use the Rectangle tool to draw a square in any color (except the movie's background color).

2. Select the square, and press F8. When the Symbol Properties dialog box appears, select Movie Clip as the behavior, and click on OK.

3. Select the new MC, and type the instance name "swatch" (without the quotation marks) in the Instance panel.

The MC's color is changed by references to the swatch MC.

Button Layer

All of the ActionScript code goes in the single button in the Button layer. The script takes the information from the text fields used as input forms and sets it in each of the eight parameters. This allows the user to test all of the possible combinations. (I think it's about a zillion or so—1.0824322E20 to be exact.)

Button: ActionScript

```
on (release) {
    transSwatch = new Color(swatch);
    transSwatchTransform = new Object();
    transSwatchTransform.ra = parseInt(raIn);
    transSwatchTransform.rb = parseInt(rbIn);
    transSwatchTransform.ga = parseInt(gaIn);
    transSwatchTransform.gb = parseInt(gbIn);
    transSwatchTransform.ba = parseInt(baIn);
    transSwatchTransform.bb = parseInt(bbIn);
    transSwatchTransform.aa = parseInt(aaIn);
    transSwatchTransform.ab = parseInt(abIn);
    transSwatch.setTransform(transSwatchTransform);
}
```

You use the same steps to create a new color variable for the MC as you do to set the RGB in hexadecimal values. However, the Object object (you're not reading double—that's what it's called) must be used to create an object to transform the eight color parameters. The object name can be named whatever you want, just as with other objects and variables. Each of the eight parameter names is appended to the object as a property to be set by the values placed into the text fields (see the next Input layer). After you have entered all of the values, the **setTransform(objectName)** actually performs the coloring. Note at the beginning of the last line that the Object name "transSwatch" is also given to the MC that has the instance name "swatch." (At the beginning of the script listing, the first line specifies that *swatch* is the name of the MC where the color is applied.) As part of the color object, the MC accepts the settings you have created by placing values in each of the eight parameters based on data entered in the text fields.

To transform the text data into useful data for the parameter values, use the **parseInt()** function. Unlike the earlier RGB example, no base value is required because the default is to decimal—which is what the parameters expect anyway.

Input Layer

You must be careful when creating the eight text fields in this Input layer. Create the first file as an Input text field defined in the Text Options panel. Then make copies of it, and rename the variables to those shown in Table 8.3. Essentially, the text field variable names are the parameter names with "In" appended.

After you are finished, run the program and see what happens when you change various parameters. For example, try placing zeros in two of the Color parameters, and 100 and 255 in the two Alpha parameters. Next, change the two parameters of a single color. Figure 8.4 shows the values with red parameters that generate a terra cotta color. Lower levels of "rb" will turn it into brown.

Getting Color

Retrieving color is a matter of getting the most recent color assigned to a target object—an MC. For example, to retrieve the last value assigned to the "eyeColor" object, you use the following statement, where "getIt" is a variable name:

```
getIt=(eyeColor.getRGB()).toString(16);
```

Notice at the end of the statement that the value is assigned to a string, which transforms base-16 numbers (hexadecimal) into a string. Because the RGB color-setting method uses hexadecimal values, the number-to-string transformation must specify "16" in the argument of the method. The **getTransform()** method works in a similar manner except that it does not require a base-16 number.

Table 8.3 Text field properties and names.

Variable Name	Border/Bg	Text Alignment	Maximum Characters
raIn	Yes	Left	4
rbIn	Yes	Left	4
gaIn	Yes	Left	4
gbIn	Yes	Left	4
baIn	Yes	Left	4
bbIn	Yes	Left	4
aaIn	Yes	Left	4
abIn	Yes	Left	4

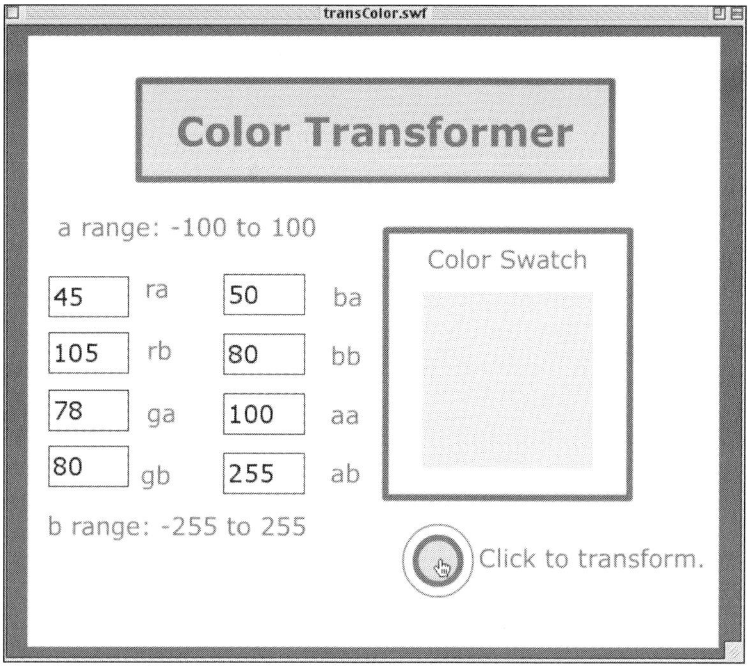

Figure 8.4

Experimenting with one color component at a time and a full Alpha shows how the colors are transformed.

Date

The Date object contains more methods than any of the others, but it breaks down into two basic methods: getting a date and setting a date. Date can be further broken down into dates and time as well as local time and Universal Coordinated Time (UTC, or Greenwich Mean Time, or what is known in aviation as Zulu time).

Web pages often open with the current time and date generated by JavaScript. With Flash pages, you can do this by getting the current time and date stored in your computer. A unique feature about the Flash ActionScript version of getting the date is that it includes UTC. For a 24-hour, round-the-world Web environment, reference to UTC makes a lot of sense. Because aircraft cross time zones, pilots have relied for years on Zulu time (UTC). All flight departure and arrival times are given in Zulu time along with local times, which is also how the Internet presents time. (To set your computer clock, see **www.time.gov**.)

The Date Constructor

The Date object has a constructor with two very different modes of construction. The first constructs an object by simply equating the object name with a new Date object. For example,

```
hotDate = new Date();
```

creates the Date object, "hotDate," with no parameter arguments. Alternatively, you can create a Date object that contains data specifying a date's exact time down to milliseconds. For example, for an e-commerce site a client may have occasion to have a countdown for the announcement of a new product. The Date object can be used to create a date for when the new product is to be introduced, and the Flash movie displays a countdown. For example,

```
launchDate= new Date (2004, 5, 6, 6, 22, 43, 998)
```

indicates June 6, 2004, at 6:22 A.M. and 43 seconds and 998 milliseconds. The breakdown for a Date object defined with arguments are the following:

1. *Year*—Twentieth-century values are from 0 to 99. All others require the full date as shown in the example above.

2. *Month*—Values 0 to 11 for January to December sequentially.

3. *Day*—1 to 31 for days of the month sequentially.

4. *Hour*—Values from 0 to 23 with 0=midnight.

5. *Minute*—Value from 0 to 59.

6. *Second*—Value from 0 to 59.

7. *Millisecond*—0 to 999.

If the above sample Date object definition were placed in a text field for display, the output would look like the following:

Sun Jun 6 06:22:43 GMT-0500 2004

The milliseconds are ignored, GMT-0500 appears as a constant with the parameters, and then the year is shown on the end.

Set and Get Methods in the Date Object

The methods, as noted above, fall into "get" and "set" categories. Each, however, is established in the same manner. A *get* method would be set as follows:

```
giveMeTime = new Date();
showTime=giveMeTime.getHours();
```

The variable, **showTime,** would then contain the current hour on a 24-hour clock. For example, 4:00 P.M. would be displayed as 16.

Setting the time and date follows the same parameters as the ones for getting the date, except that you must include a value in the arguments. For example, the following script uses seconds to show the difference between setting the seconds and getting the seconds. When you *set* a Date object's time, that time becomes the object's value until it is changed. Using a *get* method, however, the time changes constantly depending on the time. If you want to see the difference, create a text field and use the variable name "show" for it.

```
anotherTime = new Date();
time2Go = new Date();
```

```
anotherTime.getSeconds();
time2Go.setSeconds(59);
show = time2Go-anotherTime;
```

You will see the differences between the two Times, expressed as factors of 1,000. The reason for this is that, when you set a Date object, only those portions you set are affected. The other elements use the clock time of your system. For example, by setting the seconds to 59, your Date object has the following value if you set it on Wednesday, August 23, 2000, at 7:41 A.M.:

Wed Aug 23 07:41:59 GMT-0500 2000

The time parameter you changed is the only one that will not be what is returned using a get method. The following shows all of the methods associated with the Date object and their parameters ("dateObj" is a generic Data object name):

- **dateObj.getDate()**—Provides the day of the month (1–31).

- **dateObj.getDay()**—Gets the day of the week (0—Sunday to 6—Saturday).

- **dateObj.getFullYear()**—Returns the fully described year (e.g., 2002).

- **dateObj.getHours()**—Gets the hour of the day (0—midnight to 23—11 P.M.).

- **dateObj.getMilliseconds()**—Gets a value between 0–999 from the system clock.

- **dateObj.getMinutes()**—Returns a value between 0 and 59.

- **dateObj.getMonth()**—Represents months from 0 (January) to 11 (December).

- **dateObj.getSeconds()**—Provides current second between 0 and 59.

- **dateObj.getTime()**—Gets the number of milliseconds between January 1, 1970, and the current time.

- **dateObj.getTimezoneOffset()**—Returns the number of minutes between your system's set time and UTC time (Universal Coordinated Time, or Greenwich Mean Time—GMT).

- **dateObj.getUTCDate()**—Returns the UTC date.

- **dateObj.getUTCDay()**—Gets the UTC day of the week (0—Sunday to 6—Saturday).

- **dateObj.getUTCFullYear()**—Returns the UTC fully described year (e.g., 2002).

- **dateObj.getUTCHours()**—Gets the UTC hour of the day (0—midnight to 23—11 P.M.).

- **dateObj.getUTCMilliseconds()**—Gets the UTC millisecond value between 0 and 999 from the system clock.

- **dateObj.getUTCMinutes()**—Returns the UTC value between 0 and 59.

- **dateObj.getUTCMonth()**—Represents the UTC months from 0 (January) to 11 (December).

- **dateObj.getYear()**—Returns the current year minus 1900 (e.g., 2004 = 104).

- **new Date(year, month, date, hour, min, sec, ms)**—Object constructor with optional parameters. (See the earlier section on the Date Constructor.)

- **dateObj.setDate(date)**—Assigns the day of the month from 1 to 31.

- **dateObj.setFullYear(year, month, date)**—Sets year in object with optional month and date.

- **dateObj.setHours(hours, minutes, seconds, ms)**—Sets the hour with optional minutes, seconds, and milliseconds.

- **dateObj.setMilliseconds(ms)**—Sets object milliseconds.

- **dateObj.setMinutes(minutes, seconds, ms)**—Sets minutes with optional seconds and milliseconds.

- **dateObj.setMonth(month, date)**—Sets month with optional day of month.

- **dateObj.setSeconds(seconds, ms)**—Sets seconds with optional milliseconds.

- **dateObj.setTime(value)**—Sets time to any entered value. (You could put in a value like 2500, which is not recognized as a time.)

- **dateObj.setUTCDate(date)**—Assigns day of the UTC month from 1 to 31.

- **dateObj.setUTCFullYear(year, month, date)**—Sets UTC year in object with optional month and date.

- **dateObj.setUTCHours(hours, minutes, seconds, ms)**—Sets the UTC hour with optional minutes, seconds, and milliseconds.

- **dateObj.setUTCMilliseconds(ms)**—Sets object UTC milliseconds.

- **dateObj.setUTCMinutes(minutes, seconds, ms)**—Sets UTC minutes with optional seconds and milliseconds.

- **dateObj.setUTCMonth(month, date)**—Sets UTC month with optional day of month.

- **dateObj.setUTCSeconds(seconds, ms)**—Sets UTC seconds with optional milliseconds.

- **dateObj.setYear(year, month, date)**—Set the year to a four-digit value (e.g., 2005) with optional month and date values.

- **toString()**—Converts object value to a string.

- **Date.UTC(year, month, date, hour, min, sec, ms)**—Assign the object the UTC year, month, date, hour, minute, second, and millisecond.

PROJECT Learning Utility: Getting the Time and Date (ShowDateAndTime.fla on CD-ROM)

This next movie uses several different time and date objects to present UTC along with a local date. Figure 8.5 shows the display; while it is fairly simple, the code in the frame is pretty interesting. The movie uses the following layers.

* Date

* World

* Background

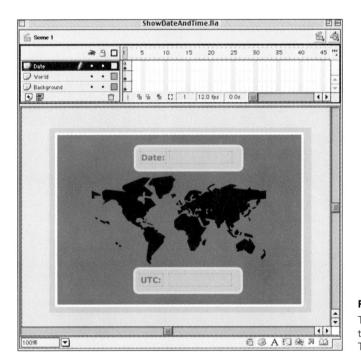

Figure 8.5
Text fields can display both local time and Universal Coordinated Time (UTC) time.

Date Layer

Everything except the background elements is on the Date layer. You can set up the World and Background layers first for format-alignment purposes. You can then test the code and text fields on a blank screen and do the backgrounds. The text field properties are listed in Table 8.4.

1. Click on the second frame, and press F5 to insert a blank frame. All of the code in this movie is in a frame. Because the time is constantly updated, especially for the minutes, you need at least two frames so that the first frame is constantly refreshed.

Table 8.4 Text field properties and names.

Variable Name	Border/Bg	Text Alignment
timer	Yes	Left
zulu	Yes	Left

2. Double-click on the first frame to open the Actions panel and Action-Script Editor. Enter the following script:

```
tellMonth = new Array("January", "February", "March", "April",
 "May", "June", "July", "August", "September", "October",
 "November", "December");
nowDate = new Date();
dom = nowDate.getDate();
month = nowDate.getMonth();
year = nowDate.getFullYear();
timer = tellMonth[month] + " "+ dom + ", " + year;
zuluHours = nowDate.getUTCHours();
zuluMinutes = nowDate.getUTCMinutes();
if (zuluMinutes<10) {
    zuluMinutes = "0"+zuluMinutes;
}
zulu = zuluHours+":"+zuluMinutes;
```

The first line in the script creates an array with the names of the 12 months. Because array objects begin with "0" instead of "1," the numbering is consistent with the Date object method—**getMonth()**—where "0" is used for the first month of the year.

After the array, using the **Date()** constructor, the script creates a Date object. Three variables store the date, month, and year for the Date object. A text field with the variable name "timer" displays the concatenated month, day, and year. Using the month variable as the array index, the correct month in the array is displayed instead of the number associated with the date.

Next, two variables—zuluMinutes and zuluHours—store the UTC time. The nowDate object is still used because it can handle all of the Date objects.

A conditional statement determines whether the value of zuluMinutes is less than 10. The reason for this is that only single digits are returned from the **getUTCMinutes()** method. For example, the output at 6:05 A.M. would read "6:5." To remedy that problem, the program concatenates a zero ("0") in front of the minutes if the number is less than 10.

Finally, the UTC time is displayed on the screen by storing the zuluHours and zuluMinutes in the text field using the variable name "zulu" (see Figure 8.6).

World Time Clock

Without a great deal of difficulty, you could modify the ShowDateAndTime.fla to create a world time clock. Use the UTC and UTC offsets to have time for the major cities in the world—London, Paris, Berlin, Moscow, Beijing, Tokyo, San Francisco, Chicago, and Bloomfield, Connecticut. So, that's your challenge. Use what you've learned to make a world time clock.

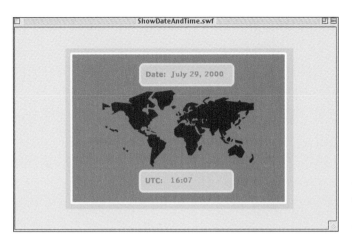

Figure 8.6.
The completed movie displays the local date and the time in hours and minutes for Universal Coordinated Time (UTC).

For modifying the movie to include the day of the week, you can add another array variable and use the **getDay()** method. The following script shows how:

```
dayRay=new Array("Sunday","Monday","Tuesday","Wednesday",
 "Thursday","Friday","Saturday");
nowDate=new Date();
dayNow=nowDate.getDay();
output=dayRay[dayNow];
```

World Layer
The World layer consists of a stylized map of the world.

Background Layer
The Background layer is made up of colored rectangles. The movie background color is set beneath the rectangles.

Math

The Math object is different from the other objects in that you do not construct it. Rather, all of the methods are initiated as part of the Math object itself. The format

```
Math.exp(8);
```

or

```
Math.PI;
```

applies to all of the methods and constants associated with the Math object. Most of the objects are self-explanatory to the math associated with them. The several trigonometry methods now available in Flash 5 remove the necessity of having to write your own. A new **Math.random()** function has replaced the old **random()** function, even though you can still use either one. Eight math constants have been added as well.

To illustrate what returns occur with the major math object methods, this next movie provides input text fields for one or two values. These values are used in the methods to show what the object method actually does. If you see a return of NaN (Not a Number), either the value entered is beyond the range of acceptable values, or the method requires a second value. For example, **atan2()** requires an X-axis value and a point, calculating the angle from the C-axis to the point. Without a second value, it returns NaN. Because the math constants are constant, they are listed along with their values and what they return.

- **Math.E**—Base of nature logarithms (2.718), Euler's constant
- **Math.LN10**—Natural logarithm of 10 (2.302)
- **Math.LN2**—Natural logarithm of 2 (0.693)
- **Math.LOG2E**—Base-2 logarithm of e (1.442)
- **Math.LOG10E**—Base-10 logarithm of e (0.434)
- **Math.PI**—Ratio of circumference of a circle to its diameter (3.14159)
- **Math.SQRT_2**—Reciprocal of square root of 1/2 (0.707)
- **Math.SQRT2**—Square root of 2 (1.414)

The remaining methods associated with the Math object are included in the following movie and script, which provide a test bench for using the Math object methods when needed.

PROJECT Learning Utility: Working Math Methods (MathObject.fla on CD-ROM)

Most of the methods for the Math object are in this single movie. The **Math.random()** function placed at the end of the list is the replacement for the older **random()** function. Rather than entering a value for **Math.random()** as an argument, the upper value is entered as a multiple. The lower limit is subtracted from the total. (See the script listed in Frame 1.) Figure 8.7 shows the initial stage and layer.

All of the objects are in a single layer, and the ActionScript is in Frame 1. Before you add your script, place the cursor in Frame 2, and press the F5 key to add a second frame to the layer.

Frame 1

```
m=new Array(18);
A = parseFloat(inputA);
B = parseFloat(inputB);
abs=Math.abs(A);
acos=Math.acos(A);
asin=Math.asin(A);
```

```
atan=Math.atan(A);
atan2=Math.atan2(A,B);
ceil=Math.ceil(A);
cos=Math.cos(A);
exp=Math.exp(A);
floor=Math.floor(A);
log=Math.log(A);
max=Math.max(A,B);
min=Math.min(A,B);
pow=Math.pow(A,B);
round=Math.round(A);
sqrt=Math.sqrt(A);
sin=Math.sin(A);
tan=Math.tan(A);
ran=Int((Math.random ())*B)
```

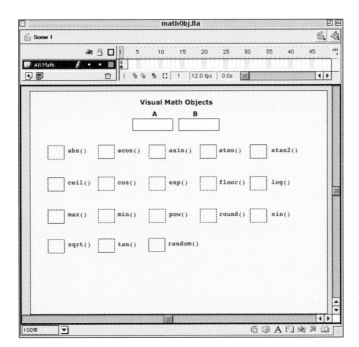

Figure 8.7

Twenty text fields provide 2 for input and 18 for displaying the methods in the Math object.

All of the output is entered into text fields with the names of the Math method. Normally, I avoid using the names of methods or other ActionScript terms as variable names; however, I did it in this example because it tied the method with the output and the output label. Table 8.5 shows the text fields used. All are Input type fields set in the Text Options panel. However, only two—labeled "inputA" and "inputB"—have a border and background and are used for actual input. Although there is no limit on the maximum number of characters in the fields used for user input, the maximum number of characters in the text fields used for output are limited to four. Otherwise, the output from the math methods overlap the other text fields. When only four characters are specified in Max. Chars. in the Text Options panel, *all* characters are included. For example, "–2.1" constitutes four characters because the minus sign and decimal point count in the four-character maximum.

Table 8.5 Text field properties and names.

Variable Name	Border/Bg	Text Alignment	Maximum Characters
inputA	Yes	Left	0
inputB	Yes	Left	0
abs	No	Left	4
acos	No	Left	4
asin	No	Left	4
atan	No	Left	4
atan2	No	Left	4
ceil	No	Left	4
cos	No	Left	4
exp	No	Left	4
floor	No	Left	4
log	No	Left	4
max	No	Left	4
min	No	Left	4
pow	No	Left	4
round	No	Left	4
sin	No	Left	4
bbln	No	Left	4
sqrt	No	Left	4
tan	No	Lcft	4
ran	No	Left	4

Figure 8.8 shows the movie's output with values in both of the input fields labeled "A" and "B." When you actually run the movie, the value for **Math.random()** will keep changing. Because **Math.random()** uses the multiple in the "B" data entry field, however, that field must have a value in it. If

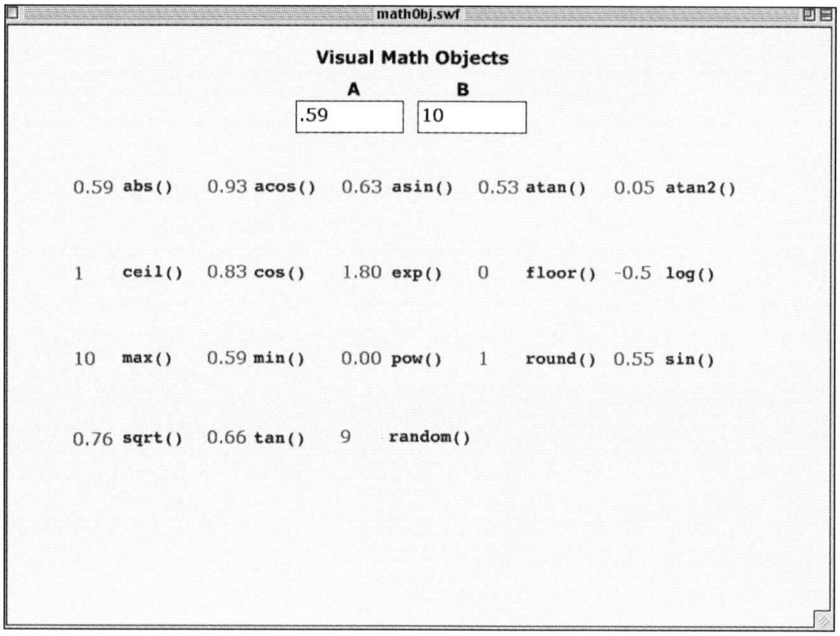

Visual Math Objects

A B
.59 10

0.59 abs() 0.93 acos() 0.63 asin() 0.53 atan() 0.05 atan2()

1 ceil() 0.83 cos() 1.80 exp() 0 floor() -0.5 log()

10 max() 0.59 min() 0.00 pow() 1 round() 0.55 sin()

0.76 sqrt() 0.66 tan() 9 random()

Figure 8.8.

By changing the values in the Input windows, you can get a clear idea of what each method returns.

you watch carefully, you will see that the value placed in the "B" field is the maximum value of the random number generated.

Number

The Number object provides two functions: translating Flash 4 scripts so that they work properly in Flash 5, and providing some methods for dealing with certain limited aspects of numbers. However, the Math object and its methods handle the bulk of the processes for dealing with numbers. Most of the methods associated with Number are constants. The Number constructors **Number.toString** and **Number.valueOf** can be useful for conversions. I've included some examples to show how they operate. Following are the Number object's constants:

- **Number.MAX_VALUE**—Largest number possible to represent

- **Number.MIN_VALUE**—Smallest number possible to represent

- **Number.NaN**—Representation of Not a Number

- **Number.NEGATIVE_INFINITY**—Representation of negative infinity

- **Number.POSITIVE_INFINITY**—Representation of positive infinity

PROJECT Learning Utility (dec2Hex.fla on CD-ROM)

To illustrate how the Number methods work, the following movie creates a Number object and turns a decimal number into a string with a base-16 value—better known as hexadecimal. The whole movie is constructed on a single layer with a compact script in the first frame. Click on Frame 2, and press the F5 key to add a second frame. In this way, the value is constantly refreshed as the movie runs between the two frames (see Figure 8.9).

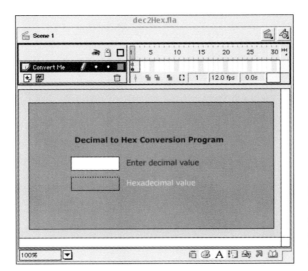

Figure 8.9

Two text fields are used to display the user-entered decimal data and the data that is then converted into hexadecimal values.

Table 8.6   Text field properties and names.

Variable Name	Border/Bg	Text Alignment	Maximum Characters
numIn	Yes	Left	0
numOut	No	Left	0

Convert Me Layer

In the Convert Me layer, add two text fields, and label them as shown in Table 8.6.

Next, add the following script in Frame 1. Note that the script creates two objects. First, it creates a Number object using one of the text fields for the source of data. Second, the script creates a String object so that characters can all be displayed in uppercase.

Frame 1

```
nuVal=new Number( parseInt(numIn));
nuHex=new String();
nuHex=nuVal.toString(16);
numOut=nuHex.toUpperCase();
```

Figure 8.10 shows the output. Because the script is continuously running, changing the initial decimal is sometimes a bit tricky, but it is not impossible. You may want to transfer the script to a button, which eliminates any problems in entering the initial value.

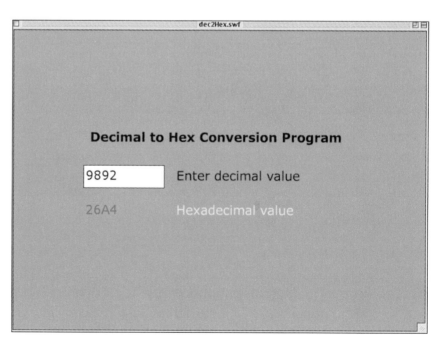

Figure 8.10
Decimal values and hexadecimal values look very different. Try entering your weight in a decimal value and look at the apparent reduction in the hexadecimal value—150 converts to an anorexic 96.

Sound

Controlling sound with ActionScript requires some planning and patience, but you can really control what the viewer hears from his computer by using the Sound object and its methods.

The Sound object works very similar to the other objects. First, you define a Sound object using the format

```
magSound=new Sound();
```

where "magSound" is the name chosen for the Sound object. Then, by attaching methods and related values to the Sound object, you can control the sound. Most of the Sound object's methods involve using a period to attach the method to the sound object, such as,

```
MagSound.setVolume(75);
```

Most of the others follow the same format. The **setTransform()** method is very different, and it will be discussed in the project at the end of this chapter. However, the others can be summarized as follows:

- **attachSound("soundName")**—Attaches a sound file from the library.

- **getPan()**—Returns the value of the last Pan setting between –100 and 100. The left speaker is a negative value, and the right is a positive value. A zero value represents equal balance.

- **getVolume()**—Returns a value between 0 and 100 representing volume level.

- **setPan()**—Sets the balance between the negative (–100 to –1) left and the positive right speaker (1 to 100) balance.

- **setVolume()**—Used to set the volume level from 0 to 100 with the default setting at 100.

- **start(off,loop)**—Starts the sound file with optional parameters for delay (seconds offset) and number of loops.

- **stop()**—Stops the sound with no arguments.

Sound.setTransform

The **set.Transform** method requires an Object object to deal with four speaker parameters. After the Object constructor has created an object to collect the values for the parameters, a Sound object is created to accept the values using the **set.Transform** method. First, the four parameters determine the percentage of input. All values range from –100 to 100.

- *ll*—The percentage of left input to be played in the left speaker

- *lr*—The percentage of right input to be played in the left speaker

- *rr*—The percentage of right input to be played in the right speaker

- *rl*—The percentage of left input to be played in the right speaker

The default setting for stereo sound is 100 for both "ll" and "rr" and 0 for both "lr" and "rl" values. Mixing the combinations can create an interesting range of sound. The general routine for setting sounds with **set.Transform** follows:

```
AlphaTransform=new Object();
AlphaTransform.ll=100;
AlphaTransform.lr=0;
AlphaTransform.rr=100;
AlphaTransform.rl=0:
AlphaSound=new Sound();
AlphaSound.setTransform(AlphaTransform);
```

For a complete example, see the "Controlling Sound in Two Speakers" project below.

XML and XML Socket Objects

ActionScript provides a number of objects to use with XML. One set of objects is for sending, building, loading, and parsing XML document trees. The other set of XML objects is for socket connections, allowing XML programmers to manage connections between XML documents and servers.

Because XML is beyond the scope of this book and these objects are designed specifically for XML users, I have not included explanations or examples of XML-related objects. The ActionScript Editor fully supports these objects, however, and will place them in the Editor window when dragged from the folders and menus of either object group.

PROJECT Controlling Sound in Two Speakers (SoundJam.fla on CD-ROM)

The movie contains the following layers:

- Components

  - Left Slider MC

  - Right Slider MC

  - Speaker MC

  - Cat MC

- Sound

- Background

This project brings several components of Flash and ActionScript together. Using the **Sound.setTransform()** object and methods, two slide levers control the left and right speakers on the computer. On the screen, two pulsating speakers thump in and out as music is played, and a cat rocks back and forth with the Cajun music supplied along with the FLA file on the CD-ROM. Figure 8.11 shows the initial stage.

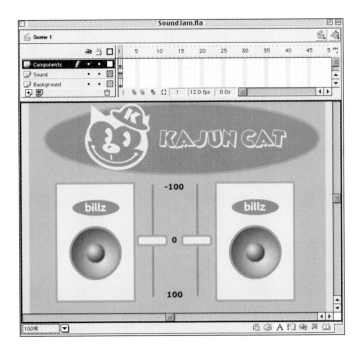

Figure 8.11

Levers are movie clips containing buttons with the ActionScript to control sound levels in the left and right speakers.

The three layers in the movie and three MCs create a movie where the motion and sound component complement one another. The speakers have a hard and fast pulsating animation, and the cat rocks back and forth to the Cajun sound loop. Two sliders increase or decrease the volume in the left and right speakers. The sliders are in the zero position, and the music is at full volume at the beginning. As soon as either slider handle is clicked on, the sound in the speaker goes off. The volume increases as the slider handle is pulled upward toward an offset of –100 or downward toward an offset of 100.

Components Layer

The Components layer has the bulk of everything in the movie. The most important components are the two slider MCs because they contain the buttons with the ActionScript that controls the sound level for each speaker on your computer.

Left Slider MC (Instance Name: left)

The left and right sliders are almost identical. The script associated with the left slider contains just the parameters for the left speaker, "ll" and "lr." Instead of using an MC as the slider tool using the **onClipEvent()** handler, I used button scripts instead. Only one drag action using **onClipEvent()** is possible. If you use MCs containing buttons, however, you can accomplish as many drag events as desired. Because the left and right sliders are so similar, only the left slider construction is handled in detail. The right slider is constructed in the same way, using a different MC name and script.

1. Press Ctrl+F8 (Windows)/Cmd+F8 (Macintosh), and create a button symbol to serve as a slider handle using the Rectangle tool. (See the slider handles in Figure 8.11.) Name the button "handle." Click on the Scene icon to return to the main timeline.

2. Press Ctrl+F8/Cmd+F8 again to create a second new symbol. In the Symbol Properties dialog box, select Movie Clip as the behavior, and name it "lSlider." Still in the Symbol Editor, drag an instance of the "handle" button to the center of the Editor. (Drag it on top of the crosshair [+] symbol on the Editor Symbol stage.)

3. Select the button. Open the Actions Panel and ActionScript Editor, and enter the following script:

```
on (press) {
    startDrag (_root.left, false, 227, 160, 227, 360);
    lSpeaker = (_root.left._y)-260;
    speakerSet = new Object();
    speakerSet.ll = lSpeaker;
    speakerSet.lr = 0;
    CajunSound = new Sound();
    CajunSound.setVolume(100);
    CajunSound.setTransform(speakerSet);
}
on (release) {
    stopDrag ();
}
```

4. Click on the Scene icon to return to the main timeline. Draw a vertical line 200 pixels long beginning at Y position 160 and X position 227 and extending downward to Y position 360. Use the Info panel to position the line correctly.

5. Drag an instance of the lLever MC to the middle of the line. Use the Info panel to place the MC at Y position 260 centered on the line as shown in Figure 8.11.

6. Open the Instance Panel (Ctrl+I/Cmd+I), select the lLever MC, and type in the instance name "left." In the second and third lines of the preceding script, the references to "left" identify the MC as the lever and handle of the slider that sets the volume.

Note: It is crucial to remember to put in the MC's instance name.

Right Slider MC (Instance Name: right)

Repeat Steps 1 through 6 with the following differences:

1. Draw a vertical line 200 pixels long beginning at Y Position 160 and X Position 310 and extending downward to Y Position 360.

2. Use the label "rLever" for the MC name when you first build it.

3. Use the instance name "right" in the Instance Panel for the MC.

```
on (press) {
    startDrag (_root.right, false, 310, 160, 310, 360);
    rSpeaker = (_root.right._y)-260;
    speakerSet = new Object();
    speakerSet.rr = rSpeaker;
    speakerSet.rl = 0;
    CajunSound = new Sound();
    CajunSound.setVolume(100);
    CajunSound.setTransform(speakerSet);
}
on (release) {
    stopDrag ();
}
```

Speaker MC

The speakers are two instances of the Speaker MC. In creating them, I borrowed a trick or two from the well-known Flash designer Hillman Curtis.

1. Press Ctrl+F8/Cmd+F8 to open the Symbol Properties dialog box. Select Movie Clip as the behavior, and use the label name "speaker." Click on OK to enter the Symbol Editor. Click on Frame 15, and press the F5 key to insert a frame.

2. Draw a 90 × 90 circle, using the Info panel to make sure you have the right size. With the circle selected, copy it by selecting Edit|Copy or Ctrl+C/Cmd+C.

3. Select Edit|Paste In Place and change the dimensions to a width of 36 and a height of 36. Because the copy is selected, this should place the second circle right in the middle of the first.

4. Select the larger of the two circles. Copy and paste it in place, and change the dimensions to W = 96, H = 96.

5. Select the Paint Bucket tool, and select the green radial from the swatches. Fill both the center circle and the second circle with the green radial (see Figure 8.11).

6. With the Paint Bucket tool still selected, click on the Transform Fill button at the bottom of the toolbox. Click on the inner circle with the radial, and pull the radial center (white dot) to the 11 o'clock position.

Note: All of the construction of the speaker cones occurs in the Symbol Editor.

Click on the Transform Fill button again and drag the center on the second circle to the 5 o'clock position.

7. To animate the speaker, select every fourth frame and press the F7 key to insert a blank keyframe. Select every frame after each blank keyframe, and press F6 to insert a new keyframe. Select the completed speaker. Copy and paste it after the keyframe after the first blank keyframe. Select Windows|Panels|Transform to open the Transform panel. Click on the Constrain checkbox, and type in "60 percent" in the scale windows. Figures 8.12 and 8.13 show how the speaker looks in the Symbol Editor, as well as in the keyframes. In the keyframe after the second blank keyframe, copy and paste the original-sized speaker. In the keyframe after the third blank keyframe, copy and paste another small speaker. Tweens were not used so that the speakers have a more definitive thumping characteristic of a subwoofer. (The tweens made it look like it was an artificial respirator.)

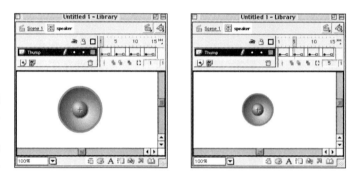

Figure 8.12
(Left) Large speaker.

Figure 8.13
(Right) Small speaker.

8. After you have completed the motion portion, click on the Scene icon to return to the main timeline. Drag two instances of the speaker to the stage, and draw "speaker" boxes around them as shown earlier in Figure 8.11.

Cat MC

The Cat MC is borrowed from Leslie Cabarga, another well-known Flash designer. Using Cabarga's Kolbalt-Kartoon font (**www.flashfonts.com**), I enlarged one of the character fonts, broke it apart, and set it to rocking in an MC.

1. Press Ctrl+F8/Cmd+F8 to create a new symbol. In the Symbol Properties dialog box, select Movie Clip for the behavior, and name it "Cat." Click on OK to enter the Symbol Editor. Place the cursor in Frame 15, and press the F5 key to bring the frame line out to 15.

2. Create the image you want to use. In this case, I took Kolbalt-Kartoon and pressed Shift+Alt+K/Shift+Option+K to put the cat character on the screen. I used a 96-point font size. Then, selecting the character, I

chose Modify|Break Apart. With the font selected, I chose Modify|Scale And Rotate and put in 150 percent in the Scale And Rotate dialog box scale window.

3. Add keyframes in Frames 5, 10, and 15. Add the following scripts in the frames:

   - *Frame 1*

     ```
     _root.kcat._rotation=-20;
     ```

   - *Frame 5*

     ```
     _root.kcat._rotation=0;
     ```

   - *Frame 10*

     ```
     _root.kcat._rotation=20;
     ```

   - *Frame 15*

     ```
     _root.kcat._rotation=0;
     ```

> **Note:** Select the Cat MC, and provide the instance name "kcat" (without the quotation marks) in the Instance Panel.

   The scripts rotate the image to the left by 20 degrees (–20), back to 0, right 20 degrees (20), and back to the center again (0).

4. Press the Scene icon to return to the main timeline. Drag a copy of the Cat MC to the stage and place it as shown in Figure 8.11.

Sound Layer

The Sound layer has a single sound loop. Here's how to set it up:

1. Select File|Import from the menu bar, and find the sound file you want to import into Flash.

2. After you import your Sound file, you may wish to rename it to eliminate the .wav or .aif extension. In the Library window, select Sound file, and click on the "i" icon at the bottom of the window to open the Sound Properties dialog box. Provide the name you want, and make any other sound file adjustments desired. Click on OK when finished.

3. Select the Sound layer, and open the Sound panel by double-clicking on the first keyframe in the layer. In the Sound pulldown menu of the Sound panel, select the sound you loaded in the Library. For Effect, select "None"; for Sync, select "Event"; and for Loop, type in "999" or any number you want to use for the number of loops to repeat.

Background Layer

The Background layer fills out the rest of the movie, as shown earlier in Figure 8.12. The color scheme was translated from CMYK to RGB using a color scheme from special effects animator and 3D illustrator Chris Cadady from Leslie Cabarga's book, *The Designer's Guide to Color Combinations: 500+ Historic and Modern Color Formulas in CMYK* (Cincinnati, Ohio: North Light Books, 1999), p. 99. With translation to RGB and the often-narrow world of 216 "Web-safe" colors, it is quite possible that the colors will appear differently on different computers. Figure 8.14 shows the running movie with the sliding levers adjusting the sounds in the two speakers. (See the CD-ROM movie to see how sound, motion, and color all work together.)

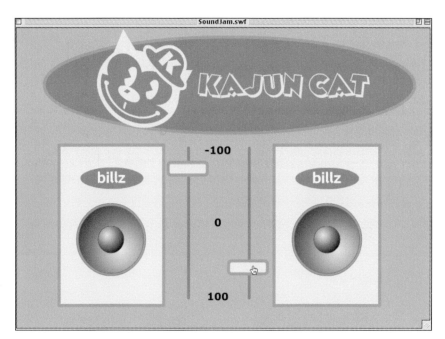

Figure 8.14

By adjusting the slide levers, you can create some very interesting sound combinations.

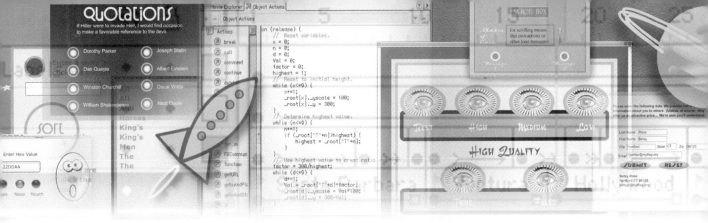

Chapter 9

Duplicating Movies, Following Paths, and Calling Functions

This chapter provides additional commands for controlling movie clips. It shows how to duplicate and remove movies, as well as how to issue commands to movie clips and how to work with user-defined functions for controlling movie clips.

Duplicating and Removing Movie Clips

You can duplicate or remove any movie clip (MC) in your movie. After creating a single MC, you can instruct your movie to duplicate it any number of times. Likewise, you can remove an MC after it is no longer needed. As always with MCs, the instance name is what is duplicated or removed—not the symbol.

The movie in this section randomly scatters stars over a black background. The stars—made up of a "twinkling" MC—are thrown against a dark night in random alpha levels to make it appear that some are nearer and others farther away. With a click of a button, you can cast another field of stars in a different random pattern. Clicking another button removes them from the stage so that it appears that the stars are disappearing and the sun is coming up. For example, the following script makes a duplicate of the MC named "star," and names it "NewStar." It places the duplicate at depth 15. It then places it in the vertical location 200, but it retains the horizontal position of the original MC. Note, in the third line of the script, how the reference to the **duplicateMovieClip()** treats it as a unique MC, referencing its instance name generated in the previous line.

```
onClipEvent (mouseDown) {
    _root.stars.duplicateMovieClip("NewStar", 15);
    _root.NewStar._y = 200;
}
```

The movie is relatively simple, but you will find it helpful to look at the parameters for duplicating a movie. Generally, you'll also want to add an X Position value to the duplicated MCs unless you want all of them in a straight horizontal line.

As seen in the previous script, the **duplicateMovieClip()** method attaches to an existing MC. The duplicate MC needs a new instance name and a depth. The new instance name can be a string literal or an expression. The depth must be a number or variable with a numeric value. Generally, if an MC is on the stage, the new MC needs a position that is not on top of the existing one. Because the script doesn't contain an X Position, the new MC adopts the X value and other properties of the original MC.

Duplicating Movie Clips (StarField.fla on CD-ROM)

To show how to fill up space with stars for your next intergalactic animated thriller, this movie employs **duplicateMovieClip()** to good effect. It uses the following layers:

- StarScript
  - MC: Star
  - Twinkle
- Buttons

The movie consists of one MC and two buttons plus a label. The scripts for duplicating and removing the MC are in two buttons. The duplicated MCs are given property values for the horizontal and vertical positions and the **_alpha** (transparency) level. The initial screen is fairly sparse, as shown in Figure 9.1. In the library window in Figure 9.1, you can see that the little star on the stage is an instance of an MC in the library. The movie needs all that blank space because it will be filled up with 30 duplicated MCs of the star. (See Figure 9.2.)

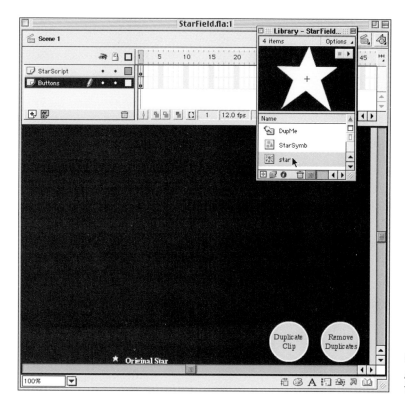

Figure 9.1

A fairly blank stage leaves room for duplicating the movie clip.

StarScript Layer

The StarScript layer is where you put your movie. To get started, change the background color to black or draw a black rectangle over the stage. Select Modify|Movie, and select black from the Swatch Palette. Follow these steps to create the Star MC:

1. Select Insert|New Symbol from the menu bar or use the Ctrl+F8 (Windows)/Cmd+F8 (Macintosh) keyboard shortcut. You are now in the Symbol Editor. In the Symbol Editor, rename Layer 1 "Twinkle."

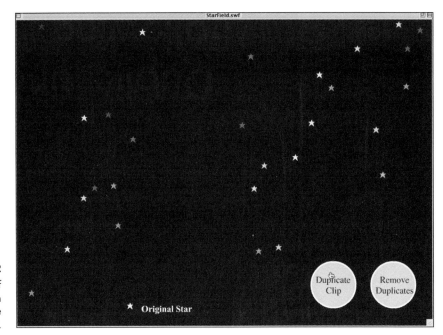

Figure 9.2
The random distribution of stars in this MC creates a different pattern each time the button is pressed.

2. Click on Frame 10, and press the F5 key. That gives you 10 frames to work with.

3. Using the drawing tools, draw a yellow star. (I magnified the stage to 800% so that I could see what I was doing, because the star is roughly 8 × 8 pixels.)

4. Select the drawing, and press the F8 key to open the Symbol Dialog box. Select Graphic as the behavior, and use the name "StarSymb." The reason for turning the drawing into a symbol is so you can change the tint.

5. Insert keyframes at Frames 5 and 10 by clicking on the frame and pressing the F6 key.

6. Select the graphic symbol instance, and select Window|Panels|Effect to open the Effect panel. Select Tint from the dropdown menu on the Effect panel and set the top slider to 100%. Select a light blue from the color swatches—something that contrasts well with the black background.

7. Repeat Step 6 in Frame 10, using a light red color.

8. Enable the Frame actions, and test it to make sure that it blinks from yellow to blue to red. Then click on the Scene 1 icon to return to the main timeline.

 Note: This step is very important because MCs cannot be addressed without instance names.

9. Drag an instance of the MC to the stage. (See Figure 9.1.) Select the Star MC and press Ctrl+I/Cmd+I to open the Instance Panel. Click on the Definition tab, and type in "stars" in the Name box. You're all set to create the buttons and their scripts.

Button Layer

The two buttons on the Button layer duplicate and remove the additional instances of the MC. Begin by drawing two circles and giving each a label. Then click on the F8 key to turn them into Button symbols. Name one "DupMe" and the other "DumpMe."

Button: DupMe

The **duplicateMovieClip()** method uses a loop to duplicate 30 MCs—the little twinkling star. The pseudo-array concatenates "newstar" and the loop index from 1 to 30 providing the Instance Names, "newstar1" … "newstar30." The X and Y Position values are random, as is the **_alpha** value. With each click of the button, you see a blanket of stars in a different arrangement.

```
on (release) {
 StarCount = 1;
 while (StarCount<30) {
 _root.stars.duplicateMovieClip("newstar"+StarCount,StarCount);
 _root["newstar"+Starcount]._x = random(550);
 _root["newstar"+Starcount]._y = random(400);
 _root["newstar"+Starcount]._alpha = random(100);
 StarCount+=1;
     }
}
```

To give the twinkling stars even more variety, you can add a random function into the script for the Star MC. Put actions for different colors in three sequential frames beyond the first frame. In the first frame, place a random function that generates three numbers [random(4)]. Use the random number and an offset to jump to different frames for different colors and then bounce back to the first frame.

Button: DumpMe

The script to remove the duplicated MCs is almost identical to the one that created them in the first place. If you use Copy and Paste from the Edit menu, you can copy the first one and paste it to the DumpMe button. You can then edit it to make changes. Delete all of the Set Property actions, and change **duplicateMovieClip()** to **removeMovieClip()**. Your new script should be as follows:

Copy and Past Scripts to Reduce Errors

In addition to saving time, you can reduce errors in scripts by using Copy and Paste. In the DupMe and DumpMe buttons, the identical names and parameters are used to duplicate and remove the MCs from the stage.

```
on (release) {
    StarCount = 1;
    while (StarCount<30) {
        _root["newstar"+starcount].removeMovieClip();
        StarCount+=1;
    }
}
```

Why does the original set of stars disappear every time the Duplicate Clip button is pressed? Each time a new array of stars is generated, an MC in one of the depths is replaced when another is placed in the same depth. Each timeline limits the number of MCs in a single depth to 1. When the same instance name is used, the old ones with the same name simply take on the properties of the new ones.

Addressing Movie Clips

The new addressing system for issuing commands to different MCs and their timelines in Flash 5 is easier to learn than the Tell Target system used in Flash 4. I suggest that you start using the new method for addressing MCs.

In the Tell Target slash system of addressing an MC, you can still use the format as shown in the following script:

```
on (release) {
    tellTarget ("/grandma/ma/granddaughter") {
        gotoAndPlay (5);
    }
}
```

However, the same script written in the dot (.) format takes less code and is clearer:

```
on (release) {
    _root.grandma.ma.granddaughter.gotoAndPlay(5);
}
```

The **gotoAndPlay(5)** method is attached right onto the path of the MC. As MCs achieve depth with one MC inside another, and yet still another inside that one, the dot format links the MCs by instance names and attaches the method, property, or variable to the end of the path. The root level is conveniently named **_root**, and the rest of the MCs and their children are linked like cars on a train. The last element in the statement is a method, property, or variable associated with the last named element in the statement.

The crucial part is the addressing—not the methods (actions). The methods are the same as those issued on the same timeline. In the preceding example, all of the actions are addressed to "Granddaughter"—a child of "Ma." "Ma" is a child of "GrandMa," which lives on the main timeline. The names refer to the instance names of the MCs. To issue more than a single command, just cut and paste the first command, and edit the method to a different method, property, or variable.

Expert Mode in Editing

When you start doing a lot of cutting and pasting, think about using the Expert Mode of the ActionScript Editor. You can switch back and forth between the two modes; for editing scripts, however, you have far more freedom in the Expert Mode—and you don't have to be an expert to do the editing.

Following Movie Clip Paths (TellMe.fla on CD-ROM)

This movie illustrates how to address MCs from different timelines. The following layers make up the movie. These layers also contain various Child layers, MCs, and buttons.

- MainLine
- GrandPa
  - MC: GrandPa
  - Button
  - Greeting
  - Pa
    - MC: Pa
    - Button
    - Howdy
    - Grandson
      - MC: Grandson
      - Button
      - Whatever
- GrandMa
  - MC: GrandMa
  - Button
  - Granny
  - Ma
    - MC: Ma
    - Button
    - Mom
    - Granddaughter
      - MC: Granddaughter
      - Button
      - Like Hello
- Lines
- Action Buttons

Paths

The following movie is a good illustration of how to use paths for addressing objects on different timelines. It has six MCs, each of which can issue orders to the others. The movie has two sets of buttons. The exterior set with dark centers is located on the main timeline. Each button sends a message to the adjacent MC indicated by a rectangle with a name inside (see Figure 9.3). The button issues a command to the MC to play Frame 5. Each MC, as well as the main timeline, has a message about itself in Frame 5. By looking at the script in each of the six exterior buttons, you can see how to access each level from the main timeline.

The interior set of buttons each has a line connected to it. These lines show how different levels communicate with one another (see Figure 9.3). For example, the button to the left of "Ma" has a line to the Main Timeline. The button to the right of "GrandPa" has one to "Granddaughter." Within the same hierarchy (for example, GrandPa or GrandMa), commands can use *absolute* or *relative addressing*.

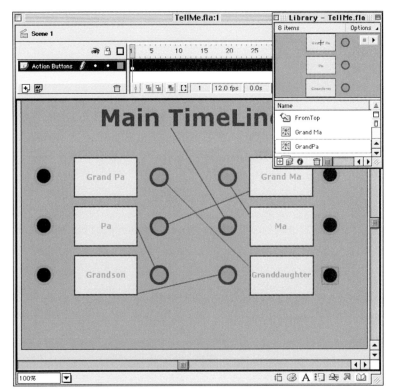

Figure 9.3

The movie clips are arranged in two hierarchies in descending order. In the library, you can see previews of the multitiered movie clips.

Absolute Addressing

In absolute addressing, the address includes the entire hierarchy beginning at the top level. The main timeline has no name, but it can be addressed as **_root** or the level for the movie, such as **_level0**, **_level43**, or any other level under any circumstances. Actually, **_root** is an alias for any top-level reference. A movie on **_level5** can be addressed as **_root** from any timeline in the same level. Any MC can be reached on any level within any hierarchy by going to the top level and naming each level from the top down within the correct hierarchy. A hierarchy consists of MCs that are contained within other MCs—all descendants of the main timeline. Absolute addressing is required to reference an MC in a different hierarchy. Chapter 10 looks more closely at incorporating different movies in Flash 5 and working with different levels.

Relative Addressing

When addressing MCs within the same hierarchy, you may use relative addressing. Relative addressing refers to the path that a command takes based on its own position. Going upward in a path can use **_parent** instead of going to the top of the hierarchy and back down. A path from "Granddaughter" to "Ma" is simply **_parent** followed by the method, property, or variable. "Pa" to "Grandson" takes the path **grandson**. However, suppose that the Granddaughter MC—which is three levels down—wants to communicate with the Grandson MC, also three levels down. In absolute addressing, the Granddaughter has to go all the way to the top of the Grandson hierarchy and then back down to Grandson in an absolute path of **_root.grandpa.pa.grandson** rather than one that goes directly across to **grandson**.

To illustrate relative addressing, we'll use our example showing that the Ma MC is below the GrandMa MC and above the Granddaughter MC. If you want to address "GrandMa" from the "Ma" level, you use the relative address of **_parent**. If you want to address "Granddaughter" from the "Ma" level, you use **granddaughter**. From "GrandMa" to "Granddaughter," the relative address is **ma.granddaughter.** From Granddaughter to Grandma would be **_parent._parent**. You use only instance names in addressing.

MainLine Layer

The MainLine layer contains a "Main TimeLine" label, one small action script, and a label on the stage at Frame 5. Always think of the main timeline as the top of all hierarchies.

Frame 1

```
stop();
```

Frame 5: At the Top (Frame Label)

The messages in the main timeline and all of the MCs in the movie are labels that appear on the main stage. Insert a keyframe at Frame 5, create a graphic rectangle on the stage, and type the following message in it:

"You have arrived on the main timeline."

GrandPa Layer

The first hierarchy begins in the GrandPa layer. As you build the layer, the GrandPa MC grows and changes in appearance. In Figure 9.3, you can see that the GrandPa MC contains three different rectangles (in the Preview panel of the Library window), representing the three MCs that make it up.

1. Select Insert|New Symbol. Select Movie Clip as the behavior and GrandPa as the name in the Symbol Properties dialog box. Click on OK to enter the Symbol Editor.

2. Using the Info panel as an aid, create a rectangle with a width of 100 and a height of 60. Place the object at 0,0 with the center point in the middle of the object selected in the Info panel. All of the other MCs use identical dimensions for their MC label boxes.

3. Using the Circle tool, create a 26 × 26 circle with an orange center and dark blue border. Select the circle. Press the F8 key, and select Button for the behavior in the Symbols dialog box and name it "SendAround." This symbol is used for all of the MC's interior set buttons.

4. With the center point in the middle of the object selected in the Info panel, place the button at x = 85, y = 0. Figure 9.4 shows the button correctly positioned relative to the label box when complete.

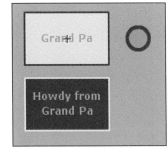

Figure 9.4
Position of the MC label, greeting, and button.

MC: GrandPa, Button Layer

The GrandPa layer contains a button. The interior set buttons for all of the MCs have one of two basic scripts. One script uses Tell Target, and the other uses Set Property. By the time you're finished with these scripts and buttons, you should have a firm grasp on using ActionScript across timelines or go stark raving mad (whichever comes first). First, look at the script and then the explanation after it.

• *Button: Instance of SendAround*

```
on (release) {
    _root.grandma.ma.granddaughter.gotoAndStop(5);
}
on (rollOut) {
    _root.grandma.ma.granddaughter.gotoAndStop(1);
}
```

If you go through the script step by step, you'll see that it is very simple:

• Using the **on(release)** option for the button, the first line tells the script the name of the target (MC with the instance name "granddaughter") using absolute addressing.

• At the end of the line, the method tells the movie to stop at Frame 5 of the granddaughter (instance name) MC. All of the MCs have label announcements that pop up at Frame 5 to identify themselves and greet the viewer.

• Beginning the next phase, the button event **on(rollOut)** is used so that when the mouse pointer leaves the button, everything can be put back to the initial state.

- Again, the path addresses the Granddaughter (granddaughter = instance name) MC and tells it to go back to the first frame.

MC: GrandPa, Greeting Layer

Each MC has a greeting so that when the MC is addressed, something can happen to show the MC has been targeted correctly. The greeting is handled by a keyframe in Frame 5.

- *MC: GrandPa Frame 5*—Figure 9.4 shows the elements in the completed MC with the time cursor on Frame 5. The greeting is set in a 100×60 rectangle positioned at x = 0, y = 75 with the center point in the middle of the object selected in the Info panel.

After you have completed everything for the GrandPa MC, continue the procedure discussed earlier with these steps:

1. Click on the Scene 1 icon in the upper left corner to return to the main timeline.

2. Select Window|Library to open the Library window. Drag an instance of the GrandPa MC from the Library window to the stage. Position it where you see it in Figure 9.3.

3. Select the MC, and press Ctrl+I/Cmd+I to open the Instance Panel. In the Name window in the Instance Panel, type in "grandpa." (I used one-word, lowercase names for all of the instance names to differentiate them from the MC labels while keeping a clear connection because of the similarity of the names.)

> **Note:** This step is very important. Remember, no instance name means no recognition in a path.

MC: GrandPa, Pa Layer

This layer is reserved for placing the MC "Pa."

MC: Pa (Instance Name "pa")

This next set of steps is to build an MC that will be placed inside another MC. Within the "GrandPa" MC is an MC named "Pa"; within "Pa" is an MC named "Grandson." You can build the additional MCs from the main timeline and then drag them into the correct MC through the Symbol Editor. Follow Steps 1 to 4 outlined earlier, and substitute the label "Pa" for "GrandPa." Use the same dimensions for the rectangles with the labels as well.

MC: Pa Button Layer

In the button layer, place the button right next to the "Pa" rectangle, as was done in the GrandPa MC shown in Figure 9.4 using an instance of SendAround. (Drag the button from the Library window.)

- *MC: Pa Button Instance of SendAround*

```
on (release) {
    _root.grandma.gotoAndStop(5);
}
```

```
on (rollOut) {
    _root.grandma.gotoAndStop(1);
}
```

MC: Pa Howdy Layer

Like the GrandPa MC, the Pa MC has a greeting in Frame 5 to identify itself. Position the greeting using the same parameters used in the GrandPa MC.

- *MC: Pa Frame*—Insert a keyframe in Frame 5. Draw a rectangle, and place the following greeting message inside the rectangle like the one shown in Figure 9.5:

  "Howdy from Pa"

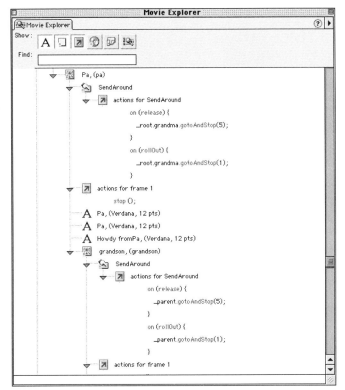

Figure 9.5

The Movie Explorer shows the hierarchy of movie clips and outlines the entire movie.

MC: Pa Grandson Layer

This layer is reserved for placing the Grandson MC.

Putting the Pa MC Inside the GrandPa MC

You have now completed the Pa MC. Now you need to place the Pa MC inside the GrandPa MC. Follow these steps:

1. Click on the Scene 1 icon in the upper left corner of the Symbol Editor to return to the main timeline (if you're still in the Symbol Editor).

2. In the main timeline, select the GrandPa MC, and select Edit|Symbols from the menu bar. Make sure that the timeline cursor is on Frame 1.

3. Drag the Pa MC from the Library window into the GrandPa MC. You will see "GrandPa" right next to the Scene 1 icon in the upper left corner. (If you do not, you are not in the Symbol Editor.)

4. Place the Pa MC in position x = 0 and y = 75 with the center position checked in the Info panel.

5. Select the Pa MC, and press Ctrl+I/Cmd+I to open the Instance Panel. Click on the Definition tab, and type the word "pa" in the Name window. (Leave out any quotation marks.)

Note: Be sure to select the Pa layer.

Note: This step is very important.

MC: Grandson (Instance Name "grandson")

The Grandson layer is the last in the hierarchy. Placing the MC inside the Pa MC is a little different because you have to drill down an additional layer.

MC: Grandson, Button Layer

In the Button layer, place the button right next to the "Grandson" rectangle, as was done in the GrandPa MC shown in Figure 9.4 using an instance of SendAround. (Drag the button from the Library window.)

- *MC: Grandson, Button Instance of SendAround*—Note that the script uses **_parent** to address the parent MC.

```
on (release) {
    _parent.gotoAndStop(5);
}
on (rollOut) {
    _parent.gotoAndStop(1);
}
```

MC: Grandson, Whatever Layer

Like the GrandPa and Pa MCs, the Grandson MC has a greeting in Frame 5 to identify itself. Position the greeting using the same parameters as used in the GrandPa MC.

- *MC: Grandson Frame 5*—Insert a keyframe in Frame 5. Draw a rectangle, and place the following greeting message inside the rectangle like the one shown in Figure 9.4:

  "Whatever...Grandson"

No third layer is reserved for another MC because the Grandson MC doesn't use an additional one.

There is a slight but important difference in placing the Grandson MC inside the Pa MC:

1. Click on the Scene 1 icon in the upper left corner of the Symbol Editor to return to the main timeline (if you're still in the Symbol Editor).

2. In the main timeline, select the GrandPa MC, and select Edit|Symbols from the menu bar. Make sure that the timeline cursor is on Frame 1.

3. *Important Difference.* In the Symbol Editor, select Pa MC. From the menu bar, select Edit|Edit Selected from the menu bar. You *cannot* use Ctrl+E/ Cmd+E as you can when you want to edit a symbol from the main timeline. You must first select the MC within the MC and then use the Edit|Edit Selected sequence in the menu bar.

4. Place the time cursor at Frame 1, and select the Grandson layer. Drag the Grandson MC from the Library window into the Pa MC. You will see "Pa" right next to the Scene 1 icon in the upper left corner. (If you do not see "Pa," you are not editing the correct symbol.)

5. Place the Grandson MC in position x = 0 and y = 75 with the center position selected in the Info panel.

6. Select the Grandson MC, and open the Instance Panel. Type the word "grandson" in the Name window. (Leave out any quotation marks.)

Note: This step is very important.

GrandMa Layer

The GrandMa hierarchy is just like the GrandPa hierarchy. However, the buttons include setting properties as well as telling targets what to do. Because this example deals with hierarchy, I thought it would be a good idea to include some complex navigation to set property parameters as well. Rather than going through all of the steps done in the preceding GrandPa layer, use the same steps, substituting the indicated button scripts and the messages.

MC: GrandMa (Instance Name "grandma")

The button script sets a property rather than using a method to issue a command.

- *MC: GrandMa, Button Instance of SendAround (Button Layer)*

```
on (release) {
    ma._visible = false;
}
on (rollOut) {
    ma._visible = true;
}
```

- *MC: GrandMa, Granny Layer: Frame*—This layer uses the message:

   "Greetings from Granny"

MC: Ma (Instance Name "ma")

The script in this button addresses the main timeline. When activated, a message appears near the bottom of the screen.

- *MC: Ma, Button Instance of SendAround (Button Layer)*—Note that **_root** alone is used as a path. You could also use, **_level0** instead of **_root**.

```
on (release) {
    _root.gotoAndStop(5);
}
on (rollOut) {
    _root.gotoAndStop(1);
}
```

- *MC: Ma, Mom Layer: Frame 5*—This layer uses the message:

  "Hiya from Ma"

MC: Granddaughter (Instance Name "granddaughter")

Note in the script how an MC at the bottom of a hierarchy addresses an MC at the bottom of another hierarchy by going to the top of the hierarchy and working its way down.

- *MC: Granddaughter, Button Instance of SendAround (Button Layer)*

```
on (release) {
    _root.grandpa.pa.grandson._rotation = 90;
}
on (rollOut) {
    _root.grandpa.pa.grandson._rotation = 0;
}
```

- *MC: Granddaughter, Ma Layer: Frame 5*—This layer uses the message:

  "Like HELLO, Granddaughter"

Lines Layer

The Lines layer is simple and involves the GrandPa and GrandMa layers. Use the Line tool from the toolbox to draw the lines from the interior set of buttons to the destination targets. Use Figure 9.3 for a guide.

Action Buttons Layer

Place the exterior set of buttons in the Action Buttons layer. Each button does exactly the same thing. It tells the target to **gotoAndStop()** at Frame 5, but each uses a different address. As you saw while building the movie, each MC and the main timeline places a message to appear on the screen in Frame 5 when the movie reaches the frame. The key use of each button is to learn how to address any of the MCs from the main timeline. When MCs are in the movie, Flash shows you the MCs from the top level. If you select an MC with embedded MCs in it, those are shown as well. When you begin to engage in more complex movies such as these with several timelines in the different MCs, you should begin using the Movie Explorer. Figure 9.5 shows a segment of what you will see in the Movie Explorer with this movie. It outlines all of the different MCs, their scripts, and the frames.

Draw a circle with an orange border and black interior. Select it, and press the F8 key to open the Symbol Properties dialog box. Select Button for the behavior, and use the label "From Top." You can use instances of this button for all of the exterior buttons in the movie. Examine closely the paths used in following clips to understand how to navigate through different MCs in Flash 5.

Button: Instance of From Top

Position this button to the left of "GrandPa" on the stage.

```
on (release) {
    _root.grandpa.gotoAndStop(5);
}
on (rollOut) {
    _root.grandpa.gotoAndStop(1);
}
```

Button: Instance of From Top

Position this button to the left of "Pa" on the stage.

```
on (release) {
    _root.grandpa.pa.gotoAndStop(5);
}
on (rollOut) {
    _root.grandpa.pa.gotoAndStop(1);
}
```

Button: Instance of From Top

Position this button to the left of "Grandson" on the stage.

```
on (release) {
    _root.grandpa.pa.grandson.gotoAndStop(5);
}
on (rollOut) {
    _root.grandpa.pa.grandson.gotoAndStop(1);
}
```

Button: Instance of From Top

Position this button to the right of "GrandMa" on the stage.

```
on (release) {
    _root.grandma.gotoAndStop(5);
}
on (rollOut) {
    _root.grandma.gotoAndStop(1);
}
```

Button: Instance of From Top

Position this button to the right of "Ma" on the stage.

```
on (release) {
    _root.grandma.ma.gotoAndStop(5);
}
```

```
on (rollOut) {
    _root.grandma.ma.gotoAndStop(1);
}
```

Button: Instance of From Top
Position this button to the right of "Granddaughter" on the stage.

```
on (release) {
    _root.grandma.ma.granddaughter.gotoAndStop(5);
}
on (rollOut) {
    _root.grandma.ma.granddaughter.gotoAndStop(1);
}
```

Whether you're building this movie from scratch or deconstructing the example on the CD-ROM that accompanies this book, remember that the movie is a learning tool for following paths. Whenever you need to look up a script for paths, this movie should help you out. Figure 9.6 shows the completed movie and how one MC can influence another.

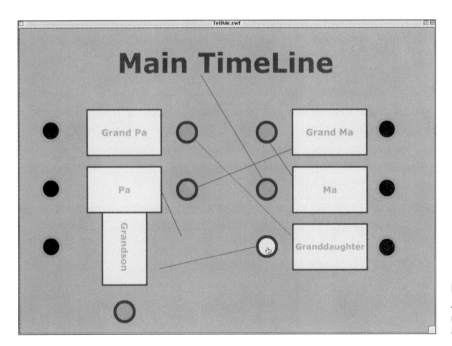

Figure 9.6
A movie clip anywhere in the movie can issue an order to another movie clip.

Passing Variables between Movie Clips

The ability to pass values in calculated variables is often the key to a good movie. In Flash 5, you can use variables with MCs in different ways. For example, the following script shows the format for using a calculated value in a variable to go to a designated frame:

```
turn = 20;
_root.flip.gotoAndStop(turn);
```

However, the following script, while placing a value into the MC with the instance name "flip" (it places 20 into the variable "turn" in the MC's timeline), will not send the MC to Frame 20.

```
_root.flip.turn = 20;
_root.flip.gotoAndStop(turn);
```

Instead, the script

```
_root.flip.turn = 20;
_root.flip.gotoAndStop(_root.flip.turn);
```

first sends the value to the variable in the "flip" MC. The second line uses the variable value that it just sent to "flip" by placing the path of the variable into the argument of the **gotoAndStop()** method—not just the name of the variable.

Calling Functions

In Chapter 7, you were introduced to user-defined functions. In this section, I want to explain briefly how to create functions that can be used by any MC on any timeline. The argument in a user-defined function can be reserved for the name of an MC. Then, by substituting an actual instance name in the argument of the function, you can use the function with any MC. An advantage of self-defined functions for animations is that once a function is created, it can be used with any MC. By assigning local variables in a user-defined function and placing the instance name in the argument, the designer just has to place the function in the MC with the reference to the MC. The learning utility in this chapter, **alienFunction.fla**, provides an example.

Most functions, though, need not address an MC. Within a frame, button, or their own script, MCs can call functions from anywhere in the movie. Because the local variables, established with the **var** keyword, are affected only by the actions within the function, several different MCs can use a single function. For example, you may want to have a function that checks a "fuel supply" that is decremented with use and has a function like the following:

```
function fuelBurn () {
    var fuel;
    var burnRate;
    var fuelCell;
    if (burnRate == 200) {
        fuel-=5;
    } else {
        fuel-=2;
    }
    if (fuel<=0) {
        fuelCell="E";
    }
}
```

To use the function, any MC can have a simple script such as

```
onClipEvent (mouseUp) {
    fuelBurn();
}
```

to initiate the script.

With 10, 20, 30, or 100 race car, airplane, or spaceship MCs, the scripting job is considerably less, and the function ensures uniformity. A great advantage of using functions is that they can return a value back to the script that called it. Moreover, in the example function, the script uses local variables. The local variables all change independently. When more than one MC uses the same function with local variables, changing the local variables in one MC does not affect any of the others that use the exact same variable names.

Learning Utility: General Function for Movie Clips (alienFunction.fla on CD-ROM)

This learning utility shows how a single function generates movement or the functional outcome of any other property. It uses three layers:

- Function Script
- Saucers
- Button

The layout for the movie is very simple. Three "alien crafts" are distinct MCs, and a single button sends them off into different directions. Figure 9.7 shows the initial stage and its features.

Function Script Layer

In the first layer, a script creates the user function. The important part of the script is how it uses the array access brackets ([ ]) as a placeholder for the argument that will be placed in the function when it is used in a script. The argument name "mc" is a word used in the function as a placeholder for the instance name of the MC subject to the function's script.

Frame 1

The script generates local variable values to be used as values for _x and _y properties. The variables (alienX and alienY) change randomly with every execution of the function. Because they are local variables, however, they never affect any other MC using the same function identified as **beam(mc)**.

```
function beam (mc) {
    var alienX = random(500);
    var alienY = random(400);
    _root[mc]._x = alienX;
    _root[mc]._y = alienY;
}
```

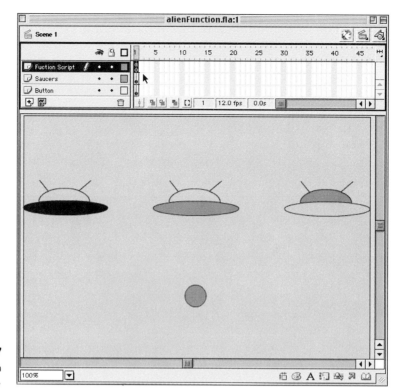

Figure 9.7
Three movie clips and a button
make up the movie.

Saucers Layer

The Saucers layer is made up of three MCs. I used three different MCs and single instances of each MC rather than making a single MC and using three instances. I wanted to use different color combinations so it would be easier to identify them uniquely. Each was given an instance name using the Instance Panel. Their initial arrangement is a line to give them a reference point, but the initial placement is arbitrary.

Button Layer

The importance of user-defined functions can be seen in the script in the single button on the stage. The button itself is simply a circle drawn with the Oval tool that is turned into a button using the F8 key. Button is selected as the behavior, with the label, "kickem."

Button: Instance of Kickem

The script uses the function **beam(mc)** where the argument expects the name of an MC on the main timeline.

Note: When entering the instance names of the MCs in the argument, be sure to place quotation marks around the names.

```
on (release) {
    beam("tom");
    beam("dick");
    beam("harry");
}
```

Each time the button is pressed, the three flying saucers go off in different random directions. Figure 9.8 shows one example of what you can expect to see.

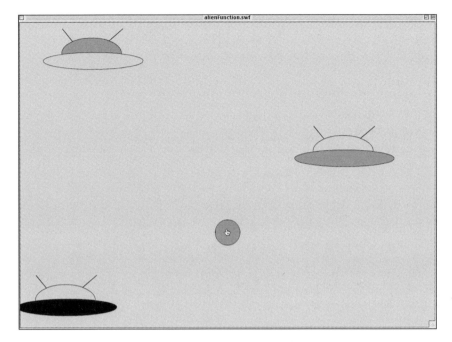

Figure 9.8
Each time the button is pressed, the movie clips move in different random directions all using the same function.

PROJECT Cartoon Factory (cartoonFactory.fla on CD-ROM)

This project evolved from a cartoon originally created by Leslie Cabarga (**www.flashfonts.com**). The purpose of the project is to show how to issue commands for controlling different cartoon character features. At the same time, however, it provides some insight into how to use Flash to create cartoon effects. It contains eight layers and six controllable MCs.

- Slider

- Buttons

- tears

  - MC: tears

  - MC: tears2

- Hat flip

  - MC: flip

- eye blink

  - MC: blink

- Kat
  - MC: lefteye
  - MC: righteye
- cartoon type
- backdrop

When I initially received the cartoon, the hat flipped, the eyes closed and opened, and the tears flew. By placing a stop action at the beginning of the MCs creating the actions, I was able to insert buttons and slide controls to show how the action scripts control cartoon motions. The buttons have "roll on" and "roll off" triggers for flipping the hat, flinging the tears, and closing one eye and then the other—a double wink—all using a path to generate actions. The sliders demonstrate three types of control: The top slider MC uses its position to send the target MC to a calculated frame based on the location of the slider. The second and third sliders set the MC properties of the scale of the tears and the rotation of the eyes, respectively. Figure 9.9 shows the initial stage and layers.

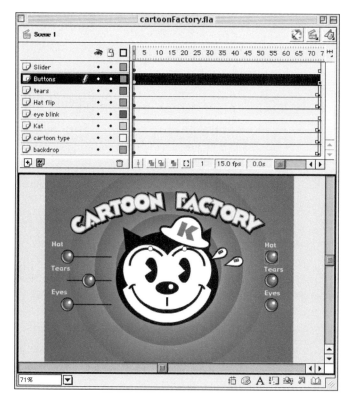

Figure 9.9
ActionScript button and slide controls for a Flash cartoon.

Focusing on the ActionScript, each of the layers contains a brief explanation of how the cartoon action occurs with an emphasis on the relevant parts used by action scripts. Some illustrations show the timelines where the animation is created, but details of each drawing and tween are general descriptions.

Tears Layer

Both of the tears are instances of Graphic symbols. In the Symbol Editor, the tears are animated to move and fade. Each instance of the Graphic symbols were changed in the Instances Properties dialog to Movie Clip behaviors so that they could be changed using action scripts. Their instance names are "tears" and "tears2."

Hat Flip Layer

The hat image is another Graphic symbol with a script created in the Symbol Editor. Using sequenced placement in frames and tweens on the Hat Flip layer, the hat flies up and back down on the cat's head. I changed the instance to a Movie Clip and gave it the instance name "flip."

Eye Blink Layer

Making a simple-looking eye blink is a complex task. Using multiple layers on the Eye Blink layer, the drawings are sequenced and tweened in the frames. Figure 9.10 shows the blink symbol timeline and layers.

Figure 9.10
The blink of an eye takes four layers and 23 frames.

Kat Layer

All of the other parts of the cat are composed on the Kat layer. I turned both eye drawings into MCs so that they could be rotated using an action script. The eyebrows (including the blink), mouth, nose, eyes, and face are all separate drawings or groups of drawings. The eye MCs have the instance names "lefteye" and "righteye."

Slider Layer

Three slider MCs (like the one in Chapter 7) control three different aspects of the cartoon on the Slider layer. Each MC contains a constrained "lever" that can be dragged 100 pixels on the X-axis and 0 pixels on the Y-axis.

MC: Lever1 (Instance Name "lever1")

All three levers have the same basic drag script but with different Y-axis constraints. The following steps can be used to create all three with the noted differences:

1. Draw a line 100 pixels in length using a width of 1 or 2. Place the line to the left of the cat image. Use the Info panel to note the Y Position of the line. The Y value will be used in setting up the constrained drag.

2. Select Insert|New Symbol. Select Movie Clip as the behavior and "lever1" as the name in the Symbol Properties dialog box. Click on OK to enter the Symbol Editor.

3. In the Symbol Editor, draw a button (H = 30, W = 30) like the one in Figure 9.9. Select it, and press the F8 key to open the Symbol Properties dialog box. Choose Button for the behavior, and label the button "lev1Button." You can use the same button in the other slider scripts.

MC: Lever1, Script Layer: Frame 1

Select Frame 2, and press the F5 key to place a frame in the second frame. In Frame 1, place the following script:

```
var a= root.lever1. x:
var b=(a-47)/4
var loc=Math.floor(b)
_root.flip.gotoAndPlay(loc)
```

The variable "loc" (for location) is set in the target timeline in the third line of the script. Because the slider line is 100 pixels and the beginning X Position for the level is x = 47, that amount is subtracted from the position value of lever1, the slider's instance name. In that way, the slider values will be between 0 and 99. The current value of the X Position is divided by 4 because the flip MC has only about 25 frames and there are 100 possible integer values that the slide covers.

4. Select the "lev1Button" Button Instance to open the Instance Properties dialog box. (You should still be in the Symbol Editor.) Open the Actions panel by selecting the arrow icon on the launcher bar.

MC: Lever1, Script Layer: Button (Instance of "lev1Button")

This next script makes the slider lever slide in a "track" defined by the upper and lower limits of the vertical position. On all horizontal slider scripts, the values of T and B must be identical. For vertical sliders, L and R must be identical.

```
on (press) {
    _root.lever1.startDrag(false, 47, 174, 147, 174);
}
on (release) {
    stopDrag ();
}
```

For the remaining two sliders, follow the preceding directions. Use the same Button symbol, but substitute the frame scripts and button scripts as indicated.

MC: Lever3 (Instance Name "lever3")

After drawing the line to be the slider groove, enter the scripts for the frame and button. Note in Figure 9.9 that the Slider MC for this lever begins in the middle of the slider line rather than at the far left as the other two do. (It is named "lever3," out of sequence, to help remind you that something is different about this lever.)

MC: Lever3, Script Layer: Frame 1

```
a = (_root.lever3._x)-47;
loc3 = Math.floor(a);
_root.tears._xscale = loc3;
_root.tears._yscale = loc3;
_root.tears2._xscale = loc3;
_root.tears2._yscale = loc3;
```

MC: Lever3, Script Layer: Button (Instance of "lev1 Button")

```
on (press) {
    _root.lever3.startDrag(false, 47, 226.5, 147, 226.5);
}
on (release) {
    stopDrag ();
}
```

MC: Lever2 (Instance Name "lever2")

Both of these scripts are similar to the other two. Note that the script rotates two different MCs at the same time.

MC: Lever2, Script Layer: Frame 1

The value in the "eyeloc" variable is multiplied by 3.6 because there are 100 values generated by the slider and 360 degrees of rotation.

```
var a=(_root.lever2._x)-47;
var eyeloc=Math.floor(a*3.6);
_root.lefteye._rotation=eyeloc;
_root.righteye._rotation=eyeloc;
```

MC: Lever2, Script Layer: Button (Instance of "lev1Button")

```
on (press) {
    _root.lever2.startDrag(false, 47, 278, 147, 278);
}
on (release) {
    stopDrag ();
}
```

Buttons Layer

All three of the buttons on the Buttons layer address movie clips to jumpstart the animations in the cartoon. The second and third button scripts use "roll on" and "roll off" to activate different actions. Create a round Button symbol to be placed to the left of the sliders. Use instances of the same button for the following three scripts. Name the button "trigger."

Button: Instance of Trigger (Hat Screen Label)

```
on (rollOver) {
    _root.flip.play();
}
```

Button: Instance of Trigger (Tears Screen Label)

```
on (rollOver) {
    _root.tears.play();
}
on (rollOut) {
    _root.tears2.play();
}
```

Button: Instance of Trigger (Eyes)

```
on (rollOver) {
    _root.blink.play();
}
on (rollOut) {
    _root.blink2.play();
}
```

Cartoon Type Layer

The Cartoon Type layer contains the page title. The font type for the page title is Kobalt-Kartoon, one of Leslie Cabarga's flash fonts (**www.flashfonts.com**). It's the perfect font for doing cartoons in Flash. The font has been enhanced in Adobe Illustrator and imported into Flash.

Backdrop Layer

Three circles with radial gradations serve as the background on the Backdrop layer. Each circle is a Graphic symbol that is resized for each layer. You use less bandwidth by using the same symbol for different tasks. Figure 9.11 shows the movie, illustrating changes in the hat flip, eye rotation, eye blink, hat movement, and tear size.

Using the path system and user-defined functions are pretty simple as far as ActionScript is concerned. It is the details in ActionScript that cause the midnight challenges. Keep an eye on the following when addressing MCs and building functions:

Figure 9.11

Buttons and sliders control character properties and behavior.

- Is the path to the target correct and complete?

- Did you remember to put in an instance name?

- Did you send variable values to the target?

- Is the function compatible with the MCs using it?

These questions make life interesting in dealing with several objects on different timelines and in multiple hierarchies in Flash.

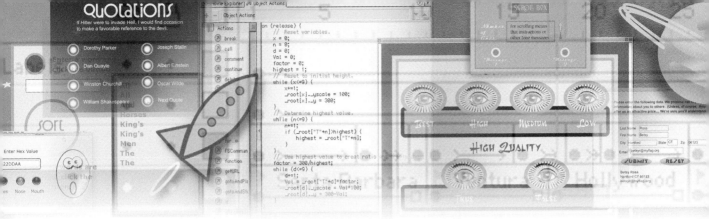

Chapter 10

Bringing It All Together

This final chapter shows how to load a Flash (Shockwave, or SWF) file from a running movie and how to load variables and text. In addition, the chapter covers how to scroll text using a special action extension. The rest of the chapter explains how to bring together a number of elements discussed in previous chapters and how Flash communicates with HTML (HyperText Markup Language).

Loading and Unloading Movies

To run movies successfully, you must know how to load and unload them. The following sections explain how to do this and why it is important.

Loading

As compact as Flash movies are when compiled into Shockwave (SWF) files, they can still be fairly large. You can reduce the load time for a movie by breaking a large SWF file into smaller SWF files and having the movie segments load when needed. Using a preloader can help considerably, especially if you have interesting material to entertain a viewer while he is waiting for the show to begin. If viewers often revisit your site, however, you should change the previews regularly or load the movie segments as needed. By loading only certain segments, you can save time for a viewer who just wants to visit a certain subsection of your site, because only the parts she needs are loaded. In certain respects, loading parts of a Flash movie in this manner is like HTML pages that load only when a link opens them. The basic format for loading a movie is

```
loadMovie ("fileName.swf", 5);
```

The file is actually a URL address. If the calling file and the file to be loaded are in the same directory or folder, using relative addressing, as in the preceding example, is perfectly fine. You can address an SWF file to be loaded from any URL, however. Thus, an action statement can also look like the following:

```
loadMovie ("http://www.sandlight.com/fileName.swf", 5)
```

You can load a movie between **_level0** and **_level15999**. The base—or first—movie you load goes to **_level0**. The levels work something like the layers in a movie with each loading on top of the other; level 0 (**_level0**) is a special case, however. When you load your first movie, it establishes the background color and frame rate. Even if you load another movie with a different background color or frame rate or unload the initial movie, the background and frame rate remains the same. You can effectively change the background only by loading a movie that uses a solid color that covers the background. In fact, you can load a movie into **_level0** to replace the movie currently there and still retain the background color of the first movie loaded. Loading a new movie to **__level0** will change the frame rate, however. Therefore, be careful what you use as a background color for your initially loaded movie.

Unloading

In addition to loading movies, you can unload them as well. By unloading a movie, you can do the following:

- Delete a movie taking up memory that may slow other aspects of the movie

- Reveal what is underneath the movie

- Change a background by removing a solid background

The Unload format is a little different from that for Load:

```
unloadMovie (0);
```

When a script unloads a movie, it specifies the movie level and unloads any movie in that level. Although the movie's name is unimportant in an Unload action, you need to remember its level. Naturally, you are going to want to plan and record when you begin loading and unloading movies. One strategy is to use a single level other than zero to sequence your movies. You unload the first movie simply by loading another movie to a level where a movie exists.

The following six movies—all with different dimensions—illustrate how the Load and Unload system works in Flash. The dimensions include movies with and without background colors, solid graphic backgrounds, and different colored fonts. However, each has the same set of buttons to load and unload movies. Because each movie stacks on top of the next, the buttons appear to be the same set, but they're just duplicates in the different movies. Each movie must be saved as an SWF file prior to running the movie. (The movies are intended to show what happens with different aspects of Load and Unload, so you may want to work with the one on the accompanying CD-ROM for a while before looking at the action scripts.)

Multiple Movies (MultiMenu Folder on CD-ROM)

Rather than a list of layers, the six movies that share a movie are listed here:

- zip.fla

- first.fla

- fifth.fla

- tenth.fla

- twentieth.fla

- hundred.fla

Because each movie is almost identical, I want to go over the first one in detail and the others just in terms of the changes that make each unique. The first one—Zip (zip.fla)—loads into Level 0 (**_level0**). It contains a total of 12 buttons: 6 load movies, and 6 unload movies. Figure 10.1 shows the initial stage.

Frame Layer

Open a new movie and change the name of the top layer to Labels. Add a layer, and name it "Frame." Save the movie as "zip.fla." It will probably be

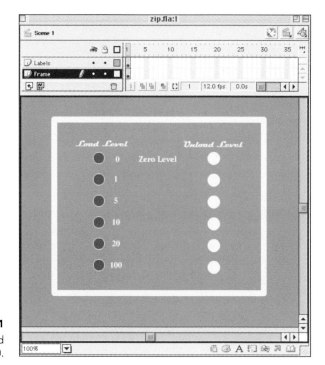

Figure 10.1
Movies are loaded and unloaded at Levels 0, 1, 5, 10, 20, and 100.

easiest to start in the Frame layer because it will provide a guide for placement of your buttons. A yellow frame will sit on top of a green background. (Use the hex value #FFF340 for a yellow that will complement the green in the Color Mixer.) Use the Rectangle tool from the toolbox to draw a yellow rectangle with no fill and a 10-stroke outline. Then select Modify|Movie to change the background color to a rich green. (Use the hex value #4C7300 in the Color Mixer to get a nice green.) That's all you have to do for the background for the time being. Lock it, and get to work on the buttons and labels in the next layer.

Labels Layer

In the Labels layer, the buttons load or unload SWF files. These Load and Unload buttons are instances of the buttons shown in Figure 10.1. Between the column of Load and Unload buttons is a label indicating the level at which the movie gets loaded. Figures 10.1 and 10.2 show how the movies are correctly labeled. The grid is turned on in Figure 10.2, but it will not appear in the movie.

The easiest way to proceed is to create the first movie, test it to create an SWF file, and then save it as an FLA file. After you've completed the first movie, use the File|Save As command to save it as the next movie, using the names listed at the beginning of this section.

Note: Save all of the files in the same folder or directory on your computer.

For example, when you've completed the zip.fla file, select File|Save As from the menu bar, and use first.fla as the file name.

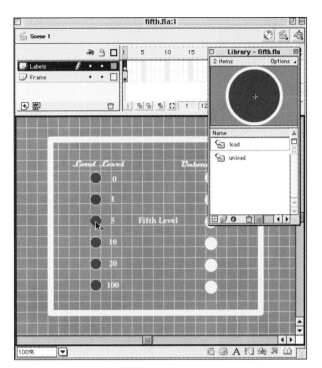

Figure 10.2
Each of the six movies are slight variations of the first one.

Compare Figures 10.1 and 10.2 to get an idea of what changes will be made. (You cannot see it because this book is not printed in color, but both figures have a green background with a yellow frame.)

Next, you create all of the Load buttons. Because the buttons are similar, select and copy the script from the first one and then paste it into the next button, making the necessary changes as you proceed. Figure 10.3 shows a **loadMovie** action being entered in the Normal Mode of the ActionScript Editor.

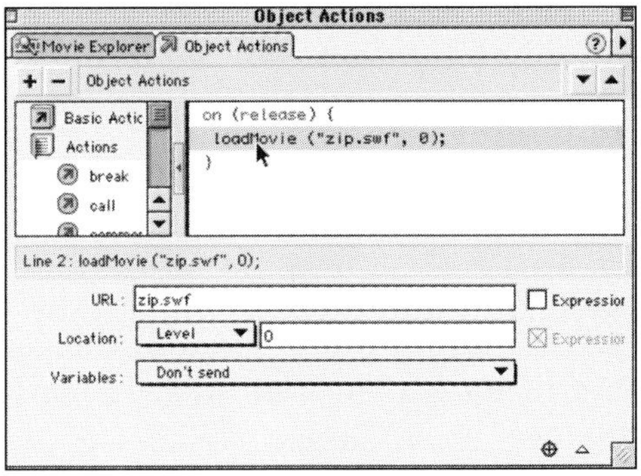

Figure 10.3
The URL is the file name and its path. The level positions the movie in a hierarchy.

The first set of buttons loads the movies. The scripts are the same except for the differences in the file names and the level on which they are loaded.

Button: Label 0 (Instance of load)

```
on (release) {
    loadMovie ("zip.swf", 0);
}
```

Button: Label 1 (Instance of load)

```
on (release) {
    loadMovie ("first.swf", 1);
}
```

Button: Label 5 (Instance of load)

```
on (release) {
    loadMovie ("fifth.swf", 5);
}
```

Button: Label 10 (Instance of load)

```
on (release) {
    loadMovie ("tenth.swf", 10);
}
```

Button: Label 20 (Instance of load)

```
on (release) {
    loadMovie ("twentieth.swf", 20);
}
```

Button: Label 100 (Instance of load)

```
on (release) {
    loadMovie ("hundred.swf", 100);
}
```

The script for unloading the movies is even more straightforward (see Figure 10.4). The script only requires the level to unload. The following buttons reflect this simplicity, and the button labels refer to the ones under the Load Column:

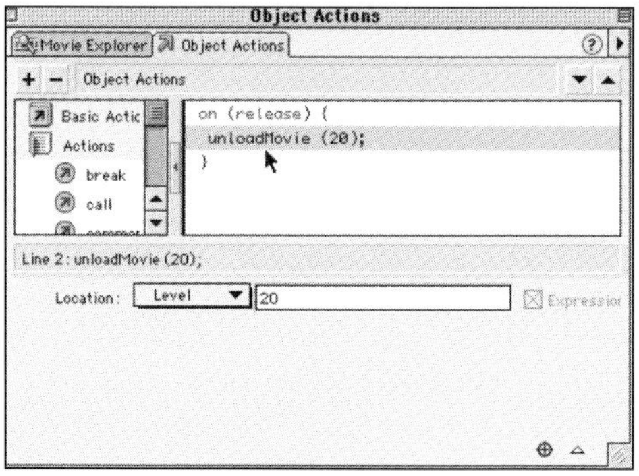

Figure 10.4
Note that no URL is required when an **unloadMovie** action is issued—only a level.

Button: Label 0 (Instance of unload)

```
on (release) {
    unloadMovie (0);
}
```

Button: Label 1 (Instance of unload)

```
on (release) {
    unloadMovie (1);
}
```

Button: Label 5 (Instance of unload)

```
on (release) {
    unloadMovie (5);
}
```

Button: Label 10 (Instance of unload)

```
on (release) {
    unloadMovie (10);
}
```

Button: Label 20 (Instance of unload)

```
on (release) {
    unloadMovie (20);
}
```

Button: Label 100 (Instance of unload)

```
on (release) {
    unloadMovie (100);
}
```

After you've completed the first movie, use Save As for the other movies. Each one should have a single label between the two columns of buttons. When you run the movie and the individual movies are loaded, however, their labels appear as shown in Figure 10.5. Some unique elements exist in the following movies, but the other movies are the same as the first one except for the label placements and names.

- *Movie: tenth.fla*—Add a deep tan background color. Select Modify|Movie from the menu bar, and select a tan swatch for the background color. You will not see this background color unless the tenth.swf movie is the first to load.

- *Movie: twentieth.fla*—Add an additional layer to the movie. Place the layer under the Frame layer, and name it "Solid Layer." Using the Rectangle tool, select a rich brown color, and draw a rectangle that covers the area inside the yellow frame. This rectangle appears as a background behind the buttons and labels.

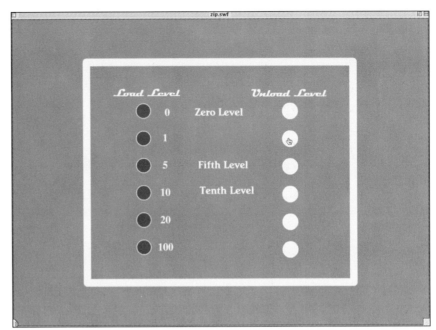

Figure 10.5

As each movie is loaded, its label appears on the screen, and the identical buttons overlay the movies already loaded.

- *Movie: hundred.fla*—Select Modify|Movie from the menu bar, and select black for the background color. Select all of the labels, and convert them from black to yellow. The yellow shows up well against a black background. Unless you load the hundred.swf movie first, however, you will never see the background color, but you will see the yellow labels.

After you've completed the movies, experiment with loading different ones first. If you unload the **_level0** movie, you get a blank screen. If you load either of the movies with a background color, that color won't go away. If you load the movie with the solid background—twentieth.swf—all of the other movie labels disappear because the solid background covers them, as shown in Figure 10.6. The keys to using Load and Unload successfully are first to see and then to understand what the actions do. The set of movies in this example is designed to help you do that.

Addressing Variables and Objects in Different Levels

Before you can begin loading different movies, you need to set them up so that they communicate with one another. The primary movie is at address **_level0**, and the others are at their specified level. For example, if you want to address a text field variable named "message" in the main timeline of a movie loaded at Level 44, your address would appear as follows:

```
_level44.message
```

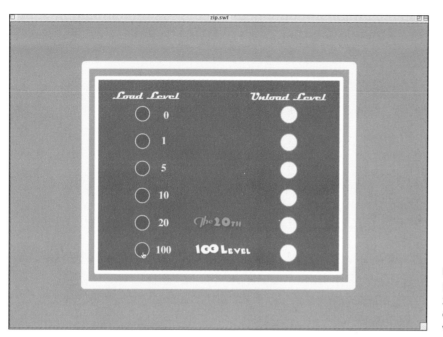

Figure 10.6
Because the movie set on Level 20 has a solid background, none of the other loaded movies are visible except Level 100.

If you need to address a more complex location—such as a variable in a movie clip (MC) inside of another MC—just follow the path as though you were addressing it from your movie and add the level specification. For example, the following addresses are doubly embedded variables on Level 5:

```
_level5.father.daughter.message
```

To get a clearer idea of how movies communicate with one another, the following example movies communicate as though they were part of the same movie (which, after a fashion, they are).

Passing Data between Levels (MovieVarTrans Folder on CD-ROM)

These two movies operating together illustrate how to pass data between levels:

- levelZero.fla

- news.fla

The movie is a simple example of how one movie loads another and then how the two movies send data between each other. The base movie is levelZero.fla. It consists of two layers, two text fields, some labels, and a button (see Figure 10.7).

Use the color palette in Table 10.1. All references to the colors are to the ones in the palette.

Figure 10.7
The first movie has one text field
for receiving data, one for
sending, and a button.

Table 10.1 Color palette for levelZero.fla and news.fla.

Color Element	C	M	Y	K
Percent				
	0	25	60	0
	0	100	80	40
	65	0	70	35
	0	55	50	5
Black				

Background Layer (levelZero.fla)

The Background layer in the initial layer is important for establishing a background—either for setting the background color of the movie or for creating one using the drawing tools. The background for this movie begins with two rectangles stacked on top of one another. Draw a rectangle using green fill and stroke. Within the first rectangle, draw a second rectangle with a light tan fill and a deep red 5-point stroke. Center the rectangle horizontally and vertically to the stage using the Align panel.

Message Layer (levelZero.fla)

Two text fields make up the Message layer (levelZero.fla). The top text field is intended to be a source of mail to the other movie, and the other text field is to be the recipient of a message from the other movie. In the top text field, type in a message to be sent to the second movie. When setting up the "fromNews" text field, select a color other than black for the text color. Table 10.2 lists the text field properties and names.

Table 10.2 Text field properties and names.

Variable Name	Border/Bg	Text Alignment
zero	Yes	Left
fromNews	Yes	Left

Label Layer (levelZero.fla)

In the Label layer (levelZero.fla), type in the labels as shown in Figure 10.7, and create a button. The sole purpose of this button is to load the other movie.

Button: Load News (Instance of loadIt)

The button loads a movie into Level 45.

```
on (release) {
    loadMovie ("news.swf", 45);
}
```

News Layer (news.fla)

After you've completed the first movie, create the News layer (news.fla). It is on a single layer, and the scripts are in the buttons. Two text fields represent the source and recipient of data from the other movie. Figure 10.8 shows the details of the second movie. When setting up the fromZero text field, select a color other than black for the text color. Table 10.3 lists the text field properties and names.

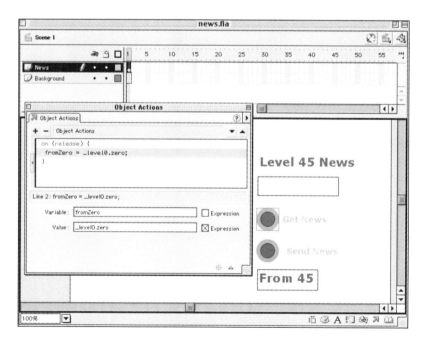

Figure 10.8
Buttons contain scripts for sending and receiving data from the other movie.

Table 10.3 Text field properties and names.

Variable Name	Border/Bg	Text Alignment
fromZero	Yes	Left
newNews	Yes	Left

To reuse the button from the first movie, select File|Save As and use the name of the second movie—"news.fla." You can use the existing materials on the page to coordinate placement of the second page and then delete all of the materials from the first page. You will need to eliminate the background graphics, however.

Button: Get News (Label) (Instance of loadIt)

The first button looks into the data in the first movie's variable, named "zero," and sets it as a variable "fromZero." Both are text fields, resulting in the same data being displayed in both.

```
on (release) {
    fromZero = _level0.zero;
}
```

Button: Send News (Label) (Instance of loadIt)

The second button reverses the process from the script in the first button. It sets the other movie's text field variable, making any data in it appear in the other movie.

```
on (release) {
    _level0.fromNews = newNews;
}
```

After you've completed the movie, the two movies fit so that they appear as a single movie. Figure 10.9 shows how the movies appear when the first movie loads the second and data is transferred.

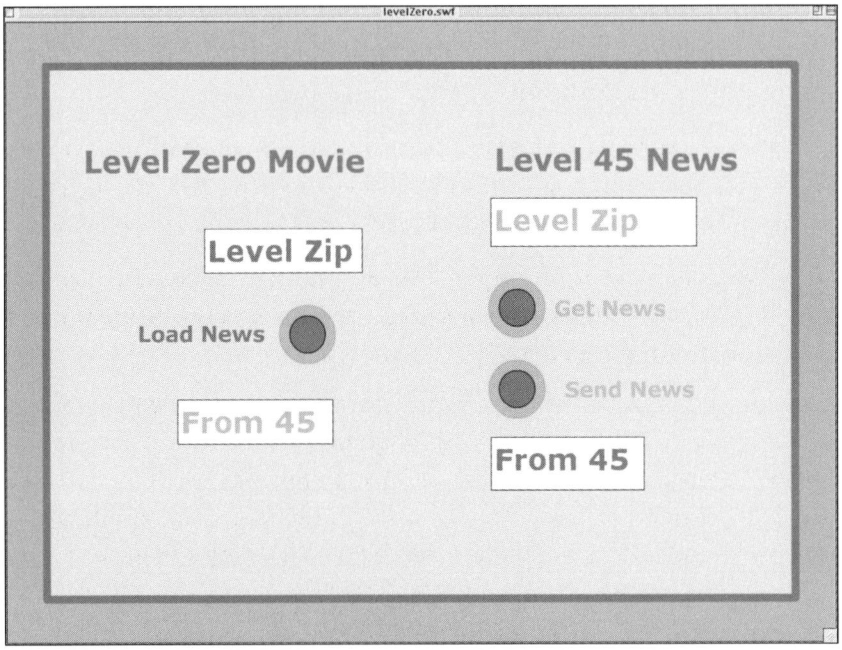

Figure 10.9

The labels help differentiate the two movies. The lighter text in the text boxes indicates that the text was sent from the other movie.

Loading Text and Variables (loadText.fla on CD-ROM)

Four layers make up this next movie:

- Text Fields

- Beam Me Up

- Frames

- Background

Passing data from other applications and sources into an SWF file is simple with Flash. You can load variables from text files or from server applications such as PHP, ASP, CGI, Cold Fusion, and other server-side languages. To illustrate how to load text and variables in a Flash movie, the next example loads two different variables from a text file. The movie uses text fields with variable names to demonstrate the source of the data and the process for separating variables in text files.

Text File

Before you do anything else, you need to create a text file to be called by the SWF file. Follow the instructions carefully because the format to recognize and call up the variable separation in the file directs the text into two different variables associated with text fields. Here's how to set up the text file:

1. Establish each variable with the format **variableName=**, and separate each variable with an ampersand (&). Leave no spaces or carriage returns between a variable's value and its following ampersand and the beginning of a new variable.

2. When you create the text file, save it in the same folder with your SWF file that calls it. Using NotePad (Windows) or SimpleText (Macintosh), create a text file named "beamMe.txt" with the following text:

   > **fromTextFile=Space exploration requires that mankind do a great deal more with less. Smaller, lighter, and more ingenious solutions also work well on earth.&buzz=4.95**

After you've established the variables in the text field, you just have to load the file into your Flash movie. I used a button for the script so that you can control the loading and see the data entering the two text fields on command. Generally, however, you should use a set of frames for checking whether a variable has been loaded. For example, if you are loading a variable named "announce," you should create a frame that checks to see if the variable has actually been loaded, using the following script:

```
announce=String(announce);
if (announce.length==0) (
    gotoAndPlay(1);
}
```

The script loops until the variable is something other than 0 (zero). Figure 10.10 shows the initial setup and layers.

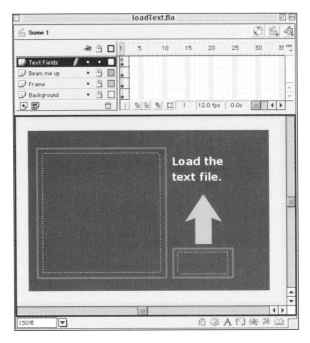

Figure 10.10
The text file is loaded into two different text fields associated with variable names.

Background and Frames Layers

First, establish a background and frames around the output windows. Two output windows have no background or border so that they can appear on top of the background rather than a white window. The frames help set off the lighter-colored text that will be in the text fields where the data will be passed. Follow these steps:

1. Select Modify|Movie and set the stage to 300 pixels × 200 pixels. The body of text is fairly short, so you will not need a great deal of room to contain it in the two text fields. Select the second frame of each layer, and press F5 to insert a second frame for all layers.

2. In the Background layer, draw a green (#00A600 color value) rectangle to cover the stage. Lock the Background layer.

3. In the Frames layer, superimpose a dark brown (#400000 color value) rectangle with a white border. Select the Frames layer, and use Edit|Cut or Ctrl+X/Cmd+X to cut the layer out.

4. Unlock the Background layer, and select Edit|Paste In Place from the menu bar. Now select the entire Background layer, and use the Align

panel to center all of the rectangles to the center of the stage vertically and horizontally. Lock the Background layer.

5. In the Frames layer, draw two reddish brown (#A10000) rectangles around the areas where the text fields are to be placed. (See Figure 10.10.) Lock the Frames layer when you're finished.

Text Fields Layer

The first frame in the Text Fields layer has the script for checking to see if the text has been loaded into the text field. With two frames in the layers, the movie loops through the script until the conditions are met.

Frame 1

The following script turns the variable "buzz" into a string and then checks to see if the length of the string is 0 (zero). If "buzz" is empty, the script sets a flag variable to 0. As soon as some text is in the text field associated with the "buzz" variable, the flag variable changes to initiate a set of actions. Once the flag is "set" (equals 1), the variable is converted to a floating point number, .17 is added to the value, a dollar sign ($) is concatenated to the variable, and the movie is stopped.

```
buzz = String(buzz);
if (buzz.length == 0) {
    flag = 0;
} else {
    flag = 1;
}
if (flag == 1) {
    buzz = parseFloat(buzz);
    buzz+=.17;
    buzz = "$"+buzz;
    stop ();
}
```

You can find more economical ways of writing the same code, but the purpose of it is to demonstrate that you can manipulate data from an external source just as you would with data from PHP, ASP, HTML, or other languages used with Web pages.

The next step in the Text Fields layer is to create two text fields—one large and one small—as shown earlier in Figure 10.10. Table 10.4 lists the text field properties and names. Select Dynamic Text for the large text field and Input Text for the small text field.

Table 10.4 Text field properties and names.

Variable Name	Border/Bg	Text Alignment	Multiline
fromTextFile	No	Left	Yes
buzz	No	Left	No

The larger of the two text fields is associated with the variable name "fromTextFile" and the smaller one with the variable name "buzz." You can see in the content of the preceding text file that both variables are assigned values and are separated by the ampersand (&).

Beam Me Up Layer

In the Beam Me Up layer, the script for loading a text file is found in a single button. Labels are provided, as well as frames for the two text fields. You will find it easier to put text fields and their graphic frames on different layers. In that way, you won't try to select one and get the other.

Button: Instance of 3 Left Arrow from Library

I used the 3 Left Arrow button from the Button library. Reducing it in size and rotating it upward provides an imagery of *loading up*. I then changed all of the arrow layer colors to #FF8CB3. The script in the ActionScript Editor has a slightly different parameter than that for loading a movie:

```
on (release) {
    buzz = "";
    gotoAndPlay (1);
    loadVariables ("beamMe.txt", 0);
}
```

Note: Although the default level for where movies are loaded is set to 0, be sure to set the level. Also, the URL in the figure is relative to the SWF file in the same folder. However, it is important that either absolute or full relative URL addresses are specified correctly.

By clearing out the text field associated with the variable "buzz" and playing the first frame, the user can reload the field as often as she wants. The text will be the same with the same file, however, so this is used more to demonstrate how to set up the script for situations where the text file is variable. Figure 10.11 shows the settings in the ActionScript Editor for loading the text file from the same directory as the SWF file that loads it.

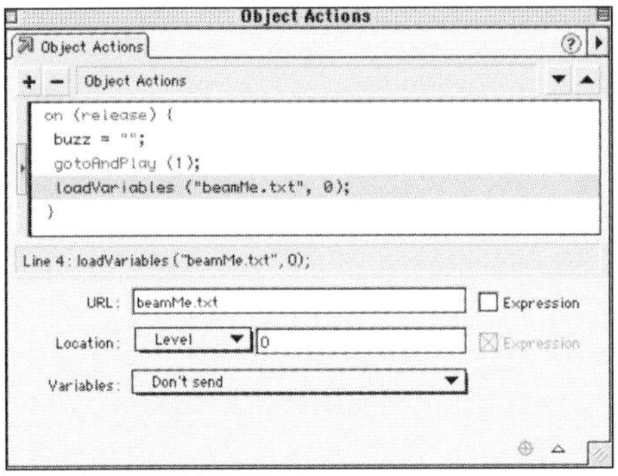

Figure 10.11
ActionScript settings for loading a text file in Level 0.

When you run the movie, the data in the text field is split and sent to the indicated text fields associated with the variables named in the text file as shown in Figure 10.12. Instead of seeing "4.95" in the small text field, however, you see "$5.12" because the script in the first frame added .17 and a dollar sign to the variable "buzz."

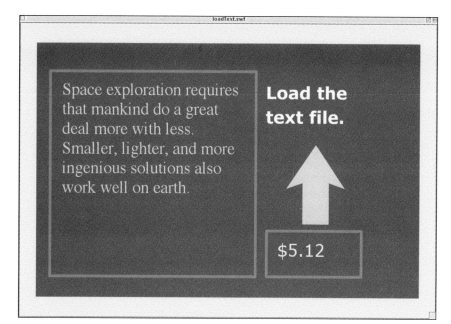

Figure 10.12
Different variables specified in
the text file receive the data in
the text fields associated with the
variable names.

Text Scrolling (scrollText.fla in ScrollFlash folder on CD-ROM)

This next movie has four layers:

- Scripts

- Buttons

- Text Fields

- Background

Scrolling text in a text field can be very useful when you have more text than space on the stage. Two properties of text fields are **scroll** and **maxscroll**. They are easy to install in your scripts and require minimal scripting. In the example movie, two different text fields off the stage contain text that is transferred to a text box on the stage. The movie demonstrates how the **scroll** property is employed. It also shows how you can store text anywhere in the movie and retrieve it when needed. Because the movie employs the **scroll** property, a text block of any size may be used.

By adding "scroll" to a variable name that contains text, you are able to specify which line is brought to the top of the text field where the text resides. For example, if you want Line 12 of a text block brought to the top, the script is

```
variableName.scroll = 12
```

The sizes of the text field and font determine the relative line in the block of text. The same amount of text in a small font size in a large text field has fewer lines than the same text block using a large font in a small text field. For example, the 101st word in a text field with 10 words per line would be in Line 10. In a smaller text field or using a larger font, however, only 5 words per line would force the 101st word to be in Line 20.

The other text field property—**maxscroll**—is read-only. Unlike other properties that use **GetProperty**, the **maxscroll** property is placed as an extension to the name of the text field. For example, to find the number of lines in a text field named "speech," you would use the following:

```
variableName = speech.maxscroll
```

For automatically scrolling text on the screen, the **maxscroll** value helps set up a loop size to show all of the text. In the following movie, note how each is employed in both button and frame scripts.

The example script shows how a single text window with scrolling can handle text blocks of different sizes. It also demonstrates how the **scroll** and **maxscroll** properties are used and what they do. Figure 10.13 shows the initial page.

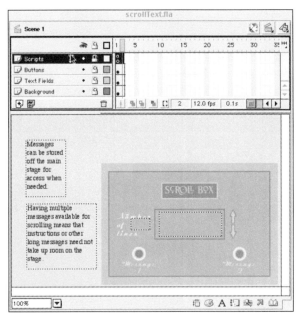

Figure 10.13

Offstage text fields can contain and hide blocks of text that can be displayed as scrolling text.

Background Layer

The stage for the movie is relatively small, 300 × 200 pixels. Add a second frame to all of the layers. Select the second frame in the first layer, and, while holding down the Shift key, select all of the others. The Background layer consists of two overlapping rectangles. The first layer is a solid (stroke and body use the same color—#FF8C66) and the second uses a 5-pixel stroke (#008000 color value) and a solid inner color (#FF6633 color value). Use the Align panel to center everything to the stage horizontally and vertically.

Scripts Layer

In the Scripts layer, a single script in the first frame looks at a flag variable to determine which off-stage text field to use. Two button scripts selected by the user control the flag values. The "scribe" variable is a text field where the text is to be scrolled. The script then finds the maximum number of lines in the selected text block and puts it into a text field variable (size) shown on the screen. Be sure to add a second frame to the layers, and place the following script in the first keyframe:

```
if (flag == 0) {
    scribe = message1;
} else {
    scribe = message2;
}
size = _root.scribe.maxscroll;
```

Buttons Layer

Four buttons make up the Buttons layer. The up and down arrow buttons shown in Figure 10.13 generate the scrolling, two lines at a time. The two round buttons have scripts that select text from the two off-stage text fields and place it into the on-stage text field where it can be scrolled. The arrow buttons are borrowed from the Button library and are scaled, rotated, and colored (use a combination of #59CC80 and #00800 color values). The bottom buttons are circles using rings of color, from outside inward (#FFD9CC, #59CC89, and #00800).

Button: Upward Pointing Arrow (Instance of 1 Left Arrow)

The scroll increments are in 2 because two lines appear at once in the scroll window. The scroll value is negative so the scroll moves to the top, which has a value of 1.

```
on (release) {
    scribe.scroll = scribe.scroll-2;
}
```

Button: Downward Pointing Arrow (Instance of 1 Left Arrow)

The scroll downward adds to the text field's **scroll** value.

```
on (release) {
    scribe.scroll = scribe.scroll+2;
}
```

Button: Message 1 (Instance of select message)

The flag variable (aptly named "flag") is set to zero to indicate that the contents of the variable "scribe" in the preceding frame script is set to "message1," the variable associated with the top off-stage text field. The script also resets the scroll to the top so that the message will not appear at the current scroll level, which could be the bottom.

```
on (release) {
    flag = 0;
    scribe.scroll = 1;
}
```

Button: Message 2 (Instance of select message)

The script is identical to the preceding except the flag variable is set to bring in "message2" as the text block.

```
on (release) {
    flag = 1;
    scribe.scroll = 1;
}
```

Text Fields Layer

The Text Fields layer contains two text fields on the stage. These text fields have graphic borders around them and labels. The larger of the two has the variable name "scribe"; the smaller is named "size." The two text fields at the side of the stage contain blocks of text to be placed in the text scroll window. Table 10.5 lists the text field properties and names.

message1 Contents

Messages can be stored off the main stage for access when needed.

message2 Contents

Having multiple messages available for scrolling means that instructions or other long messages need not take up room on the stage.

Try experimenting with different size scroll boxes and font sizes for the "scribe" text field to see how it affects the **maxscroll** property. I also found, quite by accident, that pushing and pulling on the SWF window while running the movie sometimes changes the **maxscroll** property. Figure 10.14 shows the SWF file. The larger of the two text blocks has six lines, and the smaller block indicated contains three lines.

Table 10.5   Text field properties and names.

Variable Name	Border/Bg	Text Alignment
message1	No	Left
message2	No	Left
size	No	Left
scribe	No	Left

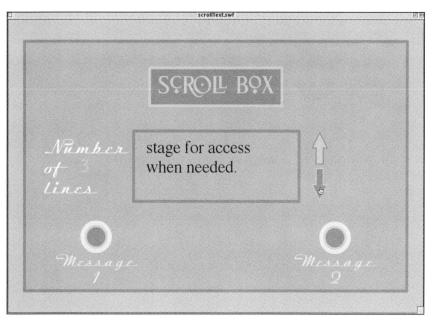

Figure 10.14
The **maxscroll** value shows there are nine lines in the scroll box. Pressing the downward button moves the lower portions of the text block into the scrolling text window.

Multibyte Functions

Multibyte functions are also available in Flash. All multibyte functions are used with strings and have specialized applications where two string characters are combined into a single value. The first character is treated as a standard ASCII value, which is multiplied by 256 and added to the second character's ASCII value. Four multibyte functions in ActionScript include:

- **mblength( )**
- **mbchr( )**
- **mbord( )**
- **mbsubstring( )**

For example, taking the initials of ActionScript—"AS"—the following statement generates those memorable characters:

```
varName = mbchr ( 16723 );
```

The value is derived as follows:

1. $A = (65 \times 256) = 16640$

2. $S = 83$

3. $A + S = 16640 + 83 = 16723$

Users do not normally need these functions. Whenever they have a specialized application that requires a multibyte value, however, values derived from these functions can be placed into variables and used just like any other function.

Passing Data among ActionScript, JavaScript, and HTML

Passing values between JavaScript and Flash is quite simple on the Flash side of the equation. By issuing a **javascript:functionName()** statement in a Get URL action, the JavaScript function fires. For example, the button script

```
on (release) {
    getUrl ("javascript:getGreen()");
}
```

launches the JavaScript function **getGreen()** in the HTML page in which the SWF file is embedded. Basically, all you need to do is to write JavaScript functions and fire them from action scripts in the frames and buttons in Flash. Use Netscape Navigator version 4.5 or newer and Internet Explorer 5 or newer to assure compatibility.

 ### Learning Utility: Moving Data from HTML to Flash (flashVar.fla in the FlashHTMLvar folder on CD-ROM)

The movie in this learning utility uses two layers:

- Border n Button

- Text Field

Moving data from an HTML page into an embedded Flash (SWF) file is a bit more involved. The key remains in the JavaScript that uses the Flash file variable names and the name for the SWF file embedded in the HTML page. In the Web page <EMBED> tag, you need to provide both a name attribute and set swLiveconnect to "true." For example, the following line provides a name that can be used by JavaScript to identify the SWF file and activate the swLiveconnect attribute.

```
Name="passFlash" swLiveconnect=true
```

In the JavaScript, you may use the FSCommand SetVariable (method) to pass a value to Flash from JavaScript. Use the format

```
window.document.MovieName.SetVariable("flashVar" , JSVar);
```

where the MovieName is the name provided in the <EMBED> tag. The FSCommand, SetVariable has two parameters: the name of the variable in Flash receiving the data, and the variable name or literal being passed to Flash. The following example illustrates how to set up and pass the variables from input on the HTML page to Flash. First, create a simple Flash movie with a text field and a button, as shown in Figure 10.15.

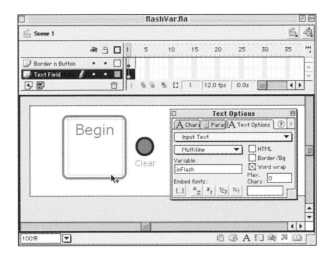

Figure 10.15
Flash text field for receiving data sent from an HTML page.

Because most of the work is done in the HTML page, setting up the Flash movie is easy. Before you begin, select Modify|Movie from the menu bar and change the dimensions to 550 × 200 pixels. You want the SWF file to fill the screen horizontally, but not vertically. The text entry box on the HTML page needs to have some room, too.

Border n Button Layer

In the Border n Button layer, draw a border around the area for the text field where data passed from the HTML page will appear.

Button: Instance of Clear

Create a simple round button using the Circle tool, select it, and press the F8 key. Select Button for behavior, and name it "Clear." The button's purpose is to clear the text field using the following script:

```
on (release) {
    _root.inFlash = "";
}
```

Text Field Layer

A single text field resides on the Text Field layer inside the graphic border. To create the field, I selected a 24-point, purple, Verdana font. The movie in an HTML page can then clearly demonstrate that the data (text) in the field is in Flash. Also, I disabled editing and included multiline and word wrap. Table 10.6 shows the text field properties and names.

Table 10.6 Text field properties and names.

Variable Name	Border/Bg	Text Alignment	Word Wrap
inFlash	No	Center	Yes

That's all there is for the movie. Publish it, open the HTML file that it generated, and make the following changes in the HTML page. Use a text or source code editor to make the additions and changes.

```
<HTML>
<HEAD>
<TITLE>flashVar</TITLE>

<script language="JavaScript">
     function getIt() {
var message=document.main.grab.value
window.document.passFlash.SetVariable("inFlash", message);
}
</script>

</HEAD>
<BODY bgcolor="#FFFFFF">
<!- URL's used in the movie->
<!- text used in the movie->

<OBJECT classid="clsid:D27CDB6E-AE6D-11cf-96B8-444553540000"
codebase="http://active.macromedia.com/flash2/cabs/
swflash.cab#version=4,0,0,0" ID=flashVar WIDTH=550 HEIGHT=150>
<PARAM NAME=movie VALUE="flashVar.swf">
<PARAM NAME=quality VALUE=high>
<PARAM NAME=bgcolor VALUE=#FFFFFF>
<EMBED src="flashVar.swf" quality=high bgcolor=#FFFFFF WIDTH=550
     HEIGHT=150 Name="passFlash" swLiveconnect=true
     TYPE="application/x-shockwave-flash" PLUGINSPAGE =
     "http:// www.macromedia.com/ shockwave/ download/index.
     cgi?P1_Prod_Version=ShockwaveFlash">
</EMBED>
</OBJECT>

<form name="main">
<input type="text" name="grab" length=12>
<input type="button" value="Press here" onclick="getIt()";>
</form>

</BODY>
</HTML>
```

Note: The JavaScript is written for Netscape Navigator version 4.7. Other versions of the Netscape Navigator or other browsers may need adjustment in the JavaScript. Fortunately, Flash is very stable across browsers.

After you have completed the HTML, JavaScript, and Flash movie, you can load the Web page in a browser, and watch it appear in 24-point, purple, Verdana font in the Flash SWF embedded in the page.

PROJECT From Pluto to Mercury (Pluto2Mercury folder on CD-ROM)

This movie employs a series of movies all tied together. The following movies and layers are included:

- neptune.fla

- uranus.fla

- saturn.fla

- jupiter.fla

- mars.fla

- earth.fla

- venus.fla

- mercury.fla

  - Common Layers

  - Plutocrats

    - MC: PlutoView

    - Planet

  - Guide: Approaching Planet (Planet Name)

  - Approaching Planet (Planet Name)

  - Leaving Planet (Planet Name)

This project involves a trip beginning near the planet Pluto and arriving at Mercury. The first movie is "neptune.fla" because the movie begins by leaving Pluto and heading toward Neptune. The ActionScript is simple enough. Each of the eight movies has a script in the last frame that loads the next movie into the same level. As a result, the memory use is kept at a minimum.

Each movie is only 4K. As a result, even the slowest modem can load it in a relatively short time. To test this daisy-chained movie, use the Bandwidth Profiler when you preview our movie. Select Control|Test Movie from the menu bar. When the SWF movie begins running, select View|Bandwidth Profiler from the menu bar. Next, select Debug|14.4 (1.2 K/s) from the menu bar to set the modem speed. Figure 10.16 shows how quickly this small SWF file loads.

An ancient 14.4K modem takes only 1.8 seconds to preload the 4K movie, as shown in Figure 10.16. A more common modem—the 56.6K—takes even less time to preload an 8K movie, as shown in Figure 10.17.

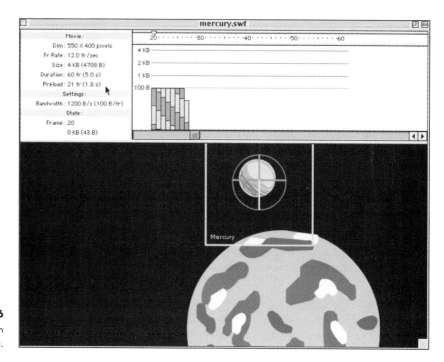

Figure 10.16

Even a very slow modem can quickly load a 4K movie.

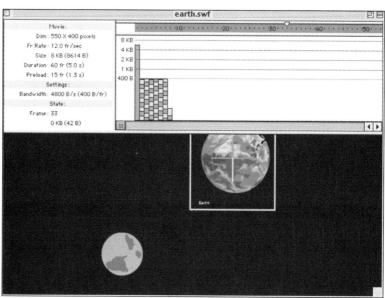

Figure 10.17

The largest movie in the set is 8K, but it takes only 1.3 seconds to preload with a 56K modem.

If you have a 4K movie in a Web page, the preloading time is negligible, especially with a fast modem or Ethernet connection. As combined movies begin taking longer to load because of their size, however, daisy-chaining movies in Flash makes more sense.

All of the movies work on a similar basis. As I finished each movie, I used the Save As command to save the next movie in the sequence. Figure 10.18 provides an idea of what the movies look like in development.

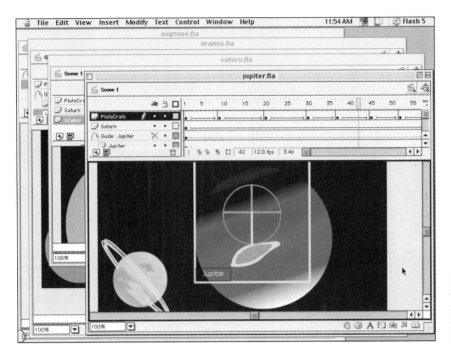

Figure 10.18
The several movies that make up the series are very similar in structure. Parts of each can be transferred to the next.

Frame Scripts

All of the movies have common features. Each movie contains two planets and an MC made up of a crosshair "guidance system" and a blinking "planet identifier." The same MC is used in all of the movies with the planet name changed, accordingly. One planet recedes in size as the other expands, simulating coming closer and moving away. (For those of you from the Institute of Planet Accuracy, only the sequence of the planets is accurate and serves as an elemental guide to planet order. For more accuracy, refer to **photojournal.jpl.nasa.gov/** where you can also find photographs of the planets in GIF format to use in your movies.) A similar ActionScript is at the end of each movie, as shown in Figure 10.19.

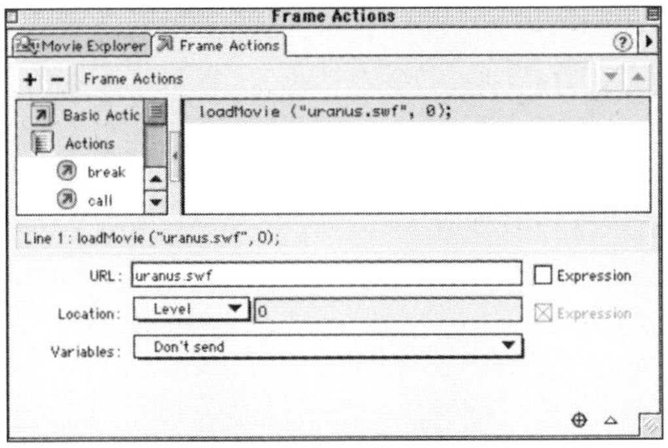

Figure 10.19
On the last keyframe of each movie, the next movie loads at **_level0**.

Use the following action scripts with the indicated movie in the last frame on any layer:

neptune.fla

```
loadMovie ("uranus.swf",0);
```

uranus.fla

```
loadMovie ("saturn.swf",0);
```

saturn.fla

```
loadMovie ("jupiter.swf",0);
```

jupiter.fla

```
loadMovie ("mars.swf",0);
```

mars.fla

```
loadMovie ("earth.swf",0);
```

earth.fla

```
loadMovie ("venus.swf",0);
```

venus.fla

```
loadMovie ("mercury.swf",0);
```

mercury.fla

Optionally, you can either use nothing else or use the mercury.fla file on the CD-ROM to see what happens when you don't want to make the trip again from Pluto to Mercury.

PlutoView Movie Clip

The PlutoView MC consists of some simple shapes and drawings. Follow these steps to create it:

1. Select Insert|New Symbol from the menu bar to open the Symbol Properties window. Choose Movie Clip as the behavior, and name it "PlutoView."

2. Draw a red 100-point circle using a 2-point stroke. Center it using the Info Panel, at x = 0, y = 0 with the center-point selected. Draw a horizontal line across the center of the circle (y = 0) and a vertical line down the middle (x = 0). That should give you a crosshair in a circle for aiming at planets.

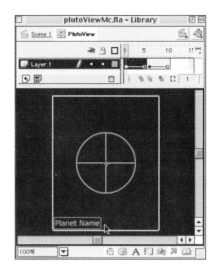

Figure 10.20
The PlutoView MC.

3. Draw a yellow rectangle with a 3-point stroke around the crosshair. See Figure 10.20.

4. Finally, in the lower left corner of the rectangle, draw a Static Text box, and write in the name of the first target planet. Because you are starting at Pluto, the next planet is Neptune. Type in "Neptune," using a light color. (I chose a light green to simulate an LCD read-out.) Click Scene 1 to leave the Symbol Editor, and you will find your MC in the Library. Drag it to the stage.

After you are finished with your first movie, save it. Then, select File|Save As to save it as the name of your second movie. In that way you can save your library with the MC and use it again. Just edit it and change the name of the target planet.

Planets

I went to the Web site **photojournal.jpl.nasa.gov/** to download images of the planets and then drew them in Flash to take advantage of the vector graphics. The one of Earth is a bitmapped version of a NASA photo with rough parameters to keep it relatively small. I saved all of the planets as Movie Clip symbols.

Movement

Your next step is to create a path for the "spaceship" to move between the planets in the middle of the screen. Then enlarge the planet by a factor of 10, and reduce the planet being left behind by the same factor. Tween both from the beginning position to the ending position. In the Mercury example, enlarge Venus, and drag it to the bottom right corner to appear being passed by closely. Use the Info Panel to resize the planets.

Options

Sound adds an important dimension to Flash movies, and one option is to include a sound loop. Very quickly, sound can take up a good deal of bandwidth, so check your file size after you put it in. Here are two tricks that will save on bandwidth and, depending on the sound file, usually will not hurt the quality:

- To have a "light" sound weight, use a small sound loop. In the Sound Panel, set Sync: to "Event," and Loops to the number of times it takes to fill the movie or portion of the movie you want.

- Reduce the Bit rate.

Another option you can add to the link of movies is a "congratulation" file in the last (mercury.fla) file. This file provides a sense of closure and lets the viewer know the movie is over. You may also want to provide an option to start from the beginning. Perhaps (for the truly gullible), you may also want to offer the first manned landing on the Sun.

Of Scripts and Ideas

The ultimate test of ActionScript is not whether you can write a script to make a movie, but rather whether you can take one of *your own* ideas and create it in Flash 5. Any scripting language, and in particular ActionScript, is a means of communicating to your computer so that it produces what is in your imagination. Ideas should not follow the route suggested by the language or the technology, but rather you should dream an idea and then see how to use ActionScript to realize what you can envision.

In all my years of programming, my best efforts always grew out of solving a problem or dreaming up an idea I wanted to see on my computer screen. The best assistance I received from friends and colleagues has not been in how to write a script, even though I've been very fortunate in receiving excellent technical help, but rather in ideas. With an idea, you have a reason to use script and to push an application to its limits, and even beyond what the designers intended. So, if you really want to learn ActionScript, dream first.

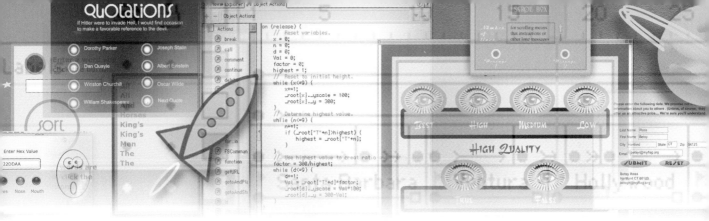

Example Glossary

The actions, operators, functions, and properties in Flash 5 all have short examples of how they would be used in a frame or button script. A short description accompanies each term. Use this Glossary for a quick look-up, not as a general description of Flash 5 ActionScript.

Actions and Statements

For all intents and purposes, the term "action" is equivalent to "statement," and the two are used interchangeably.

Basic Actions

FS Command—Issues an FS Command to Player.

```
fscommand ("allowscale", true);
fscommand ("fullscreen", true);
```

Get URL—Opens specified URL in optionally stated window.

```
on (release) {
    getUrl ("http://www.sandlight.com", _self);
}
```

Go To—Go to a specified line number or label and either play or stop.

```
gotoAndPlay (7);
gotoAndStop ("Score");
```

If Frame Is Loaded—Determines whether a specified frame is loaded. The action is often used in early frames as a preloader.

```
ifFrameLoaded ("Scene 1", 14) {
    gotoAndPlay (4);
}
```

Load Movie—Loads a specified movie at a URL in a stated level or into a specified target movie clip. If the load is at the same level as the movie that loads it, the loading movie is replaced.

```
on (release) {
    loadMovie ("whistlingSmith.swf", 1);
}
```

On Mouse Event—Triggers a script when the mouse or keyboard event occurs. The statement between the curly brackets ({}) execute on the mouse event.

```
on (release) {
    unloadMovie (44);
}
on (press) {
}
on (releaseOutside) {
}
on (rollOver) {
}
on (rollOut) {
}
on (dragOver) {
}
on (dragOut) {
}
```

Green Highlights

In the menus in the Action panel, some actions, operators, functions, and properties have green highlights. The highlight indicates that the word is in the process of phase-out and may have been decremented. For example the function **int()** is being replaced by the **parseInt()**, the **random()** function is being replaced by the **Math.random()** object, and the property **_highquality** is being supplanted by **_quality**. The replacement words are less likely to work in Flash 4, while the green highlighted terms work fine. Throughout the book you will see both used, but you should learn and use the newer formats and words as Flash 4 is phased out. Pay special attention to objects and their uses. If you are creating movies primarily for Flash 4 compatibility, however, use the green highlighted terms.

```
on (keyPress "B") {
}
```

Play—Plays movie. No parameters.

```
play ();
```

Stop—Stops movie. No parameters.

```
stop ();
```

Stop All Sounds—All sounds are turned off.

```
stopAllSounds ();
```

Tell Target—Gives a command to a movie clip. Issues a command to a different timeline. (This action has been deprecated, and the second example below shows the preferred addressing to accomplish the same task. Also, the **with** statement is replacing **tellTarget**—see **with** in the the Actions section.)

```
on (release) {
    tellTarget (_root.Mccool) {
        gotoAndStop (10);
    }
}

on (release) {
    root.Mccool.gotoAndStop (10);
}
```

Toggle High Quality—Toggles between anti-aliasing on (high quality) and off. No parameters.

```
on (press) {
    toggleHighQuality ();
}
```

Unload Movie—Removes all movies from the specified level. The movie URL need not be specified.

```
on (release) {
    unloadMovie (1);
}
```

Actions

break—Stops a repeated action in a loop. In the following example, the value in the variable "box" would be 7.

```
on (release) {
    do {
        k = k+1;
        if (k>6) {
            break;
        }
    } while (k<9);
    box = k;
}
```

call—Initiates an action in a specified frame but does not open the frame. The frames script is essentially "borrowed" by the calling action. The only parameter is the name of the movie clip and frame name. The frame name is preceded by a colon. (The user-defined function is recommended, and **call** has been deprecated.)

```
on (release) {
        call ("_root.script:fade");
}
```

comment—Allows remarks in a script without any action taken. Double forward slashes mark the beginning of a comment.

```
// This should be changed if new MCs are added
```

continue—Similar to a break. Instead of stopping the loop, however, it breaks the current iteration in a loop. The variable box would equal 9.

```
on (release) {
    do {
        k = k+1;
        if (k>6) {
            continue;
        }
    } while (k<9);
    box = k;
}
```

delete—Deletes the specified variable or object and returns a **true** if successful.

```
delete (k);
```

do while—Loop until the termination condition is met. Commands in the do container [do {....}] are executed to the point of the condition set in the parentheses following the **while** condition. The loop sets the loop condition at the *bottom* of the loop so that the loop conditions will be met at least once. (See also **while**.)

```
on (release) {
    do {
        k = k+1;
    } while (k<9);
    box = k;
}
```

duplicateMovieClip—Creates a copy of the specified movie clip using an instance name. Requires a level and a new instance name for the duplicate movie.

```
on (rollOver) {
    _root.mcCool.duplicateMovieClip ("moreCool", 1);
    moreCool._x=10;
}
```

else—Provides an alternative action in situations where an **If** condition is not met.

```
if (k != 8) {
    gotoAndPlay (1);
} else {
    gotoAndPlay (7);
}
```

else if—Provides a second condition in situations where the first **If** condition is not met.

```
if (k != 8) {
    gotoAndPlay (1);
} else if (name=="George") {
    gotoAndPlay ("King");
}
```

for—Loop from an initial set value to a termination condition at an increment level. Increment with **Var++** increments after the loop and with **++Var** increments before the loop.

```
on (release) {
    for (k=1; k<10; k++) {
        box = k;
    }
}
```

for...in—Loop through an object returning all *variables* in *object*.

```
on (release) {
 dog = {breed:'Springer Spaniel', class:'senior', name:'Bogee'};
 for (breed in dog) {
 out += dog[breed]+newline;
    }
}
```

The output to variable would be:

```
Springer Spaniel
Senior
Bogee
```

FSCommand—See **FS Command** in the Basic Actions section.

function—Defines a set of actions for launch upon command. The function definition establishes the actions but does not launch them. (Replaces **call**.)

```
function tiltIt (tiltV) {
    _root.myclip. _rotation=tiltV;
}
```

To execute a function, put the function's defined name in a button, movie clip, or frame script. Provide argument if required in the form of a literal or variable.

```
on (release) {
    tiltIt(35):
}
```

getURL—See **Get URL** in the Basic Actions section.

gotoAndPlay—See **Go To** in the Basic Actions section

gotoAndStop—See **Go To** in the Basic Actions section.

if—Establishes a condition to launch other actions.

```
if (k==44) {
    gotoAndPlay (4);
}
```

ifFrameLoaded—See **If Frame Is Loaded** in the Basic Actions section.

include—Calls and executes external text file containing ActionScript. Recommended extension for text file is **.as**.

```
on (release) {
    #include "remote.as";
}
```

loadMovie—See **Load Movie** in the Basic Actions section.

loadVariables—Loads text files as variables into the specified level or target. In the text file, the variables must have the format, "varName=varValue" (no quotation marks). If more than one variable is placed in the text file, an ampersand (&) must separate the variables with no spaces or carriage returns.

```
loadVariables ("message.txt", 0);
```

nextFrame—Go to the next frame. (Expert Mode only.)

```
nextFrame ();
```

nextScene—Go to the next scene. (Expert Mode only.)

```
nextScene ();
```

on—See **On Mouse Event** in the Basic Actions section.

OnClipEvent—ActionScript associated with the selected movie clip. This event detects nine different events.

```
onClipEvent (load) {
    score = 1;
}
onClipEvent (enterFrame) {....
onClipEvent (unload) {....
onClipEvent (mouseDown) {....
onClipEvent (mouseUp) {....
onClipEvent (mouseMove) {....
onClipEvent (keyDown) {....
onClipEvent (keyUp) {....
onClipEvent (data) {....
```

play—See **Play** in the Basic Actions section.

prevFrame—Go to the previous frame. (Expert Mode only.)

```
prevFrame ();
```

prevScene—Go to the previous scene. (Expert Mode only.)

```
prevScene ();
```

print—Sends a specified bounding box in the named level or target to a printer as a vector graphic. The bounding box may be a movie, frame, or max area.

```
on (release) {
    print (0, "bmovie");
}
```

printAsBitmap—Sends a specified bounding box in the named level or target to a printer as a bitmapped graphic. The bounding box may be a movie, frame, or max area.

```
on (release) {
    printAsBitmap (3, "bframe");
}
```

removeMovieClip—Deletes a specified movie clip from a movie.

```
on (release) {
    removeMovieClip (_root.shorts./orangeShorts);
}
```

return—When executed, this optional expression returns a value of function or **null** if no expression is included.

```
function doTax(price,rate) {
    return price + (price*rate);
}
```

Using **return** generates a calculated outcome in the function that may be passed to the variable. Using the above script, the variable **out** in the following script would contain the calculated values of the literals used as arguments.

```
on (release) {
    out=doTax(39,.08);
}
```

setProperty—Changes the property of the specified movie clip. The path is to the instance name of the clip—not to the symbol's label. This older format can be used in scripts for Flash 4.

```
onClipEvent (mouseDown) {
    setProperty ("/mcCool", _rotation, 44);
}
```

The replacement format for the above **setProperty** script is,

```
onClipEvent (mouseDown) {
    _root.mcCool._rotation=44;
}
```

set variable—Establishes and/or changes a variable's value. Variable values can be any legitimate data type or compound expression. If selected from the action menu, it appears as:

```
set (name,value);
```

and can be written as:

```
set(k,(x/k)*100);
```

However, the recommended way to set variables in Flash 5 is the following:

```
k = ((x/k) * 100);
```

startDrag—Sets the conditions to begin dragging a movie clip. May be constrained to left and right parameters and top and bottom parameters. A Boolean option of **true** locks mouse to center.

```
onClipEvent (mouseDown) {
    _root.mcCool.startDrag( false, 100, 250, 200, 250);
}
```

stop—See **Stop** in the Basic Actions section.

stopAllSounds—All the sounds currently playing are stopped without stopping the movie. Sounds set to stream, however, resume playing when playhead moves over the frames that contain them.

```
If(enoughAllready==7) {
    stopAllSounds();
}
```

stopDrag—Sets the conditions to end the dragging of a movie clip. No parameters.

```
onClipEvent (mouseUp) {
    stopDrag ();
}
```

tellTarget—See **Tell Target** in the Basic Actions section.

toggleHighQuality—See **Toggle High Quality** in the Basic Actions section.

trace—Debugging statement that shows the "traced" variable's value in an Output window.

```
do {
    var k=k+1;
} while (k<=10);
trace (k);
```

unloadMovie—See **Unload Movie** in the Basic Actions section.

var—Establishes a variable as a local variable. It is especially valuable in functions where more than a single button, frame, or movie clip are included in a script.

```
function counter() {
var k+=1;
}
```

while—A loop that establishes the loop condition at the top of the loop and executes until the condition is met. If the condition is met on the initial iteration of the loop, it exits the loop without executing statements inside the loop. (See also **do...while**.)

```
on (release) {
while (k<9){
        k = k+1;
    }
    box=k;
}
```

with—The **with** statement addresses an object, and the object is subject to the statements within the curly brackets ({}) after the **with** object is identified. (Replaces **tellTarget**.) Multiple statements can accompany the **with** action.

```
on (release) {
    with (_root.show) {
        _rotation=56;
        _alpha=76;
    }
}
```

Operators

!—The exclamation point is used for logical NOT. Under conditions to reverse a Boolean (**true** or **false**), the NOT operator tests for the absence of a condition.

```
If (!Key.isDown(Key.ESCAPE)) {
  Display="Press escape key to exit.";
}
```

!=—Tests for inequality.

```
k=10 ;
j= 11;
if (k != j ) {
box = "It is not equal" }
```

%—Returns modulus. In division when a remainder exists, it is called the "modulus." In the following example, the modulus in the variable "box" is 6. (50 ÷ 11) = 4 remainder 6.

```
k=50 ;
j= 11;
box= k % j;
```

&&—Logical AND used in a decision statement. TRUE && TRUE evaluates to True. TRUE && FALSE and FALSE && FALSE evaluates to False. Widely used to test more than a single condition.

```
k=50 ;
j= 11;
x= (k > j);
y= (j > 5);
if (x && y) {
box="Totally correct!" ;
}
```

In a multiple conditional statement, the following shows the correct use of logical AND.

```
if ((total==all) && (total>=lastQ)) {
output="Books balance and it was a good quarter!";
}
```

( )—Group expressions and reset precedence with parentheses.

```
k=(5 + w) * (34-v);
```

*—Multiplies two numbers or variables with real number values.

```
k=12 * x;
```

+—Adds numbers or variables with real number values or concatenates strings.

```
k=a + 7;
wow="Speed" + "memory";
```

++—Increments variables and is generally used in **for** loops. "++variableName" increments before the loop, and "variableName++" increments after the loop.

```
for ( k=1; k<=521; k++ ) {
box=k;
}
```

-—Subtracts the value or variable with a real number on the right from the value on the left.

```
k= k - 2
```

- -—Decrements variables and is generally used in **for** loops. A "- -variableName" decrements before the loop, and a "variableName- -" decrements after the loop.

```
for ( k=1000; k>=521; k-- ) {
box=k;
}
```

/—Divides the value or variable with a real number on the left by the value on the right.

```
k = 250 / 50
```

<—Evaluates "less than" to be True if the value on the left is less than the value on the right.

```
var k=20;
```

```
var j=15;
if (j< k) {
box="You're still younger.";
}
```

<=—Evaluates "less than" or "equal to" to be True if the value on the left is less than or equal to the value on the right.

```
var k=1;
do {
    k = ++k;
    box = k;
} while (k<=50);
```

<>—Evaluates "not equal to" to be True if the value on the left is not equal to the value on the right. (This operator is still available for use in ActionScript, but the != operator is preferred.)

```
var k=15;
var x=51;
if (k <> x) {
box="They have nothing in common.";
}
```

==—Evaluates "equal" to be True if the value on the left is equal to the value on the right. *Important!* A single equal sign is used for assignment, whereas the double equal sign is a test used in loops and conditional statements.

```
var k=29;
var x=29;
if (k == x) {
box="Identical twins.";
}
```

>—Evaluates "greater than" to be True if the value on the left is greater than the value on the right.

```
var kid=15;
var parent=40;
if (kid > parent) {
box="You're not the boss of me now!";
}
```

>=—Evaluates "greater than" or "equal to" to be True if the value on the left is greater than or equal to the value on the right.

```
var k=17;
var x=17;
if (x >= k) {
box="Bigger or better?";
}
```

and—Logical AND is evaluated as True if both conditions are true. The logical AND is very useful for evaluating more than one condition in a single conditional statement. (See also &&.)

```
var k=15;
var x=40;
if ( (x > k) and (x=40)) {
box="Got em both.";
}
```

not—Logical NOT is evaluated as True if a condition is NOT true. It works something like a double negative, but it can be used when filtering in unwanted conditions. (See also !.)

```
var k=15;
var x=40;
if (not( k > x)) {
box="Two nots make a nut?";
}
```

or—Logical OR is evaluated as True if one of two or more conditions is true. Note in the following example that only one of the conditions is true. (See newer operator ||.)

```
var k=15;
var x=40;
if (( k = 15) or (x = 99)) {
box="Either one";
}
```

typeof—Evaluates the type of variable value as a string, number, or Boolean.

```
var k=(3>6);
if (typeof k == "boolean") {
box="It's a Boolean";
}
```

void—This operator voids an expression and is used to test for undefined objects. May be used to reset variables:

```
counter += counter
void(counter);
```

or it can be used to test for undefined values, using the following format:

```
if (j==void(j)) {
    display = "Variable is undefined";
}
```

||—Boolean operator for logical OR operation or conditional statements. If one of two or more Booleans is True, it returns a true value. (Double pipes.)

```
k=37 ;
j= 27;
if ((k>j) || (j<26)) {
box="All I need is one!"
}
```

Bitwise Operators

Successful programming does not require the use of bitwise operators any longer. (As a bitwise operation, floating point numbers are converted into 32-bit integers. Using bitwise operators, you can evaluate each integer in a floating point number.) If you are one who dabbles in the binary world of 0s and 1s, however, the following brief descriptions should suffice.

&—Bitwise AND.

<< >> >>>—Binary shift operators.

^—Bitwise XOR.

|—Bitwise OR (single pipe).

~—Bitwise one's complement.

Compound Assignment

Use the preceding examples to see how the compound assignments work as shortcuts. All of the operators combine, performing the operation of the left half of the compound assignment with assigning the resulting value to the left variable. For example,

```
X = X * Y;
X +=1;
```

is the same as

```
X *= Y;
X= X + 1;
```

You will find compound assignments a clear and handy shortcut once you are used to using them.

%=—Compound modulus.

&=—Compound bitwise AND.

*=—Compound multiply.

-=—Compound subtract.

/=—Compound divide.

<<=—Compound bitwise left.

>>=—Compound bitwise right.

>>>=—Compound bitwise unsigned right.

^=—Compound XOR.

|=—Compound bitwise OR.

String Operators

String operators are the string equivalent of the comparative operators used for numbers. (Most of the string operators are being replaced by general operators that work on both string and non-string expressions.) String comparative evaluations are based on a letter's position in the alphabet, with "A" having the lowest number (1) and "Z" having the highest (26). Therefore, "Z" is greater than "A." Lowercase letters have higher values than uppercase letters, however. Therefore, "a" is greater than "Z." If you are creating movies primarily for Flash 4, use these operators.

add—Concatenates two or more strings. The "box" variable's value is "Howdee!" *Important:* Replaces the ampersand (&), which is used for the same purpose in Flash 4. (May use + instead.)

```
k="How" ;
j= "dee!";
var welcome = k add j;
box=welcome
```

eq—Tests for equality between two strings. When you assign a string to a variable, however, use = as shown in the example. (May use == instead.)

```
var A = "apples";
var O = "oranges";
if (A eq O) {
box = "They're the same";
}
else {
  box = "They're different!.";
}
```

ge—Tests for "greater than" or "equal to" between two strings. Remember that the value of the variable contents is evaluated—not the name of the variable. (May use >= instead).

```
var Z = "Antelopes";
var A = "Zebras";
if (A ge Z) {
box = "The value of the variable is what counts!";
}
```

gt—Tests for "greater than" between two strings. (May use > instead).

```
var lc = "a";
var uc = "W";
if (lc gt uc) {
box = "LowerCase is higher than UpperCase.";
}
```

le—Tests for "less than" or "equal to" between two strings. (May use <= instead).

```
var SameO = "Twin";
var OsameO = "Twin";
if (SameO le OsameO) {
box = "Double your fun!";
}
```

lt—Tests for "less than" between two strings. (May use < instead).

```
var Fatso = "Gigantic Bulk";
var TooSlim = "Anorexia";
if (TooSlim lt Fatso) {
box = "Eat something!";
}
```

ne—Tests for "not equal" between two strings. (May use != instead).

```
var A = "apples";
var O = "oranges";
if (A ne O) {
    box = "They're still different!.";
}
```

Functions

Boolean—Converts expression to Boolean (True or False). The value of the variable "box" is True.

```
var a="Andy"
var k="Kate"
var j=Boolean (a != k);
box = j
```

escape—Returns the ASCII encoding value ISO Latin-1 character set. For example, the following returns the code "%21" in variable "a."

```
var a=escape("!")
```

eval—Returns the value of the variable or property or the reference in an object. In setting up pseudo-arrays in Flash 4 (for example, clip1, clip2, clip3, and so on), the name and number (usually a number variable) are concatenated into a variable name. In Flash 5, using the Array object is recommended instead of pseudo-arrays. The first example returns the value of the object's **_alpha**, and the second returns the address.

```
out=eval("_root.boat._alpha");
display=eval ("_root.boat");
```

false—Sets to a Boolean value of False. Note in the example that the word "false" does not have quotes around it.

```
var n=false
```

getProperty—Returns the value of the specified property of the specified target.

```
var k=getProperty ("/mcCool", _x );
```

The suggested manner for finding an object's property value would be,

```
var k=_root.mcCool._x;
```

getTimer—Returns the number of milliseconds since the movie started playing.

```
timer = getTimer ();
```

int—Returns a value with the decimal values truncated. The following example returns 34. (Being replaced by **parseInt** function.)

```
Var k=34.964
Var lob=int(k)
```

isFinite—Tests for a finite number. Returns Boolean True or False. The example returns True in the variable "box" because 56 is a finite value.

```
var k = 56;
var j=isFinite( k );
box=j;
```

isNaN—Tests for a value not being a number. If the value is not a number, a Boolean True is returned. The following example returns True because "Flash on" is a string—not a number.

```
var k = "Flash on";
var j=isNaN( k );
box=j;
```

maxscroll—Read-only property associated with a text field through a variable name. It returns the maximum value based on the size of the associated text field. For example, the text field variable is named "display," and its **maxscroll** value is placed in a variable named "topScroll."

```
topScroll= _root.display.maxscroll
```

newline—Inserts a new line (or carriage return).

```
var k="Top"
var b="Bottom"
var c=(k + newline + add b)
box=c
```

number—Converts an expression to a floating point or Boolean number. Returns a 0 if it is not a number. (This is not recommended for general use. It was intended to help convert Flash 4 files to Flash 5 files. Use **parseFloat** or **parseInt** instead.)

```
k="145.76"
j= Number (k)
box=j *2
```

parseFloat—Converts a string into a floating point number. If the string is not a number, the return is "NaN." The following example shows how **NaN** may be generated. The dollar sign ($) is not a number. Because it is part of the string "n," the "NaN" value returns when an attempt is made to change it into a number. (You can use the **NaN** function to error-check this type of occurrence.)

```
n="$874.87"
j= parseFloat (n)
box=j * 3
```

parseInt—Converts a string into an integer and truncates any decimal value. The following example returns 874:

```
n="874.87"
j= parseInt (n)
box=j
```

random—Generates a random number between "n" and "n-1" where "n" is a positive value. The following example generates values between 0 and 8:

```
var vague= random(9);
box=vague;
```

scroll—Sets the top scroll line value associated with text field through variable name. Basically, this property sets the line number for the top line in a text field that you can update by using a higher value each time you want to scroll the text upward and a lower value each time you want to scroll downward. For example, the following script uses an incremented variable to jump four lines with each encounter.

```
on(release) {
_root.bigText.scroll=x+4;
}
```

string—Converts a number into a string variable. The conversion can be useful for adding monetary symbols to financial values.

```
var bucks=782.21
var signbuck=string(bucks)
var showsign="$" + signbuck
box=showsign;
```

targetPath—Returns the target path of an MC as a string. Allows indirect addressing of a target.

```
targetPath(_root.fender[j+2]) {
....
}
```

true—Boolean value of True.

```
var flag=true
```

unescape—Opposite of **escape**. Use unescape to convert ASCII encoding value into ISO Latin-1 character. The following example returns an exclamation point (!) because %21 is the symbol's ASCII encoding.

```
var a = unescape("%21");
```

updateAfterEvent—Provides screen updates in clip actions independent of the frame rate. It helps to smooth drag operations.

```
onClipEvent (mouseDown) {
      startDrag (mcCool, true, 100, 250, 200, 250);
updateAfterEvent(mouseDown)
}
onClipEvent (mouseUp) {
      stopDrag ();
updateAfterEvent(mouseUp)
}
```

String Functions

chr—Returns a character associated with the ASCII value in a function. Upper- and lowercase characters have separate ASCII values. The following example shows the ASCII value for an uppercase "A" in the "chr" function.

```
v=chr(65)
```

Note: All string functions are now available using the string object. Most are deprecated in Flash 5. See Chapter 7 for a discussion of string objects.

length—Returns the length of the string.

```
K=length("SandLight")
```

ord—Returns the ASCII value of a character. The following example would give "v" a value of 97:

```
v=ord("a")
```

substring—Returns the partial string defined by ("stringName," index, length). The index is the starting point in the string *after* the index value. The length is the number of characters to be included in the substring. In the following example, "Light" is the substring of "SandLight":

```
k=substring ("SandLight", 4, 5 );
box=k;
```

mbchr—Multibyte **chr** function.

mblength—Multibyte **length** function.

mbord—Multibyte **ord** function.

mbsubstring—Multibyte **substring** function.

Properties

_alpha—Level of transparency. The lower the alpha, the higher the transparency. May be read or set as a percentage. Accepts values 0 to 100.

```
setProperty(mcCool,_alpha, 50)
```

_currentframe—Read-only property of the current frame of the specified movie or movie clip.

```
k=_root.McCool._currentframe;
```

_droptarget—Read-only property indicating the name of the movie clip on which another movie clip has been dropped.

```
k = _root.seeker._droptarget;
```

_focusrect—Sets a property to have a yellow rectangle around buttons when a tab is used to navigate. This is a global property with True or False settings.

```
_root.seeker_focusrect=true;
```

_framesloaded—Read-only property returning the total number of frames in a movie clip that has been loaded.

```
k=_root.McCool._framesloaded;
box=k;
```

_height—Returns the height of a movie clip (Example 1). It may also be set (Example 2).

```
a=_root.seeker_height;
box=a;

onClipEvent (keyDown) {
    _root.seeker._height=104;
}
```

_highquality—Like the High Quality toggle, this property has Boolean values to turn this global property on and off.

```
_highquality=false;
```

_name—The "_name" property works more like a "rename" because it renames the selected movie clip's instance name. The following example changes the name of the movie clip from "seeker" to "sam." Then it uses the new name to rotate the movie clip 55 degrees.

```
_root.seeker._name="sam";
_root.sam._rotation=55;
```

_quality—A global property that has four settings for the quality of bit-map smoothing and anti-aliasing. The settings, which must be set in all caps, are LOW, MEDIUM, HIGH, and BEST. This property will likely supplant **_highquality**.

```
_quality=BEST;
whatQual=_quality;
```

_rotation—A rotation quality has values between 0 and 360. Negative values rotate counterclockwise. They must address a specific movie clip.

```
_root.seeker._rotation=200;
```

_soundbuftime—Global property used to set the time for a sound prebuffer. The default is five seconds.

```
_soundbuftime=12;
```

_target—A movie clip's instance name. You may change it if you wish. In the following example, the movie clip with the instance name "seeker" is changed to the name "magicTap."

```
_root.seeker._target="magicTap";
```

_totalframes—Returns the total number of frames in a movie clip.

```
on (release) {
tf=seeker._totalframes;
box=tf;
}
```

_url—Read-only property returning a movie clip's URL.

```
location=_root.seeker._url;
```

_visible—Returns the Boolean value for whether a specified movie clip is visible. The visibility may also be set. The following example hides the movie clip named "seeker."

```
on (release) {
_root.seeker._visible=false;
}
```

_width—Sets or returns the width of a specified movie clip. (See also **_height**.)

```
on (release) {
_root.seeker._width=50;
}
```

_x—Sets or returns the horizontal position of a specified movie clip. (See also **_y**.)

```
on (release) {
_root.seeker._x=250;
}
```

_xmouse—Mouse horizontal value from the center of the specified movie clip (MC). If the MC moves, so does the relative value of **_xmouse** on the screen. For example, if the MC is at x = 50 and the **_xmouse** value is 60, when the MC moves to x = 100, the **_xmouse** value in the same screen position is 10. (See also **_ymouse**.)

```
var mposX=_root.seeker._xmouse;
```

_xscale—A percent scale of a specified movie clip on a horizontal plane. The following example sets the horizontal scale to 200 percent. (See also **_yscale**.)

```
_root.seeker._xscale=200;
```

_y—Sets or returns the vertical position of a specified movie clip. (See also **_x**.)

```
on (release) {
_root.shootMe._y=114;
}
```

_ymouse—Mouse vertical value from the center of a specified movie clip. If the mouse clip moves, so does the relative value of **_ymouse** on the screen. (See also **_xmouse**.)

```
on (release) {
yHere=_root.seeker_ymouse;
}
```

_yscale—A percent scale of a specified movie clip on a vertical plane. The following example sets the horizontal scale to 50 percent. (See also **_xscale**.)

```
on (release) {
_root.shootMe._yscale=50;
}
```

Index

If you like this book, you'll love these...

LOOKING GOOD ON THE WEB
Daniel Gray
ISBN: 1-57610-508-3 • $29.99 U.S. • $43.99 Canada
224 Pages

Speaking from the user's perspective, this book provides a comprehensive, non-technical introduction to Web design. You'll learn how to design and create friendly, easily navigable, award-winning Web sites that please clients and visitors alike.

PAINT SHOP PRO™ 6 VISUAL INSIGHT
Ramona Pruitt and Joshua Pruitt
ISBN: 1-57610-525-3 • $29.99 U.S. • $44.99 Canada
350 Pages

With concise instructions and screenshots on every page, *Paint Shop Pro™ 6 Visual Insight* teaches the most useful elements of the program to get you started. You'll get straight to work producing everyday effects, such as touching up photos, sprucing up colors, and creating eye-catching text effects.

ADOBE® LIVEMOTION™ F/X AND DESIGN
Daniel Gray
ISBN: 1-57610-676-4 • $49.99 U.S. • $74.99 Canada
352 Pages with CD-ROM

Presents step-by-step projects for creating dynamic effects with Adobe's latest Web program. A 32-page color studio illustrates the program's advanced capabilities, including animation. Working in conjunction with other popular graphics and Web software, such as GoLive®, Pagemill®, Freehand®, and Illustrator®, is covered.

FLASH™ 4 WEB ANIMATION F/X AND DESIGN
Ken Milburn and John Croteau
ISBN: 1-57610-555-5 • $49.99 U.S. • $74.99 Canada
400 Pages with CD-ROM

Dedicated chapters and real-world projects highlight key features of Flash™ 4, including editable text, automated publishing, and forms capability. World-renowned Flash expert John Croteau provides added insight to teach you the most professional Flash effects being used today.

The Coriolis Group, LLC   Telephone: 1.800.410.0192 • www.coriolis.com
Coriolis books are also available at bookstores and computer stores nationwide.

Look for these books, coming soon...

FLASH™ 5 CARTOONS AND GAMES F/X AND DESIGN

Bill Turner, James Robertson, Richard Bazley
ISBN: 1-57610-958-5 • $49.99 U.S. • $74.99 Canada
390 pages with CD-ROM • Available: March 2001

Covering Flash™ 5 from a cartoon and gaming aspect. Learn how to cohesively pull together and create all the necessary elements for an entertaining cartoon show. Create cartoon characters for television and music videos; then discover how to use those cartoon elements when scripting and programming interactive games on the Internet. This book goes beyond the general description of the various Flash tools by showing what can be done with them!

FLASH™ 5 VISUAL INSIGHT

Sherry London
ISBN: 1-57610-700-0 • $24.99 U.S. • $37.99 Canada
368 pages • Available: January 2001

Flash™ 5 Visual Insight provides an illustrative, simple approach to this leading web development program. The format grabs the readers' attention with screenshots and caption-like text teaching the applicable and useful fundamental elements of this program, such as tools and their options. Then, building on that base to guide readers through creating their own movie!

FLASH™ 5 F/X AND DESIGN

Bill Sanders
ISBN: 1-57610-816-3 • $49.99 U.S. • $74.99 Canada
416 pages with CD-ROM • Available: January 2001

Helping Web Designers create aesthetically pleasing, interactive Web sites. Animation, tweening, using the timeline, coordinating sounds, shape, color, scenes, movement, and sequences, as well as scripting actions and interfaces are covered in this book. Readers gain an understanding of Flash's underlying conceptual framework for creating movies.

DECIPHERING FLASH™ GRAPHICS

Jon Warren Lentz
ISBN: 1-57610-812-0 • $49.99 U.S. • $74.99 Canada
352 pages • Available: March 2001

This easy-to-read, richly illustrated book appeals not only to the Flash™ novice but also to the accomplished Flash artist who seeks inspiration and guidance with the higher capabilities of the program. Each chapter is devoted to a specific Flash site by targeting at least one Flash functionality. It provides inspiration through in-depth, case-study explanations with real-world examples of cutting-edge Flash design.

The Coriolis Group, LLC   Telephone: 1.800.410.0192 • www.coriolis.com
Coriolis books are also available at bookstores and computer stores nationwide.

What's on the CD-ROM

The *Flash ActionScript*'s companion CD-ROM contains elements specifically selected to enhance the usefulness of this book, including:

- All of the Flash 5 learning utilities and projects from the book (more than 50) in both source code (.FLA) and ready-to-play (.SWF) formats.
- Macromedia Flash 5—30–day limited trial version. You can enter all of the .FLA file source code and create your own animated movies with Flash 5.
- Freehand 9—30–day limited trial version. Make vector graphics that can be imported and used in Flash 5.
- Dreamweaver 3—30–day limited trial version. Macromedia's Web site creation tool lets you import Flash 5 .SWF files right into a Web page.
- Fireworks 3—30–day limited trial version. Create and import PNG files with preserved vectors for use in Flash movies.
- "How to Make a Font"—Flash movie by Leslie Cabarga.

System Requirements

Software

- **Windows:** Windows 95, 98, NT4, 2000, or later.
- **Macintosh:** MacOS 8.5 or later.

Hardware

- 133 MHz Intel Pentium processor for Windows or newer.
- Power Macintosh processor or newer (G3 or G4).
- 32MB of RAM is the minimum requirement.
- 40MB of available disk storage space.
- 256-color monitor capable of 800 × 600 resolution.